INTERSECTING GENRE

INTERSECTING GENRE

A SKILLS-BASED APPROACH TO CREATIVE WRITING

Jason Olsen

BLOOMSBURY ACADEMIC
LONDON • NEW YORK • OXFORD • NEW DELHI • SYDNEY

BLOOMSBURY ACADEMIC
Bloomsbury Publishing Plc
50 Bedford Square, London, WC1B 3DP, UK
1385 Broadway, New York, NY 10018, USA
29 Earlsfort Terrace, Dublin 2, Ireland

BLOOMSBURY, BLOOMSBURY ACADEMIC and the Diana logo are trademarks of
Bloomsbury Publishing Plc

First published in Great Britain 2023

Copyright © Jason Olsen, 2023

Jason Olsen has asserted his right under the Copyright, Designs and Patents Act, 1988,
to be identified as Author of this work.

For legal purposes the Acknowledgements on p. vii constitute an extension of
this copyright page.

Cover design: Rebecca Heselton
Cover image © Vince Cavataio/Getty Images

All rights reserved. No part of this publication may be reproduced or transmitted in any form
or by any means, electronic or mechanical, including photocopying, recording, or any information
storage or retrieval system, without prior permission in writing from the publishers.

Bloomsbury Publishing Plc does not have any control over, or responsibility for, any third-party
websites referred to or in this book. All internet addresses given in this book were correct at the
time of going to press. The author and publisher regret any inconvenience caused if addresses
have changed or sites have ceased to exist, but can accept no responsibility for any such changes.

The author and publisher gratefully acknowledge the permission granted to reproduce copyright
material in this book. The third-party copyrighted material displayed in the pages of this book is
done so on the basis of fair use for the purposes of teaching, criticism, scholarship or research
only in accordance with international copyright laws, and is not intended to infringe upon the
ownership rights of the original owners.

A catalogue record for this book is available from the British Library.
Library of Congress Cataloging-in-Publication Data

Names: Olsen, Jason, 1974- author.
Title: Intersecting genre: a skills-based approach to creative writing / Jason Olsen.
Description: London; New York: Bloomsbury Academic, 2023. | Includes bibliographical
references and index.
Identifiers: LCCN 2023002903 (print) | LCCN 2023002904 (ebook) | ISBN 9781350288652
(paperback) | ISBN 9781350288645 (hardback) | ISBN 9781350288669 (pdf) |
ISBN 9781350288676 (epub)
Subjects: LCSH: Creative writing. | Literary form.
Classification: LCC PN187 .O47 2023 (print) | LCC PN187 (ebook) |
DDC 808–dc23/eng/20230505
LC record available at https://lccn.loc.gov/2023002903
LC ebook record available at https://lccn.loc.gov/2023002904

ISBN: HB: 978-1-3502-8864-5
PB: 978-1-3502-8865-2
ePDF: 978-1-3502-8866-9
eBook: 978-1-3502-8867-6

Typeset by Deanta Global Publishing Services, Chennai, India

To find out more about our authors and books visit www.bloomsbury.com and
sign up for our newsletters.

CONTENTS

Acknowledgments vii
Note on Pronouns viii

1 Question Everything 1

2 The Genres in Brief 13

3 Stories and Song: Intersections between Fiction and Poems 29

4 The Stage on Which We Stand: Intersections between Creative Non-Fiction and Plays 43

5 Structure of Action/Action of Structure: Intersections between Screenplays and Fiction 55

6 The Uninvented: Intersections between Poems and Plays 69

7 The Self and the Screen: Intersections between Screenplays and Creative Non-Fiction 83

8 Wants and Perspectives: Intersections between Plays and Fiction 97

9 The Smallest Building Block in the Universe: Intersections between Poems and Screenplays 111

10 Voice and Perspective: Intersections between Fiction and Creative Non-Fiction 125

11 Know Your Audience: Intersections between Plays and Screenplays 139

12 The Lyrical Self: Intersections between Creative Non-Fiction and Poems 157

Contents

13	**Playing Tennis without a Net: Further Genres**	173
14	**Sixteenth Thought: Revision and Editing**	181

Glossary	189
Works Cited	193
Index	196

ACKNOWLEDGMENTS

I wish to thank Utah State University for support in completing this project. Specifically, I am grateful for the help provided by Phebe Jensen, Greg Dart, Rich Etchberger, and Nathan Straight, among many others.

I will be forever grateful to Lucy Brown for believing in this project and helping me shape it into existence. I also extend thanks to Aanchal Vij and everyone at Bloomsbury who assisted me along the way, including the readers who went through earlier stages of this manuscript and provided essential advice and direction. I am also grateful to each of the writers, editors, publishers, and creative minds I interacted with during the various stages of this project.

I'd also like to thank the writers who were kind enough to meet with me to discuss genre and craft: Michelle Bonczek, Kevin Drzakowski, Gregory Delzer, Jody Keisner, Katie Manning, Liz Marlow, Carrie Oeding, Robin Runyan, Kory M. Shrum, and Ashley Wells. In addition to their guidance, the conversations with those listed above were invaluable for guiding me in writing this book, and I could not have written it without their help. I am also grateful to Scott Poole, Catherine Schuller-Gruenwald, and Kenneth Witzgall.

Throughout my life, I have had the fortune of studying with a number of remarkable creative writing teachers, including Nancy Eimers, Christopher Howell, Mark Jarman, Jonathan Johnson, John Keeble, Claudia Keelan, William Olsen, Alicia Ostriker, Douglas Unger, Nance van Winckel, and Richard Wiley. Each of these teachers helped shape me into the teacher and writer I am today, and I am forever grateful.

I also wish to thank my mother, Tina-Marie Olsen, for nurturing my lifelong love of reading and writing, and my wife, Chapel Taylor-Olsen, and our children, Eliza and Tate, for their love and support during the research, writing, and revising stages of this project.

NOTE ON PRONOUNS

To the best of my ability, I have reduced gender-specific language in this book to make it more inclusive, including the frequent use of the non-gender-specific pronoun "they." However, many of the quotes I provide are from writers (mostly from earlier eras) who used terms such as "men" and "he" instead of more inclusive, non-gender-specific language. I have kept these quotes in their original forms in order to maintain the integrity of their thoughts on writing, and the non-inclusive choices are made by the original writers. Further, the inclusion of a quote from a writer should in no way be seen as an endorsement of that writer's overall beliefs and behavior.

CHAPTER 1
QUESTION EVERYTHING

Good writing begins with inquisitive writing. What we write develops from the questions we ask. Often, these questions are functional. *What do I need at the grocery store? When am I supposed to meet my friend for lunch?* Inquisitive writing also benefits creative writing. *Why does my protagonist so desperately need to return home? Why does this line need to break on this word? What is it about this childhood memory that makes me want to share it in an essay? Now that my character has overcome this obstacle, what happens next? What does this setting mean for the conversation my characters are having?* Inquisitive writing begins with—and is propelled by—questions.

Questions (and their answers) are the heartbeat of good writing. These questions are not always conscious in the writer's head as they write, especially not with an experienced writer. That experienced writer might be confident enough with their writing that these questions and their subsequent answers happen simultaneously during the process. This is not the rule, however—very often, a writer at even an advanced level must stop and ask themselves questions about a work in progress. This does not mean the writer asks these questions aloud or writes them down, but the inquisitive writer always thinks about questions.

Writers must train themselves to be inquisitive because an inquisitive writer is a successful one. Good writing does not come from mere inspiration—it requires careful thought about what will best benefit a given piece of writing. The writer is always the one making those choices at every stage—from idea conception to drafting to revising and editing.

This sounds obvious, but the writer is always in control. The "muse" is the idea that something outside the writer is their main inspiration. In mythology, muses were goddesses who inspired creativity. While we do not think of muses in this way today, the concept endures with the myth of ideas (and text) coming less from the writer and more from mythical inspiration. This concept takes agency away from the writer. Writers need to take that agency back.

This is not to say that inspiration has no place in writing—but overvaluing inspiration devalues effort and inquisitive work. The world around them should inspire a writer, but they should not rely on that inspiration in favor of the work of drafting and revising. A writer who sits around waiting for inspiration may wait a remarkably long time. A writer who asks the questions that get a piece moving forward is a writer in control of their craft. Inspiration and inquisitive writing can work together, but the writer must ask questions to enable a work to approach its fullest potential. Inquisitive writing begins with inquisitive thinking.

Intersecting Genre

Successful writers must be conscious observers of their world, and ask questions about the things they see and why they matter. A writer needs to ask these questions during the writing process, but they should also ask them before putting any words on the page.

> #### Going Further
>
> Question-asking is a critical part of all writing, creative or otherwise. The questions asked will depend on the type of writing, but there are questions that always matter:
>
> - Who is the audience? What is the audience's reading level, maturity level, and experience?
> - What is that audience expecting? A writer never has to provide everything an audience expects, but writers need to put themselves in the potential reader's perspective to understand expectations.
> - What does this audience already know about the subject of this piece of writing? Are there things that they do not know but should?
> - As the writer, why are *you* writing this? What are your personal goals?
>
> As these questions illustrate, two of the most important aspects of writing involve audience and purpose. When a writer begins drafting a piece of writing with a clear sense of individual purpose and an understanding of who it is for, they are ready to move forward.

Why Write?

The best question to start with is a simple one—*why write?*

There are many reasons: to remember something, to convince someone else of your point of view, to educate, to charm. Creative writers try to engagingly convey something that matters. The goals of a specific piece of writing will vary, but the general objective is to create something—regardless of your initial intention—that deserves to be read. When you are writing a shopping list, the motivation is practical. When we write creatively, it is less about function and practicality, and more about creating something engaging. Creative writers write to remember. We also write to encourage others to remember us and the things we have written.

Writing stems from the writer's (or reader's) need to remember, learn, or feel something. Creative writing is the best method for a person with something personal and urgent to say, and it can also be the last resort for a creative voice yearning to be heard. As you continue your creative writing journey, one of the most important discoveries you will make is about your motivations. The more you write, the more you will understand your reasons for writing creatively.

Writing Warm-Up

Think briefly about the different reasons you write in your day-to-day life, and how writing fits into your various roles (including as a creative writer, an employee, a student, and a friend, for example). Write down at least five different reasons you write.

After you have come up with those five reasons, think about the type of writing you do for each, and the time and value you put into each. As you write your answers, you will think more about why you write (and what you prioritize).

What Is Creative Writing?

The next logical question is *what exactly is creative writing*? It is a difficult concept to define. The term is vague—*any* writing can be creative, whether a poem, a blog entry, or even a witty recipe. This vagueness makes creative writing challenging to teach and learn. Looking up the term in Oxford's *Lexico* dictionary yields a seemingly functional yet insufficient definition for our purposes: "Writing, typically fiction or poetry, which displays imagination or invention (often contrasted with academic or journalistic writing)." Some of this definition is useful—while "imagination" and "invention" are not precise terms, they are central to creative writing. Including these words in a relatively dry definition is encouraging.

Other parts of the definition are less valuable. While fiction and poetry are creative writing genes, it is limiting to omit so many others (and a disservice to exclude genres that will make a writer more complete and successful).

The parenthetical at the end of this definition—"(often contrasted with academic or journalistic writing)"—is where it loses its way. First, it is dangerous to define something by what it is not. Creative writing is difficult enough to define—exclusionary examples muddle it further. But much like singling out fiction and poetry limits the writer's ability to explore diverse creative writing opportunities, introducing genres as definitively *not* creative will only restrict the potential of those types of writing.

Maybe the most helpful strategy is to forego formal definitions altogether. Everyone sees creative writing differently. One writer may enthusiastically say creative writing is all about storytelling, and another might say it has less to do with the story and more about style and voice. To one reader, "creative" means fantasy and science fiction; to another, it means finding a way to tell their personal story. There is no perfect creative writing definition because there is no single approach to or style of creative writing. There are countless creative writers, and each one has something to say. No two people think the same, so no two writers should follow the same approach to writing.

> ### Going Further
>
> Just because we choose not to settle on a formal definition does not mean we cannot include more creative explanations. Writers have always come up with rather unique and compelling ways to describe their crafts. For example:
>
> "The novel is the one bright book of life."—D. H. Lawrence
>
> "If I read a book and it makes my whole body so cold no fire can warm me, I know that is poetry."—Emily Dickinson
>
> "All good poetry is the spontaneous overflow of powerful feelings."—William Wordsworth
>
> "The sound of language is where it all begins."—Ursula K. Le Guin
>
> These are not definitions in the way we expect. Instead, they cut to the heart of whatever an individual writer sees as an essential aspect of creative writing. They prioritize metaphor over logic. As a writer grows in their craft, they not only improve their writing but also better understand their own definitions of what they do.

The inquisitive writer who asks for clear-cut definitions will be disappointed. While Chapter 2 will provide further insight into individual genres, pithy definitions will not serve us there either. This should not discourage a reader—not having pat definitions reveals how many possibilities exist in each genre. There is no *one* way to look at anything. Writers have many opportunities to find their unique paths into creative writing. Importantly, this is "paths," not the singular "path." There are multiple entry points—and ways to succeed—in creative writing. Never trust someone who says there is only one way to succeed. Understanding as many styles and approaches as possible is crucial to path(s)finding.

Think of Walt Whitman's words in "Song of Myself": "Do I contradict myself?/Very well then I contradict myself./I am large, I contain multitudes." Whitman is explaining that human beings (and he uses himself to speak for everyone) are complicated and filled with feelings, beliefs, and philosophies that might not make sense when taken together. People are allowed to contradict themselves because humanity is complicated. If creative writing is the stuff of humanity—the stories of who we are as people—then creative writing gets to be a bit messy, too.

Expect messiness in your writing. Do not run from it, and do not let it overwhelm you. Genres can help. As complicated as creative writing is, having categories that encapsulate (and identify guidelines for) certain types of writing is essential in making the difficult task of creative writing more accessible. It also expands the universe of possibility one genre at a time. These seemingly divergent genres are how writers find their paths into (and through) creative writing.

What Are Genres?

Throughout this book, the term "genre" is used interchangeably with "form" to discuss types of creative writing, including fiction, poetry, creative non-fiction, screenwriting, plays, and other non-traditional creative categories (known in the book as "Further Genres"). For our discussions, consider **genre** a classification—an individual writing type requiring a particular approach. The word **form** can refer to the genre, but it is often more precise, specifying approaches within a genre (like sonnets, lyric essays, or novels). Even if they differ in tone, style, or content, two disparate short stories would still fit into the fiction genre. Same for two poems. Perhaps one of those poems might have more in common thematically with a fiction story than another poem. Still, the two poems are considered part of the same genre.

The world is built on genre, even if we do not always notice it. Streaming services suggest future binge-watching based on the genres viewers have already watched. Music services create playlists based on the genres listeners have enjoyed most. Grocery stores even send customized coupons for things related to items customers have purchased in the past. Perhaps the word "genre" is an odd fit for separating fruits and vegetables, but it helps illustrate categories overall. Genres and categories fill a basic need of identifying groups or styles of things. However, if the sole purpose of genre is to separate, the concept is not being used to its full potential.

Why Are Genres Useful?

Genre is about categories. This book is about genre's importance in creative writing, but discussions about other categorizable things, like music and movies, often employ genres. Genre both specifies and excludes. We can use it to indicate what we like, and we can also use it to show what we do not like. While this exclusionary use of the term is common and might seem innocuous, it can harm our growth as writers.

It seems innocuous, though, and for non-writing purposes, it might be. If someone wants to express their movie preferences, they can say they like one genre best, but they might also be more exclusionary and state that there is another genre they do not like—"I like all movies *except* horror," for instance. This is not harmful—preferences matter. Perhaps this hypothetical horror movie hater has emotions triggered by horror film tropes and chooses to stay away to protect their mental health. Allowing our preferences and needs to be dismissed devalues us as people, and could be harmful. Genres help reveal personal values through preferences and exclusions. This is good.

Perhaps the person who tells others they enjoy all genres except one or two is on the brink of understanding the value of genres but does not realize it. Using music as an example, different genres of music require various mental states from the listener. On a long drive where the driver feels comfortable and in control, the music choice could be of a slower tempo. Maybe a driver who finds themselves distracted needs thoughtful music with provocative lyrics. Perhaps a driver feeling sluggish (but not so tired as to need to stop the car altogether) should listen to some high-energy hip hop to revitalize themselves. Is the traffic stressing the driver out? Perhaps they should turn the music off completely. In these examples, all genres are valid because each has a specific purpose.

Listening to different musical genres requires different mindsets and also *creates* different perspectives. This is true of musicians too. A musician must be aware of different genres because each requires a unique approach, instrument, and technical method. A piano player must know how to play differently if asked to play classical or jazz. Genres do not exist simply to create borders to keep categories apart—genres exist to give people insight into what makes genres different, not to confirm superiority. We can create amazing things by combining genres. Artists willing to merge previously separate genres have created some of the most memorable pieces in music history.

When presented with a genre, we instinctively know some of that genre's expectations. Maybe the knowledge is unconscious, and perhaps we do not know every rule, but we know some. If a friend asks you to watch a movie together, your first question is likely, "what movie?" This is an inquiry into genre. If the friend asks to watch a horror movie, you know what type of movie it will be: emotional with a sense of unease and discomfort, even if it also presents thrills. If the movie is a comedy, the stakes are lower, even if the movie will likely be less thrilling. Sometimes people want something light and escapist. Other times, the mood calls for something else. Genres help choose what is suitable for a particular occasion.

Going Further

The term "genre" can be problematic. When asking what "genre" means in creative writing, some people will define it as discussed above: fiction, poetry, creative non-fiction, plays, and screenwriting. Others will define "genre" as styles within those above categories: sci-fi, fantasy, realism, and magical realism, for example. Fiction, poetry, creative non-fiction, plays, and screenplays are often called "forms" rather than "genres." While this text will primarily use "form" and "genre" interchangeably, there will also be references to the categories within these forms/genres.

Genre fiction refers to works that fit into the categories of sci-fi, fantasy, and others within the broader scope of fiction (these can also be called **subgenres** of fiction). This will be the case with poetry as well. Instead of labeling "genre poetry" (which, based on the above definition, would be poetry that deals with science fiction, fantasy, or some other approach), the discussion will address "forms" of poetry (such as the sonnet form); thus, the term "poetic form" will be used rather than "poetic genre." Try to see it less as confusing and more as an interplay between these approaches. All of these genres and forms are interconnected—it makes sense that the terms used to describe them are also interconnected.

What Makes Genres in Creative Writing So Important?

Genre expectations help us understand how to approach a given genre or form. Whether a writer realizes it or not, basic instinctual impulses guide them when they begin to write in a new genre. Poetry is emotionally driven, fiction is story-driven, and creative nonfiction is about the writer's experiences. A screenplay needs to have dialogue and action that pushes it forward. A writer must consider how a play's characters will interact with each other and the setting. Not knowing every nuance of a genre is fine—the knowledge builds with additional exposure, knowledge, and practice.

Comprehending these various genres helps you become a better writer in the genre you most favor (if a writer does indeed have a preferred genre, something not required). In this book, genres are complementary, not isolated. Genres are opportunities to find intersections; what we learn at these intersections is crucial for writing growth. No one genre or form leads to success; success comes from understanding all possibilities of creative writing.

In this book, all genres are equal. Poetry is equal to fiction is equal to creative nonfiction is equal to plays is equal to screenplays is equal to any other possible creative writing genre. Later in a writer's life, genres might not be equal. A time may come when a writer does favor one genre quite specifically and does not feel the need to study much else, but even those writers can benefit from reading works out of their areas of expertise. The multigenre writer is better versed and more thoughtful because they look at writing from myriad possibilities at all stages. The time to settle on a single genre in favor of all others is not at the beginning of the journey. This book helps writers understand relationships between genres and use those relationships to see patterns and strategies that will help in whatever genres they eventually choose to explore.

Learning about these genres educates our ability to write in all of them. A writer interested enough to write creatively does not enter any genre blindly—some knowledge accompanies primary interest. Knowing a bit about a specific genre or form explains how to start in that genre. A writer might initially not understand the intricacies of a particular genre, but they will likely know enough. For example, if a writer jumps into a memoir essay, they will begin aware that the genre asks for a first-person narration of a story that happened to them. The writer does not know as much as they will after more experience writing in that genre, but they enter with the basics taught by the genre itself. The writer will learn even more by writing and reading creative works from the genre. A writer begins a poem knowing it should be musical and usually has line breaks. These are "rules" that a writer knows through intrinsic understanding. There are more "rules" to be learned, but the genre is informing the reader about these "rules" even if the writer is not fully aware.

A writer does not need to obsessively follow every "rule," but these introductory "rules" set writers up with a basic understanding of a genre. The "rules" are essential whether a writer is just beginning or wants to break the "rules" to try something new. If a writer wants to write a very formal sonnet, a sonnet's specific "rules" will be essential.

If that writer wants to subvert the sonnet form by writing something that willfully challenges what a sonnet is, the "rules" need to be firmly in mind for that too. You cannot break "rules" if you do not know what they are in the first place.

What "Rules" Are We Talking About?

Each time this book has mentioned "rules," the word has been accompanied by quotation marks. Each time you see that word snug inside its quotation marks, think of this moment from a 1932 profile of American business person Thomas Edison by Russian-American chemist Martin André Rosanoff:

> As soon as we were installed in our ménage, I approached [Edison] in a humble spirit: "Mr. Edison, please tell me what laboratory rules you want me to observe." And right then and there I got my first surprise. He spat in the middle of the floor and yelled out, "Hell! There *ain't* no rules around here! We are tryin' to accomplish somep'n!" And he walked off, leaving me flabbergasted.

In creative writing, "rules" are essential tools for our success. "Rules" allow us to jump between genres and learn from each. "Rules" should not restrict a writer; they help us understand what is possible. Rules, on the other hand, are restrictive. Rules force us to write in an unforgiving manner. "Rules" are guidelines; rules are not. "Rules" are the expectations for genres—short stories have a beginning, middle, and end; poems have line breaks; creative non-fiction is about a writer's experiences. Rules, on the other hand, are structured and seemingly unbreakable.

The difference between "rules" (with quotation marks) and rules (without) is that "rules" are what a genre can teach us that will inform our decisions. A "rule" is flexible, while a rule is not. A "rule" can be a necessary guidepost that leads us in the directions we can go. A "rule" is breakable. A rule is a roadblock; a "rule" is an opportunity. If writers break the rules, they are in trouble. If they break "rules," they are creative. We just have to be aware of why the "rule" breaking has occurred and how the different genres can expand our potential to approach these creative writing "rules."

The most effective way to use genre to become a better creative writer is to learn from the intersections between genres. Think of these genres as teachers. Each genre is a different type of teacher. Some help us understand sounds and silence, and some help us define characters. All genres teach stories.

Learning poetry—or any of these forms—is valuable in its own right, but understanding certain aspects and principles of poetry will absolutely make for a better fiction writer (and non-fiction writer and screenwriter, and so on). These intersections are the backbone of this book—it explores these convergences and why they matter. The more a writer understands these relationships between genres, the more that writer will understand the craft and know-how to succeed as a creative writer.

Going Further

Creative writing requires craft. **Craft** in this book refers to the "nuts and bolts" of creative writing—a technical understanding of certain aspects (plot, character-building, detail, line, and stanza structure, for example). It is easy to think that creative writing is just about coming up with brilliant ideas and magically watching them become fleshed out, but writing is more work than that. Without craft, an idea will never reach its potential.

Getting value from studying these intersections is not possible without knowing the genres in the first place. The next chapter will discuss the basics of each genre featured in this book. No one approaching creative writing is likely walking into it without *some* knowledge of these categories, so these introductions are not wholly basic. Still, these brief discussions will provide essential tools to understand each genre and how each form can educate the others. Never forget—none of these genres exist in a vacuum.

Writing Practice

What do you know about these five major genres? This writing exercise will show you. For each of the following genres, write down five representative words that come to mind. Just write down whatever comes to mind for each of these genres as quickly as you can:

Fiction
Poetry
Creative Non-Fiction
Drama
Screenwriting

Now, review the twenty-five words in front of you. What stands out? Do you see words repeated for more than one genre? Do you see words that surprise you? Think of these twenty-five words as a preliminary mission statement about how you view creative writing. What story do your words tell? What are your creative writing instincts?

Specific genres are only the beginning. While the focus in this book is on the most frequently used creative writing forms, remember that what we learn while writing fiction can help us with a play or a poem, but it can also help us create content for a podcast. Learning screenwriting can lead to better blogging. Those types of writing not encompassed with the five primary genres are called "Further Genres."

The "rules" change, of course, but writing is writing. No single form of writing is inherently superior or inferior to another, though there could be certain occasions that

Intersecting Genre

would call for a specific genre. In the same way a mother might prefer a handwritten birthday card to a text message, a play might be a better fit for an idea than fiction (and vice-versa). There is a reason certain plays make for lousy movies, and some plays lead to great ones.

Audiences matter, too—an audience might find a writer's intimate exploration of feelings off-putting in a screenplay but utterly appropriate in a poem. Most mothers would likely enjoy receiving an original poem slipped into that handwritten birthday card, but some mothers may enjoy a simple rhyming love poem more than an abstract non-rhyming poem.

Something to remember is that you should have two goals for your reader—do not confuse them and do not bore them. Keep things clear and engaging. Sometimes writing can be complicated and dense—this is not necessarily the same as confusing. Creative work is typically confusing because it is unfocused and sloppy. Complexity in writing is a goal—confusion is not.

What Is So Important about Reading?

At a public literary reading, after a published writer has read from their book and the audience has expressed their approval, a question-and-answer session often follows. During these question-and-answer sessions, some audience member will inevitably ask, *how do I become a better writer?* The response will almost always be some version of the following: *A writer needs to do two things—write a lot and read a lot.* This is good advice.

The first part—writing—is obvious. Practicing is crucial when improving anything, whether skateboarding, baking, or writing. The more one practices, even without concern for doing it perfectly, the more one grows in their craft. Being a better writer requires a lot of writing. No surprise there.

But it is the other part of this advice that some writers underestimate. It is not necessarily surprising that avid reading can help a writer grow, but it is also perhaps advice often misunderstood or overlooked. According to his biographer, Scottish writer James Boswell, eighteenth-century English writer Samuel Johnson said, "the greatest part of a writer's time is spent in reading." He adds that a writer "will turn over half a library to make one book." Most aspiring writers would agree that reading is essential, but they still might feel a little lost with this advice. The two questions writers need to ask are: *What* am I supposed to read, and *how* am I supposed to read it?

What Am I Supposed to Read?

What to read starts with what the individual enjoys reading and continues with recommendations from friends and mentors. If writers are most interested in writing in specific genres (including genre fiction categories), it follows that those writers must read a lot within the genre that interests them. Want to write fantasy fiction? You better read as much as possible. If a writer is interested in many genres, that writer should read a great variety of things. *What* should never be limited to solely works within genres of the writer's interest—being a voracious reader of whatever they can get their hands on will make for a better writer.

A writer must be willing to slip outside their reading comfort zone. A person who typically reads realistic fiction, for example, might recoil at the idea of taking on a 1,000-page science fiction opus but may find insight and ideas they did not expect. The person who loves science fiction novels might think there would be no way they could love a memoir about a writer's struggle with substance use disorder, but they might find themselves proven wrong. Ultimately, when it comes to being a better writer, all reading is worthwhile, just so long as the reader reads it correctly.

How Am I Supposed to Read?

While knowing *what to read* makes sense, the *how* of reading might seem a little strange. You know *how* to read, of course, but writers are not always taught how to approach different kinds of texts. We learn how to analyze literature and understand its purposes and methods. We talk about character motivations or the historical context of a given work, which is helpful for students and scholars analyzing a text. Creative writers need to read differently. Sometimes we read for pleasure. Other times, we read as students, trying to learn from the text. At other times, we read as writers. It might take time to learn, but once engrained, reading as a writer will allow for a new world of inspiration and possibilities.

When reading as a creative writer, you should not bother analyzing the meaning of a given work. Instead, try to figure out why a piece of writing succeeds. Think about what you like about a piece and why you like it. What about the sound of this poem is so appealing? Is it something haunting about the tone? Is there a character description that succeeds in painting a vivid picture? A creative writer must think about why certain work thrives and other work does not.

This book does not contain as many examples of creative work as other books might, but there is a reason for that. These examples are often included with extensive detail in terms of questions and ideas to lead to further thought ("Explorations"), along with writing prompts that will expand a writer's creative work ("Creative Response"). Reading for writers is different than for students in more analysis-based settings, and we will discuss what it means to read like a writer and then do precisely that.

The book is primarily structured in chapters focusing on two genres and the relationship therein, but nothing should be that narrow. The chapters contain value beyond the two primary genres discussed in a chapter because the strategies will also relate to other genres (sometimes directly and often indirectly). Everything is connected. For example, the chapter that discusses the intersections between fiction and screenwriting will have discussions that will benefit other genres too. The two-genre structure of the chapters is a convenient way to establish connections between the two forms under discussion, but everything in this book will tie in with everything else.

Intersecting Genre

This is true even in Chapter 2, which is set up differently than what follows. That chapter contains introductory discussions of each featured genre. These introductions begin our understanding of these genres (and later chapters will discuss each genre more thoroughly) and will help ground readers as they progress.

When reading through this book, remember that everything is connected in writing, always. Your goal should not just be to become simply a better memoirist, short story writer, play writer, screenplay writer, or poetry writer. You should be striving to become an overall better writer. This book will lay out the paths—and intersections—that will make that possible.

CHAPTER 2
THE GENRES IN BRIEF

In his book *Genre*, Australian academic writer John Frow explains that genre's "structuring effects are productive of meaning; they shape and guide." By using the word "structuring," Frow recognizes that genre can provide a template for similarities between certain things. Genre gives creative writing *structure*, and we can get a better sense of something by comparing it to something similar. This way, we can understand Frow's guidance about how genres "shape and guide." Genre shows us why specific works fit into different categories.

As meaningful as genre identifications are, they can create challenges in literature and writing. Genre identification can often discourage readers or writers from thinking about work outside a specific genre. The wall separating two creative writing genres can often seem impenetrable. It may be easy to compare one poem to another, but a reader might feel less capable of comparing a poem to a screenplay or short story. Breaking down those walls is a key to excelling as a complete writer. When these walls collapse, we find valuable intersections within the rubble.

But before understanding the possible intersections, we must gain a basic understanding of each of the primary creative writing genres. The following genre descriptions are starting points for more extended conversations that will continue throughout the book. This chapter will provide the necessary background to begin your journey.

Nomenclature of Writing within Genres

Some of the language used in the book may feel awkward, but it is deliberate and essential. The terms "poet," "playwright," and "screenwriter" are avoided because they insinuate a mastery of a particular genre and lack the flexibility of genre-switching that is so important to a writer's growth. In a book that values learning from all genres, terms that evoke mastery are potentially restricting and harmful.

To use "fiction writer" and "poet" side-by-side makes "poet" feel like a vocation while a "fiction writer" is exploring a hobby. Calling a writer a "poet" or "playwright" leaves little room to grow outside that genre, defeating this book's purpose. So, while those writing fiction and creative non-fiction will be called "fiction writers" and "creative non-fiction writers" (as is common), "poetry writer" replaces the term "poet," "play writer" replaces "playwright," and "screenplay writer" replaces "screenwriter." Employing these different terms is a step toward demystifying the genres themselves. There is a sense of

Intersecting Genre

mysticism in words like "poet" and "playwright"—they are old terms that tie writers to the genres as if they were tradespeople. That sense that only experts can write within a specific genre is stigmatizing.

Using the word "writer" exclusively eliminates the need for these terms but, if we acknowledge genres, we must identify them differently. While this book celebrates how one genre can help us excel in another, there is no illusion that genres are interchangeable. Writers learn from each genre, and there is no benefit in pretending the genre divisions are irrelevant. Having the language to help think about how writers switch from one genre to another will make such leaps easier to reach.

Fiction

Fiction is prose work of variable length in which a writer has taken liberties with truth to create something compelling. Fiction can be a short story or a novel (or something in-between), but the writer must imaginatively generate the content. This does not mean fiction must be pure fantasy (though it could be). It can have many real-world elements—it just means that the writer has imaginatively created the core contents for artistic purposes. Creative non-fiction comes from fact and history (whether that history is personal or collective); fiction comes from imagination.

> **Going Further**
>
> The words "imagined" and "imagination" are used purposefully here—fiction can be accurately described as a "lie," but that emphasizes deceit over creativity. In a way, all writing (even work based on truth) is a lie because of the artificiality of writing. Describing a thing is never the same as that thing itself. Singling out fiction as a lie is unnecessary. The most proactive way to excel in fiction writing is to embrace the imaginative aspect and deemphasize deceit.

One of fiction's greatest strengths is its ability to create emotional responses despite the "lie" at the center of a work of fiction, but fiction is perhaps as capable—if not *more capable*—of conveying the *truth* of certain situations than is reality. On the surface, this is a contradiction. How can fiction—something that is not *true*—do such a thing? A fiction writer uses real-world emotions and situations but has complete control over the direction those beginnings take them. Being unburdened by truth allows the fiction writer to move in any direction, thus having the freedom to create something reality would not allow.

A fiction writer can feel like they have the freedom that a writer steadfastly attached to truth does not have. If history and reality do not move the way a story requires, a fiction writer can change those facts into something new—something fiction.

Fiction is the cumulation of many truths, and the result is something that is not entirely true but *feels* real. Fiction is story and plot. Fiction is character. The first word that starts a piece of fiction is an invitation, and the reader might not be prepared for what follows. That is okay. The reader knows that fiction is not true, but that does not mean it is a deception. Fiction is a prose exploration of an idea that typically employs characters and plot to create an emotional resonance with the reader.

Expectations for Fiction

What is the most important aspect of fiction? Some say fiction is primarily about storytelling and plot, while others think characters matter most. Others tell us good fiction is dependent upon compelling world-building. Someone else might focus on the power of great fiction's emotional impact.

All of these answers can be right. Every writer is different, and each story, novel, or novella has a different focus. There is simply no way to know what matters most in a particular work of fiction until the writer has explored the world of the piece enough to figure it out.

A writer should strive to do it all—build compelling characters who do interesting things in a well-developed world that leaves the reader feeling something authentically emotional. Some of this work can happen in the idea development stage, and some can occur during drafting. Most importantly, the writer must be conscious of achieving these multiple goals.

Misconceptions about Fiction

Emerging writers often worry about what to write about in fiction because they feel that the story will not be compelling to anyone else if they do not write about something extremely high stakes. This can be a problem—if someone chooses not to write about something because it does not seem "exciting" enough, it can cost the world worthwhile fiction. Many writers start with big ideas, often inspired by adventure-driven novels or film series. Being inspired by popular media is fine, but if the action-packed high-impact world of popular culture impacts our storytelling, it can make it feel like everything needs to be big, action-packed, and loud. Where does this leave a writer who wants to create something more intimate?

Fiction writing is big enough to embrace all perspectives. Those smaller-scale stories—the ones that reflect people's lives more than something action oriented—matter. Realistic fiction is not inevitably boring (in the same way fantasy fiction and science fiction are not automatically exciting). Writers must realize that there is room for everything. Writers who think that fiction (or any genre) *has* to be about a particular thing presented in a certain way may start their writing lives well, but as they continue to write, they will realize the creative world they have constructed is impossibly small.

Intersecting Genre

Some fiction writers may also have an inconsistent view of audience. They may try to reach an audience that is simply too broad—no matter how much a writer tries to be something for everyone, they cannot satisfy every reader. Besides, a piece written to make everyone happy runs the risk of appealing to no one.

Say a writer shares a short story with ten people, each an experienced writer and reader of fiction. These ten people each provide clear and detailed notes, complete with thorough suggestions about the next steps for revision. Will each of those ten readers have the same suggestions? Of course not. Each will come at the story (as they would for all stories) with personal experiences, biases, and values that make their opinions uniquely theirs. Some may agree with others on some points (and there may be areas where everyone agrees), but there will also be certain aspects on which they will disagree. To follow every suggestion, a writer would follow threads that lead to contradictions and inconsistency. It is the same with an audience—a writer should never write to please everyone, but it is a good idea to think of an **idealized audience** (a hypothetical audience that would most appreciate a given work) and write fiction with that audience in mind. If that audience is ultimately the writer themselves, that is not the worst thing in the world—if a writer likes what they have written, there is a chance someone else will too.

It is often smart for a writer to write in a particular way for a specific audience. If the writer delves into a fiction subgenre such as fantasy, that writer needs to know an audience's expectations for that genre. That does not mean the writer cannot challenge those expectations, but some key aspects of a subgenre like fantasy are what make it fantasy. If a writer tries to write a fantasy novel and does not know the expectations of that genre, no reader who loves that genre will engage with the text for long. To know a particular audience, a writer must start by reading and understanding the kind of work that the audience expects.

A writer needs to write for themselves too. If the writer is bored with their work, what hope do other readers have? The work does not have to be wildly personal (though it could be), but the writer has to find something that matters to them when they write.

Poetry

Poetry is a creative writing genre that is typically broken in lines and stanzas (as opposed to simply paragraphs of sentences) and is known for its emphasis on musicality, emotion, and imagery. Of the creative writing genres discussed in this book, poetry is the most challenging to explain, and it is undoubtedly the one that has caused the most anxiety for writers and students. A prose paragraph is approachable because a reader can see it and know that the sentences will explain whatever the writer wants to get across. A reader knows the words in a prose paragraph create the overall intention of that paragraph. The words add up to meaning.

Going Further

Unlike prose, which is presented in paragraphs, poems are typically presented in **lines**. A line is a unit of poetry that ends before the right-hand margin at a point chosen specifically by the writer. A line **break** (where the writer has chosen the stop the line) can, but does not have to, correspond to sentence endings or punctuation pauses—it is completely up to the writer.

Lines can be arranged in **stanzas**—sections that contain lines and are separated (typically by extra spaces) from each other. When talking about poems in prose discussions, a line break is typically depicted with a backslash, and a stanza break with two backslashes. For example: "I love my dog/with the love//of a child."

Readers come to fiction and non-fiction to be entertained or informed (or both). Those same readers approach poetry as if it will be, well, hard. Perhaps poetry in the twenty-first century needs better public relations people. A reader who can excitedly and gleefully begin a long novel series might recoil at a much thinner volume of poetry because of how much work they perceive poetry to be.

Some of this rests on how schools often teach poetry. Poetry should be a joy, but schools often teach students to decipher poems and provide definitive interpretations even when there are many different ways to read a single poem. When readers receive a poem (especially in the classroom), they often tense up as if a poem is a logic problem with one difficult-to-find solution. A poem should be an opportunity for a writer to express themselves in ways impossible in other forms. A poem should be an invitation for a reader to feel something. A poem should never be a problem.

But the idea of "poetry as a problem" persists because of "rules." While the rules in creative writing are really "rules," writers can be intimidated by the fact that, for centuries, formal poetic rules were far less flexible. While most poetry writers today use fewer strict formal structures than in the past, those structures are still influential. Understanding these structures is vital to knowing the historical context of poetry, and that historical context is valuable. Writers learn from all kinds of writing—things written hundreds of years ago and today.

Because they write with an anticipation of performance, play and screenplay writers compose with the idea of *hearing* what is said, but what separates poetry from these other genres is that it is not simply heard—good poetry contains a musicality that transcends mere oral comprehension. There is also no one way to do this. Some poetry writers create musicality through strict adherence to syllabic consistency and rhyme, and others do it through alliteration (repeating constant sounds) or assonance (repeating vowel sounds). Others use approachable and conversational language.

Poetry can be intimating because of an overabundance of "rules," but the reality is that the challenge of poetry comes from an abundance of freedom. Poems are vehicles of endless potential. A poem can be a political gesture or a personal cry, and it can be both or neither. A poem can be anything; freedom is as intimidating as seemingly endless "rules."

Intersecting Genre

Misconceptions about Poetry

Some of the intimidation writers (and others) feel about poetry comes from misconceptions about what a poem must be. Too many writers assume that poetry must be obtuse and complex and that, when read aloud, it must sound affected. Poetry is verbal art, so almost all poems benefit from being read aloud, and all poetry writers are free to read their poems in whatever way feels right. Some think spoken poetry is pretentious, but that is unfair to all writers and poems. Just as a writer needs to write a poem in a style that fits them and the poem personally, the writer should have the freedom to read that poem aloud however they choose. Some writers read their work aloud quickly, some slowly, and some read a poem in the same cadence they would use in everyday conversation. What matters is that each writer finds their poetic voice both on the page and aloud.

Another critical misconception is about formal structure. As stated above, poetry is a genre that allows immense freedom. However, many writers approach poetry from the opposite mindset. Instead of seeing poetry as a place of infinite possibilities, they see it as the genre with the most restrictions. Considering that so much of what English and literature classes teach are rhyming poems from centuries past, a writer's first poems often start with attempts at rhyme and classical structure. While contemporary poems can have rhyme schemes, consistent meter, and a set number of lines (and whatever specifics a form requires), they do not have to do so.

Writers also assume that emotions drive poems, and abstract poems that sacrifice images and specificity for emotional intensity are the norm. Good poems give readers something to visualize and hold on to—a poem without images will be difficult for a reader to latch onto and, while it can still matter deeply to the writer, it might not have the same resonance for a reader.

Expectations for Poetry

While writers can begin writing poetry feeling handcuffed because they think that poems must fit into specific structures and styles, the reality is that poems can be whatever a writer wants them to be. In his introduction to the 1997 *Best American Poetry* collection, American writer James Tate writes that "it doesn't matter" if a poem is "written about a mite or the end of the world." There are brilliant poems written about big and small things. Tate continues in this essay: "One of the things that matters is the relationship of all the parts and elements of the poem to each other. Is everything working toward the same goal?" Any topic can make for a good poem—or a lousy one. What matters most is that the poem's parts—whatever they are—fit together toward a common goal. One thing for poetry writers to remember is that poems, like other forms, do not *have* to sound like anything.

The lack of expectations can be freeing for a writer but also intimidating. Every writer needs to approach poetry in a way that makes them feel most comfortable. A writer's work—regardless of genre—is continually strengthened by reading the works of others.

This is true of fiction and plays and everything else. There is such an immense variety of poetry that it is easy to feel overwhelmed. Writers, especially beginning writers, often imitate what they like. One unique challenge for poetry writers is that so much of the poetry read and taught in schools is often from hundreds of years ago. If a writer taking a nineteenth-century British poetry class wants to write poems, they may start writing poems that imitate Alfred Tennyson rather than a more contemporary voice. This is not a knock on Tennyson—a brilliant nineteenth-century English poetry writer—but Tennyson's approach to form and language, while wildly popular in his day, is less immediate in our current age. The solution is never to take away the book of Tennyson from the writer—all writers should read whatever they want and need to read—but perhaps to slide a copy of something more current into their poetry collection as well. Poetry is alive and well—even if too many people assume it stopped being vital sometime in the twentieth century.

Creative Non-Fiction

If fiction is made-up, then **creative non-fiction (CNF)** is the truth. CNF is typically seen as a creative writing genre that revolves around personal or historical events. So, yes, CNF is about things that have happened, but where do we go from there? Does it have to be about the person writing the piece? Can it be about something or someone else? Does it have to feel like a fiction story, just true? Or can it weave and move in different formal directions?

One of the significant challenges with CNF is that, while it is a genre that allows great freedom, many writers find themselves stifled by not knowing what they should write about. Often, that block comes from wondering if anything is interesting enough about themselves and their personal experiences to warrant sharing. They have difficulty knowing where to begin. Some writers would rather do anything but write about themselves.

Much of what we see in CNF takes the form of a prose memoir, often with an eye toward serious and challenging periods in the writer's life. A **memoir** is CNF work (either essay or book-length) where the writer discusses a period, theme, or relationship from their life. These types of essays are valuable for both a writer looking to therapeutically discuss a pivotal time in their lives and a reader who wants to learn and grow from the experiences of others. But not every example of CNF is built around heady and challenging experiences—writers can explore the humorous and the mundane, often in ways that test the limits of standard prose.

CNF rivals poetry for the sheer range of material within the genre. Certainly, memoir is a common way to approach the genre, but writers can explore memoir in myriad ways. It can be about a specific episode (perhaps a recollection of a battle with substance use disorder) or a significant relationship (the writer could explore their dynamic with a parent). A memoir is not an **autobiography**—a recollection of a writer's entire life. That does not mean it cannot follow a long period of that writer's life—it just does so from a specific angle. Perhaps a book-length memoir about the author's relationship with their father follows that writer's entire life but does not discuss episodes that do not directly involve the relationship with their father.

The different range of memoirs provides limitless opportunities for a writer, but that barely reveals the types of exploratory essays that fall under the umbrella of CNF, including lyric essays, creative journalistic essays, and travel writing, among many others. Some forms of non-fiction not typically associated with CNF, like reviews or analyses, could also fit within the genre with enough creativity.

Misconceptions about Creative Non-Fiction

The main misconception about creative non-fiction is about the emotional weight a topic needs to possess. Some writers feel insufficiently capable of writing CNF because they do not feel they have endured enough hardship in their lives to warrant it. CNF does not have to be about difficult times (though it could). If a writer decides they cannot write CNF because of their self-perceived lack of significant personal experience, they are not thinking widely enough. When writers at any level of personal experience unfurl their histories, they will find extensive material—as long as they realize that any interesting memory is a potential building block for a CNF essay.

Memory or experience can never be the only factor in a successful CNF narrative. A great piece of creative non-fiction is a product of a writer who puts compelling characters into relatable and fascinating situations. Sometimes writers feel—especially when starting in CNF—that an interesting story is all they need to write something great. This is not the case. The most enthralling story imaginable will allow a writer to begin a potentially successful piece of writing, but without craft, it will just be a lost opportunity.

Expectations for Creative Non-Fiction

An expectation for CNF is truth, but we need to unpack that concept. A writer needs to share the primary events depicted within a given piece of CNF in a way that protects the integrity of truth. But within the unfolding of scenes, a writer can take liberties. The reader acknowledges and accepts this fact, at least subconsciously. A reader has expectations of truth in a work of non-fiction and would not immediately admit that any bending of the truth is acceptable, but the reader knows the writer's primary goal is to compellingly capture the memory.

Here is a short scene in which speaker remembers a moment with their grandfather:

> Much like we did every day after I came home from school, I placed my backpack by the back door and joined him in the backyard, sitting at the wide patio table under the giant yellow umbrella that jutted from the center of the table. He was listening to big band music on the radio. It was Los Angeles, so the time of year didn't matter much as far as the weather was concerned, but it was late March 1989.

He smiled as I sat down. He slid a lemonade toward me. The ice clicked in the glass, so I knew he had it ready for me just as I came home.

"How was school?" he asked.

I shrugged. "I got to write a lot," I said. "I like writing. It's so much better than other subjects."

He smiled. The dog barked.

Is this scene true? The writer would assuredly say it is—an interaction between the grandfather and grandchild (with lemonade) occurred. But is it *true*—did everything the writer claims to take place happen? Probably not, right? The writer specifies the story takes place in 1989, decades ago. The speaker also recalls memories from childhood, which are difficult to depict accurately. The event described is also mundane—it is easier to remember specific events that are personally notable. The memorable moments of our lives lead to vivid details. This story also contains dialogue. Does the reader assume that dialogue in a CNF piece will be word-for-word precise? Of course not—it is difficult enough to remember something immediately after it is said and nearly impossible to do so years (or even decades) after the fact.

So there are moments where truth is not verbatim, but the essence of a story and its major events need to be as accurate as possible, even if the details are amalgams of events and times. For example, a writer might not specifically remember the shirt they were wearing when their favorite toy fell into the lake, but the feelings that were true to that moment are what matter. If there was a shirt that the writer wore a lot during that time (but maybe not at the moment of a specific memory), that is still an effective detail that will pull the reader in further.

Play Writing

A **play** is a creative writing work written in a specific standardized format to eventually be performed on a stage. Writers in other genres will often read their work aloud in front of others, but those genres do not have a specific home the way plays do. If a play makes it to production, performers will present the play on a **stage**. A stage can be any open area with an audience, usually (though not always) with a physically elevated space. A play writer writes a play with the intention of its performance in front of a live audience in a formal area known as a stage.

While this may seem like common sense, it is crucial. If a play writer is not thinking about space and movement (and the confines of a stage), the play will not work. There is no parallel in any other creative writing genre (including screenplays because settings in a movie work much differently). While the presence of a stage is limiting, it is also grounding. Other genres seem to allow unrelenting freedom, but play writers have this one specific thing to tether them. In many ways, it is a gift.

Writers who love writing dialogue will find a special connection to plays. For dialogue practice, there is no better genre. This includes screenplay writing which emphasizes dialogue but in a way that matches sound and movement, two things in plays that are, in contrast, differently explored. Plays can have sound effects and music, but the main sounds on the stage are dialogue. Characters move and act, but their actions are always tethered to the stage.

A good play needs to sound good (and dialogue is vital), but it must also be active and appealing. A play is a blueprint that allows collaborating artists to eventually stage a play. A completed play is not just dialogue, character development, stage instructions, or setting descriptions—it is a how-to manual for the director, performers, and everyone else involved. A play is a text that collaborators use to construct an artistic event on stage. The play writer is the instigator of collaboration.

Of course, the path to writing a successful play moves through other genres. Suppose fiction and creative non-fiction are exercises in storytelling, and poetry explores the best possible use of language. In this case, plays exist in-between and away from those other genres. A play tells a story, but the story does not exist only in the reader's head. Instead, a play is a more tangible sensory experience, one where the produced play provides sounds and actions that engage the audience. The audience *sees* the action in ways impossible in fiction.

This also means that reading a play differs from reading a work of prose because the reader knows that the ultimate form of a play is in performance and, therefore, the play's text is merely a prelude to that intended form. The words on the page are silent, but the reader subconsciously brings them to life in an imaginative pseudo-performance.

A good play is about movement and resonance. All creative writing begins with an imaginative burst, but for a play writer, that burst must linger because the more a writer allows the characters and actions of the play to move around their mental stage, the more successful the eventual creative product.

Misconceptions about Play Writing

When watching from the audience, a play seems almost entirely dialogue-driven. This is an understandable conclusion—the characters usually communicate through frequent dialogue. Unlike fiction or creative non-fiction, there is no narrative way to let the audience entirely into a character's mindset without characters specifically communicating those thoughts. In fiction and CNF, characters can talk and move, just like in a play, but they can also think, remember, and imagine in ways that are organically conveyed. It is possible to express a character's inner thoughts in a play, including with a character who speaks directly to the audience and "breaks the fourth wall" to provide further information. Suppose the only way to convey information in a play is through dialogue and character actions. In that case, a play writer does not necessarily have the same creative freedom to show the reader a character's inner thoughts, right?

Of course not—it just requires creativity and innovation. While it is common for writers unaccustomed to plays to stick mostly to dialogue (with some attention to setting and character actions), this strategy is limited. Speaking is not the only things play characters can do. They act. They react. The performers and director of a play can make decisions that help shape a character, but they are not solely in charge of such character-building. A play writer must include directions of physicality (including desired facial and overall physical reactions) to help the reader (and eventual collaborators) understand what is happening.

One thing to remember with plays is that they move clearly and deliberately. This is true for characters and how they move on the stage, and also for the plot itself, which will also move in precise ways. Plays are dialogue-driven, but the dialogue does not matter if the rest of the play is not moving effectively.

Expectations for Play Writing

As stated above, plays should have a clear sense of movement. When writing a play, it is wise to think carefully about scenes and acts. Think of scenes as building blocks for the story and that subsequent scenes are required for the story to proceed (and for the characters to develop). Scenes occur in other creative writing genres but are a virtual currency in plays. In fiction, a scene can exist with specific settings, actions, and dialogue, but a fiction writer's ability to get into a character's thoughts can make a scene start in a literal location and end up in a character's head. This works differently in a play—other methods are required to show what happens in a character's head (like a "dream sequence" with altered lighting to alert the audience to a different mindset). So a play informs the audience of what needs to be known and then continues to move.

If a poetry writer feels like writing a sonnet in iambic pentameter, they are more than welcome to do so. If not? Well, no need to count those stressed and unstressed syllables. When writing plays, that choice of form is less available. The formatting of a play (and screenplay, as discussed in the next section) is formally structured and consistent. This is important. If a writer decides to share work for professional purposes, it is crucial to abide by formal guidelines. This established format is standardized when writing a play, so potential collaborators must see the proper layout. The formatting is standardized to create uniformity for all collaborators, complete with easy-to-read headings for characters and immediately-understood actions and settings. A director and performers (along with other collaborators) need to know precisely where something is in a script. Proper formatting allows that.

Screenplay Writing

Screenplays are creative works written in a standardized format to eventually be produced for the screen (film, television, or internet). Creative writing does not always feel like a collaborative art form. After all, most poetry writers compose alone. Fiction writers, too. A single author usually writes CNF, and that author is usually writing about their experiences or relationships. Non-writers (and some writers) imagine a writer taking their deepest, most personal thoughts and putting them on the page in deep and complete solitude. While this is not exactly true, it is not always untrue, either.

Intersecting Genre

Writing for the stage and screen is different. These are inherently collaborative forms. As discussed in the previous section on writing plays, the play writer must consider the stage (and how performers, directors, and set designers will interpret their work). All of those elements are true with a screenplay but magnified. While many people are involved in producing a play, a film almost always has more (especially in full-length films). Just watch through the credits of a recent big-budget movie. It takes a while to get to the end of the credits because a major movie is a serious collaborative effort.

This book is not interested in discussing all of the jobs necessary for creating a film but even in the case of *just* writing the screenplay, there is often collaboration. Between 2000 and 2020, a little under 40 percent of the movies nominated for the Academy Award for Best Screenplay (combining the categories for both "Original" and "Adapted") were by more than one writer. During the same period, the Tony Awards (awarded for excellence in stage production) nominated 92 plays for "Best Play," and a collaborative team wrote only about 2 percent of those. Collaborative screenplay writing is normal.

Why, exactly? According to Pamela McClintock of *The Hollywood Reporter*, 2018 saw $41.1 billion in global movie theater ticket sales. Most of the highest-grossing films also cost a fortune to make—if a screenplay is going to serve as the blueprint for a movie (on which millions could be either made or lost), those risking financial capital will need as many hands on their investment as possible. This is not a recommendation to find someone else to collaborate with on screenplays—it is a call to consider what the predominance of screenwriting collaboration represents.

Misconceptions about Screenplay Writing

When it comes to the creative writing genres, fiction, poetry, and creative non-fiction are universally accepted as the primary forms taught and explored in creative writing programs. These are the three genres most typically taught by creative writing instructors in English departments at the university level. While not as canonized as the other three, writing plays is also often taught in English departments (regularly in conjunction with theater departments). Screenplay writing, however, is not often in this company. Therefore, the first misconception is that screenplays are not as essential a genre as the other four. This is untrue. The skills obtained by learning how to write better screenplays will unquestionably lead a writer to more success overall.

A reason for screenplay writing's secondary status may be its proximity to writing plays. While both genres involve a writer creating something intended to be performed and produced by somebody else, writing plays and screenplays are different experiences. Chapter 11 will discuss this further, but for now, it is notable to emphasize that each genre's physicality and overall scope are different. There are limits to what a play can do on stage and, thanks to special effects and wide-ranging settings, the screenplay could be made into something with less restriction. Plays can also have impressive sets and special effects, but concerns over sets and effects are less likely to compromise a screenplay.

Writers may also see the task of writing a screenplay as more of an earned vocation than they do with the other genres. With a short story, a poem, or a piece of CNF, the writer can independently craft and create the final product. There is no other step to presenting it to an audience. A play typically reaches its more complete form when performed on stage, but even performing a play somehow may feel more approachable to a writer. But the screenplay is an artifact of professional filmmakers. How does an inexperienced writer expect to write a screenplay that can become a Hollywood blockbuster? This is a fair point, perhaps, but also a meaningless one. There are avenues for writers outside the film industry to find a way to get screenplays made into films, including independently with like-minded collaborative groups.

Even if a film version of a screenplay seems out of reach, writing screenplays is something any writer can—and should—try. Like plays, they are fantastic tools for practicing dialogue, and, unlike plays, they provide an infinite sandbox in which a writer is allowed to play, even when based on previously written material. Take, for example, the book and movie versions of *Jurassic Park*. The book, written in 1990 by American writer Michael Crichton, is darker and much more violent than the 1994 movie directed by American filmmaker Steven Spielberg. The character of John Hammond, the park's founder, is eccentric and kindly in the film but much less likable in the book. As for the ending, the book resolves with Jurassic Park's (and Hammond's) destruction after the protagonists escape. The movie concludes with the escape and assuredly more hope than what follows the destruction of the creator and his dream in Crichton's novel (both left intact in the film). These differences illustrate how audiences perceive a movie and how many different directions a screenplay can take.

Since collaboration is key and other people will assuredly be involved in creating a film out of a screenplay, a darker screenplay might be harder to convince others to collaborate on, especially if the final product could be a crowd-pleasing, family-friendly adventure film (which the *Jurassic Park* novel is not). A dark cautionary tale about the dangers of "playing God" by recreating creatures long since dead works well for a novel. The film still functions as a cautionary tale, but by making John Hammond less villainous and more kindly, the movie can focus on adventure without as many of the novel's philosophical interests.

Expectations for Screenplay Writing

Ultimately, a screenplay should be whatever the writer thinks is best for a given piece. There can be many expectations about what a film should be, but ultimately, the screenplay writer comes up with what best serves the particular piece in question. It is essential to think here of audience expectations. While all creative writing genres depend on emotion—the emotional goals of the writer and the audience's emotional reaction— the expectations of emotional responses for each genre are different. All genres, of course, can be funny, but comedy is more expected in screenplays than poems, for example. We also may expect many novels to be serious. Once again, using an example from a film adaptation, the original 1952 novel *The Natural* by American writer Bernard Malamud is about a baseball player who attempts to overcome adversity to play baseball again in his mid-thirties. The 1984 film, directed by American filmmaker Barry Levinson,

Intersecting Genre

follows roughly the same story. The endings deviate, perhaps even more dramatically than *Jurassic Park*.

In the novel, the main character (Roy Hobbs) accepts a bribe to lose the last game of the season. While at bat in a climactic moment, he decides to do his best to win the game after all but fails, striking out. The book ends with the reader assuming that Hobbs' act of taking the bribe will ultimately ruin and shame him forever. It is a depressing ending, but it fits a serious novel. The film takes a different route. In the movie, Hobbs refuses the bribe. Hobbs does not strike out when he has his climatic at-bat with the game on the line. Instead, he hits a home run that smashes the stadium lights. It is a cinematic celebration of resiliency and heroism.

The novel and movie formats bring very different expectations—if someone reads a serious novel that resolves with a "happy ending," they might think, "I read 300-some pages in this book, and everything works out? That doesn't feel believable." Suppose a movie that presents itself as an inspiring depiction of the human spirit ends with abject failure and defeat (with no way to grow from that defeat). In that case, the audience might think, "I spent two hours watching this movie just to feel miserable at the end?" The audience's expectation of what a movie should provide can never be the writer's only guide, but it can indeed be one of their guides.

Further Genres

It would be a mistake to insinuate the five genres presented here are the only ones worth writing and studying. Creative writing is about finding opportunities, and limiting ourselves to any finite number of genres would harm our efforts to reach our full potential. In a world built on digital communication and seemingly limitless media access, the possibilities of writing are also unlimited. While this can be overwhelming, it is truly an opportunity. The idea of **Further Genres** is not about identifying every possible type of creative writing that does not fit into the five major categories. Instead, it is a call to the writer to think outside of the typical formats.

Some writing genres are not typically considered "creative"—journalism and academic writing, for example. Some readers may immediately equate "creative" with "made up," but our discussion of creative non-fiction reveals that this is not the case. Instead, it is instructive to think of "creative" as the process of crafting work and not necessarily just the final product. Creative writing emphasizes imagery and storytelling over the more straightforward approaches traditionally taken in journalism or academic writing.

Journalism or academic writing (and countless other genres) have as much potential for creativity as the primary genres discussed in the book. While it is difficult to see a direct news story as creative writing, there is creative potential in a profile of an important figure or a unique approach to a research topic. A writer in any genre—especially Further Genres—must see creative potential in everything. A successful creative writer finds creative avenues in unexpected places.

Think of Further Genres as opportunities. What can fit in Further Genres that will not fit anywhere else? Is a text message creative writing? Usually not—typically, texts are limited to terse accounts of information, but does that have to be the case? What about a recipe? How might that be rendered creatively? It might be best to think of Further Genres as an empty backpack—what are ways to fill that backpack with folders full of ideas of what could be? Further Genres, like all genres, are best considered as opportunities to find ways to write something that matters so it can resonate with someone else. Creativity benefits all forms of expressive writing.

Summary

The overall world of creative writing is vast and intimidating. This is why writers often consider themselves in terms of a single genre rather than the broad label of "creative writer." While people certainly identify as "writers," there is often a push toward more specific clarification. If a writer tells a new acquaintance at a dinner party that they are a writer, the new acquaintance will likely want more clarification—"What kind of writer?" At this point, a journalist may say, "I'm a journalist—I write about local government and politics." But, likely, a fiction writer would not say, "I'm a creative writer of novels and short stories." They would likely never say, "I'm a creative writer." But the reality is that "creative writing" is clear and defining. There are many genres within that broad umbrella, each of which can be used by a creative writer when seen fit.

Each creative writing genre has its own voice, features, and potential. A writer who understands multiple genres and learns how best to write in many of them is someone who will better understand their potential as a writer.

Writing Wrap-Up

After reading through an introductory discussion of each of these genres, what stands out to you about these genres overall? The first chapter has a question about what you knew about each genre before reading this book. Now that you have more information about each genre, have your ideas evolved? What genre feels most comfortable? Why? Which genre is the most intimidating? Why?

CHAPTER 3
STORIES AND SONG
INTERSECTIONS BETWEEN FICTION AND POEMS

All writing is story-based. The most imagistic poem tells a story even if that story lacks familiar narrative tools. It is still a story. For something to be a "story," it needs characters and meaningful actions. The image-based poem might not seem like it fits this description, but a narrator describing something is still telling a story (even if it lacks some of the depth we expect in a work of fiction). Without compelling stories, there is nowhere for a piece of creative writing to go.

What exactly is a **story**? The most straightforward definition is that a story is a collection of real or imaginary events resulting in a reader's (or listener's or viewer's) emotional reaction. That "emotional reaction" can be delight, sadness, excitement, frivolity, or any other possible response. Everything that occurs within a story is in the service of other parts of the larger piece of writing. While similar to story, **plot** is somewhat different: the story is the larger world of your characters, and the plot is the specific sequence of events within a particular piece of writing. Story is everything that exists in the world you have created; the plot is what happens within that larger world in your novel, short story, or another creative writing piece.

A lyric poem (discussed further both later in this chapter and Chapter 12) builds from story if all the parts logically fit together—even if it does not have the beginning-middle-end structure that we often equate with plot. If the sequence of events in the poem pays attention to a larger world, it is a story. We can confidently say this because storytelling is not just about the story but also about the *telling*.

If all writing builds around stories, then all forms of creative writing are expressions of storytelling. These stories pass down through generations and become cultural touchstones. Before print, oral storytelling was the tool to pass stories down from one generation to another. Even though oral tradition is not the only form of storytelling in modern cultures, every person reading to children at bedtime is part of that tradition.

Telling stories is not where storytelling begins and ends—it also requires *storylistening*. Eudora Welty, the American fiction writer, explains, "Long before I wrote stories, I listened for stories. Listening for them is something more acute than listening to them." Welty rationalizes that this skill develops in childhood but cannot end there.

Regardless of genre, writers need to be great storytellers. Great storytellers need to be great listeners. The process of storytelling cannot thrive without listening. Storylistening can be the impetus that drives a young person's love for reading and writing, but it cannot only be the stuff of childhood. We all must listen.

Intersecting Genre

However, there are too many voices to hear all of them. So what voices must a great storyteller listen for exactly? This is a crucial question and, ultimately, difficult to answer. There are too many valuable voices for anyone to know for certain which deserve an audience and which do not. A writer needs to seek out the voices and stories that will matter to them, and that takes careful listening.

Writing Warm-Up

A **found poem** is a poem created out of words found somewhere in the world. These can be words found in newspaper articles, comic books, political speeches—anywhere. If we find words, we can make a found poem. Sometimes these found poems are accidents—for example, a library in Stratford-upon-Avon printed this gem by listing off a patron's borrowed books:

> Holding you
> I found you
> In deep water
> Before we say goodbye

Sometimes the words are presented in the order they were found (like in the previous example). Often, writers rearrange the words to find new relationships.

For this writing warm-up, seek out some news articles, and find some compelling words and phrases. Piece them together however you like. Found poems are a great way to see how the world is full of poetic potential.

Oral Tradition

While oral tradition is ubiquitous worldwide, Native American cultures are ideal for studying these traditions. Telling stories ensures preserving stories. The storyteller affects the story. Oral tradition teaches us the importance of voice in the same way that a dozen different joke tellers can put a dozen unique spins on the same joke with the same punch line. Voice is the personality conveyed in a piece of writing. A story is not just about the plot—it is also about voice and storytelling. Stories are passed down from one generation to the next for many reasons—to share legends, explain the universe, and entertain. These are things inherent in all writing. Many of these Native American stories are direct. Some versions of these stories are in print in various forms—poetry and prose—for audiences ranging from children to adults. Here is an excerpt from "Coyote and Rabbit," translated by Hildegard Thompson from Navajo:

> One day Coyote was out walking.
> He was walking in the forest.
> He saw Rabbit.

> He started to chase Rabbit.
> Rabbit ran in a hole.
> Coyote said,
> "I'll get you out of that hole.
> Let me think."
> Coyote sat down to think.

The language is simple—in Navajo culture (and all cultures that value story as something sharable through time), there is significance in telling the story *and* remembering the story. Simplicity and directness lead to acute remembering—this is the case with oral tradition, lyrical poems, and popular songs.

Like similar tales, the basic story of "Coyote and Rabbit" leads to a moral lesson. The simple, short sentences and lines have power and authority. Imagine the words read slowly, the tale unfolding one word at a time. Perhaps the directness makes it feel less musical, but these words are resonant. The repeated words ("Rabbit" appears in three straight lines) add authority. These lines are not overflowing with resplendent images, nor is the story particularly complex. What is effective is the gravity of the voice driving the piece. There is confidence in this simplicity.

Understanding storytelling puts the writer in control of both "story" (how to shape a narrative) and "telling" (how to use musicality and voice to create a compelling creative work). As crucial as they are to all types of creative writing, these elements help shape the unique relationship between fiction and poetry. This relationship provides a path for us to better understand and learn about both genres. It even creates a separate genre—the prose poem (as examined at the end of this chapter).

Writing Practice

Think about a specific event that happened to you recently. It does not have to be a particularly noteworthy event, just something that happened.

Now, write it down with an ear toward the oral tradition. Keep your sentences short and authoritative, mimicking the sound of a steady drumbeat.

When you have finished describing this story, read it aloud. How does the simplicity and pattern of what you have written come across?

What Fiction Teaches Us about Poems

Poetry is intimidating to many writers, even those who have successfully written prose, plays, or screenplays. To these writers, poetry is an almost mysterious genre—difficult to read and write. It feels like a genre apart from and uninterested in other genres. This is both untrue and a problem. How can we better understand a genre if it does not feel approachable? The solution is to simply relax. A poem does not have to follow any rules to be successful, nor does it need to tie back to Chaucer, Shakespeare, and Dickinson. It simply needs to exist. Writers often worry about sullying the good name of poetry but rarely think about doing the same with fiction. There is nothing to sully; as with any genre, just write.

The best way for writers to think about poetry is to consider how they would write anything else. A fiction writer has ideas, and then, thanks to the magic of paragraphs, those ideas develop. With poetry, a writer describes something—an image, a moment, or a feeling—and the poem progresses thanks to lines and metaphors. When writing a fiction piece, a writer thinks about story and characters, and likely does not dwell upon the romantic idea of being a "writer of fiction." This is smart—a fiction writer should not linger on their identity as a fiction writer. The writer should simply write. The word for a person who writes fiction is "writer." When we write fiction, we are simply writing.

The word for someone who writes a poem is not traditionally "writer." It is "poet." "Fictionist" is a word but not used often. And while "novelist" is a description for those who write novels, calling a writer of novels a "writer" does not feel jarring. This is not so for "writer" and "poet," two words that feel less synonymous. This book avoids the word "poet," and, while "poetry writer" may seem clunky, this book is about intersecting and celebrating genres—not creating valueless distinctions. The genres matter, but writers should not limit themselves to a single genre.

Admittedly, this is semantics—there is not much at stake in the word choices for describing certain genre writers. Unless, of course, there is. One of the first things we can learn from fiction is that writers are writers. When people share the names of their favorite fiction writers, the answers are limitless and incredibly subjective. These replies will emerge from personal preference and, often, on preferred fiction genres (like fantasy or science fiction). If asked to list great poetry writers, the answers are typically less subjective—Shakespeare, Dickinson, Yeats, and other oft-taught writers. The list of great poetry writers comes from canonical work; the favored fiction writers come from subjective experience. Knowledge of poetry often comes from a limited range of exposure—too many developing poetry writers simply have not read enough poetry. Too many writers lack confidence in poetry—both in study and in composition—thus defaulting to famous names rather than what they have personally discovered. Certain fiction writers also carry larger-than-life mystiques, but the work is always what matters—fiction is, after all, about characters and stories. Writers benefit from reading as much as possible. Poetry writers must realize this too. Simply reading work from the early twentieth century and prior is not enough to understand the craft—nor is it sufficient to read only recent Twitter poems. All writers need balance.

A crucial balance is between *story* and *telling*. Great fiction provides a great story, compellingly told. A short story or book can have a fantastic plot idea, but it will fail if it lacks effective storytelling. How does one compellingly tell a story? First, through language that comes alive on the page. Writing should have unexpected and exciting language that sounds good when read aloud. Boring language makes for dull fiction.

While we may equate this kind of compelling language to poetry, it is a disservice to fiction to assume that poetry always has interesting language and fiction does not. Good fiction can have the lyric swagger that we should expect from poems. Here is an excerpt from the novel *Kalyana*, by Indo-Fijian Canadian writer Rajni Mala Khelawan:

> I could see the sun rise from our kitchen window. It always started with a speck of deep orange far in the distance. Slowly the speck would become larger and larger, at last spreading across the sky in a brilliant fan. Then it seemed as though all of Fiji would light up. Birds would chirp. Caterpillars would awaken, stretching and yawning, wriggling their little bodies along leaves and twigs. Frogs would croak to clear their throats. Butterflies would spread their wings as the lizards disappeared into their holes. And the newspapers—they would lay claim that theirs was the first newspaper published in the world that day.
>
> When I was younger, I thought this meant that *The Fiji Times* was the first newspaper ever published in the world. Mother had always said, "News reporters, Kalyana, have the best job in the world. Through the mighty power released from their pens, they can bridge the gap between solace and pain." Because of mother, I never doubted that news reporters were important people who were granted the duty to change humanity and erase its suffering. It made me so proud to have been born in a country that had discovered the business of printing news, the trade of exchanging stories. As I grew older though, I began to realize that I was terribly wrong: *The Fiji Times* did not discover the business of printing news. It was merely insisting that Fiji was the place that saw the first light of day.
>
> Worse, years later, when all the timekeepers joined together to measure exactly which place on the globe saw the first morning light, a small island by New Zealand took the centuries-old title. The Fiji Islanders wept and scrambled to modify their timekeeping sheets, but alas! The truth was clear: Fiji was not the place where the first day of the entire world began.

This excerpt tells its story in unexpected ways: with a catalogue of creatures to give the reader a glimpse of life in Fiji, a story of something the speaker heard when she was younger, and a series of realizations that caused her to question things she thought she knew about her home island. There is a beginning (the dawn of day), a middle (the things the speaker believed to be true), and an ending (the reality of what she had believed). The *story* part of this excerpt is clear.

But the *telling* is where things come alive. First, the piece begins with a clear indication of the morning: "I could see the sun rise from our kitchen window." The language here is simple and straightforward. That does not mean it lacks lively language. Even in this seemingly simple sentence, Khelawan delivers language that emphasizes sound. Listen for those "S" sounds that start the paragraph: "see," "sun," and "rise." These are three of the first six words and that sets up a repeated lulling sound to show us how the speaker's day begins in Fiji. There is a relaxed and leisurely nature to the word sounds. While "could" and "kitchen" both have harsher sounds (think of how both words begin with a clicking sound), the rest of the sentence lulls with softer "S" and "W" sounds. This continues with the second sentence: "It always started with a speck of deep orange far in the distance." More of those "S" sounds—"it always started with a speck" is lulling and lively. Clicking sounds (like "K" and "T") appear in this sentence, but "speck" is softened by both the "S" sounds at the beginning and the slow movement of "deep orange" that follows. The language invites us into a lazy morning.

As the excerpt continues, the lulling language shifts. At the beginning, the language is intoxicating—the descriptions of animals and creatures on the island are musical and active, with verbs that dance across the page, allowing the reader to visualize the creatures' appearances and movements. As it progresses, however, things shift. By the third paragraph, the language loses some of its grace when the speaker acknowledges the loss of innocence that comes from realizing that so many of the things she believed were untrue. Instead of harsher sounds softened by constant lulling "S" sounds, the final two sentences reverse the sound patterns. The "S" sounds are present but less lulling because of harder sounds and punctuation choices. For example, the second-to-last sentence in this excerpt ends with "sheets, but alas!" There are three "S" sounds here in four syllables—this should create that same lulling sound we traced at the onset. But it does not. Why not? First, because "T" sounds in "sheets" and "but" overwhelm the "S" sounds. The "K" sounds discussed earlier blended into the softer sounds, but the comma after "sheets" forces the reader to pause before "but," not allowing the lulling sounds to gracefully continue. That forces us to pause on "but," making it a harsh sound. Finally, the exclamation point at the end forces us to accentuate the "s" at the end of "alas" more dramatically. Khelawan asks us to yell the word. There is not a lull—it is a cry. The tonal shift helps us understand the emotional weight of the final sentence—the speaker is not only realizing the lie behind what she thought was true, but the entire island population is learning the same. This is not just a coming-of-age revelation for a single character—it is an island full of people dealing with this revelation. The stakes are high; the leisurely morning is no more.

We expect to examine poetic language with a careful and in-depth eye, but good fiction also stands up to such scrutiny. Good poetic fiction still maintains storytelling elements and builds characters, and is a pivotal tool for writers of poetry. Beautiful language is not for poetry writers alone, but compelling storytelling is not unique to fiction. Poetry and fiction both should tell great stories with the type of beautiful language they both deserve.

Explorations

- What does Khelawan gain from the long description of the morning in this excerpt? In what way does this description benefit the piece?
- We get a clear sense of how the speaker's mother celebrated the value of writing and journalism. Why do you think Khelawan spends time describing this perspective and how does it affect the speaker?

Creative Response

- This excerpt shows examples of things the speaker believed as a child but realized eventually in life were untrue. Write a few paragraphs that explore a character who similarly discovers that beliefs they held as a child are not what they originally thought. Make sure to show how this revelation affects your character.

- Write a piece that begins with the dawn. Think about the specific location of this sunrise (it can be a place you know well or one you have imagined) and, using Khelawan's excerpt as a guide, provide specifics of what makes mornings in this place unique.

What Poems Teach Us about Fiction

Explicit and implied **cues** give the reader insight into how something should be read. They are common in fiction and poetry, and guide the writer. In fiction, the writer composes in paragraphs, knows characters make conscious choices, and creates a plot to carry things forward. Knowing each of these things *cues* the writer on how to write fiction.

In poetry, these cues are often viewed as obstacles. Instead of seeing genre expectations as tools to accomplish great things, poetry writers often see these equivalent cues (line breaks, stanzas, musicality) as hurdles. If a fiction writer thinks *I've got a great idea for a story—I'm going to jot down my thoughts,* why should the poetry writer think, *I've got a great idea for a poem—now, let me mentally scroll through a dozen possible formal structures and then meditate on where this poem fits canonically?* Poetry writers need not put unnecessary pressure on themselves during the drafting stage.

All writing is part of a longer journey. Mary Oliver, the great American poetry writer, explains, "Poetry is a river; many voices travel in it; poem after poem moves along in the exciting crests and falls of the river waves." It is intimidating if that river is filled exclusively with the voices of writers who lived 100 years prior (at the most recent). Fiction writers do not always think this way—they may think, yes, I am writing novels like Virginia Woolf before me, or short stories like Anton Chekov once did, but they will also think of more contemporary work that inspired them. The mystique of poetry often causes writers to overlook the present in favor of the past. This is a mistake that, typically, fiction writers do not make. This is a crucial lesson to learn.

It is important to admire the work of other writers but we should *learn* from those writers, not feel inadequate because they existed. We learn from the writers around us, both from earlier eras and from our own. We find our own voices, but we should never hesitate to listen to the voices around us. When we read a writer who impresses us, whether a contemporary romance writer or seventeenth-century English metaphysical poetry writer, we should never think, *this other writer is so good, there's no reason for me to write anymore*! Instead, we should think, *what is it that I like so much about this, and how can I find a way to fit that into my work?* One of the most effective ways to accomplish that is through imitation.

Imitation is taking some aspect of another's work to learn how to write in a new way. When we imitate, we use someone else's work as a blueprint for our creations. Imitation can feel like cheating to some writers, but it is not. An imitation poem is not about copying what is most apparent about another writer. After reading several poems from a writer who has earned the reader's adoration, that reader should try to write an imitation poem and write their way into understanding what they admire about the work.

Imitation poems are simple—take and use something from someone else's poem as an inspiration for your own. It could be a similar theme, topic, or structure. If an imitation poem is simple, writing an imitation story should be too. All writers begin from the shadows of work they admire. As writers continue in their field, they will forge a unique and independent voice, but finding that voice does not need to happen quickly. Instead, a writer should find threads in the work they admire and find out how to weave those into something uniquely their own. A successful imitative work may have similarities to the original but will be unique to the writer.

If a writer is imitating ideas to create something new, that is not plagiarism—it is a journey to finding one's work through the experience of other writing. Remember, imitations are not necessarily a method for creating outstanding unique work—they are ideal practice for trying something new. Everything you write is important because it leads you to whatever you write next. Imitation poems are a great tool to help your journey.

Here is a poem by the Canadian writer Kathryn Mockler:

The Seance

—The spirits at my seance are not allowed to talk about the 1960s or how cellphones have changed the way we communicate. In fact, there should be no discussion of technology at all. The colour schedule for my séance will be yellow and red.

—Are you at all worried people won't come to your séance and that in the end no one really cares?

—Even murderers are interested in spirits. Even murderers will take the time to talk to the dead. Sometimes they'll leave a tip or a little note with their phone number on it.

—Do spirits get worked up if they don't like the menu or don't feel up to having something to eat?

—Spirits are always courteous to the waitress. They almost never slap her ass or attack her on the way to the car from the parking garage.

—Do spirits mind telling you how much money they make in a year or how often they get paid?
—Sometimes spirits are snobs, but don't let that discourage you.

Mockler's poem provides multiple jumping-off points for imitation. There is a formal structure (prose stanzas that each begin with a dash), personality in the poem's voice, humor, social commentary, and a clearly defined narrative situation, just to name a few possible places. Any of these things (and assuredly others) could serve as a viable inspiration for an imitation poem.

The scenario of the poem (which begins with rules about what spirits at the speaker's séance are not allowed to discuss) is unexpected and absurd. An imitation poem of this piece could start with a ridiculous scenario somewhat related to the poem (like a poem set at a zoo where guests are not allowed to read poetry to the animals) or something equally absurd and seemingly unrelated to Mockler's poem.

Or maybe a writer will take a section of the poem and be inspired that—for example, the fifth stanza talks about the spirits being "courteous to the waitress" and not physically assaulting her. Perhaps this socially charged stanza inspires the imitation writer to follow that thread. Short of copying the poem verbatim, there is no *wrong* way to imitate. Read the poem, find a place to enter it, and try something new. That is the only expectation.

Writing Practice

Write an imitation poem of Mockler's "The Séance."
Again, there is no wrong way to do this—you can follow her subject matter, her formatting, her sounds—you just need to create something uniquely yours that uses this poem as its starting point.

Embracing the Narrative

Poems can be about anything. And if poems can be about anything, it follows that they could be about stories. Two of the most common structures for contemporary poetry are **lyric** and **narrative** poems. The lyric poem is typically short and focuses on a single (or limited) image or idea. A narrative poem generally is longer and more interested in storytelling. Understanding what makes for a good story in fiction will logically lead us to know how to tell a good story in a narrative poem.

Poetry is difficult to define, but one of the most appropriate definitions is that poetry is a verbal art form. Unlike other forms of writing, poetry is almost always meant to be read aloud. Some writers will be conscious of this, reading their drafts aloud to understand how the musicality of a piece is developing. However, even the writers who do not do this think in terms of sound, ensuring the poem's words are coalescing so that the poem benefits. Maybe these writers only hear sounds in their heads as they write, but

Intersecting Genre

the effect is the same. When writing a poem, a writer constantly *listens* to the words, even when not saying those words aloud.

Fiction is different. A fiction writer is not necessarily thinking of sounds—instead, they develop their characters and plots. The sound of the words, so integral in writing a poem, seems less essential to a prose writer. Poems need to sound good, and fiction needs to tell compelling stories. But *everything* should sound good and be compelling.

When writing, it is entirely normal to *feel* something. It would be strange if a writer constructing a creative work were unemotional as they did so. What types of things does a writer feel as they write? They can feel frustrated if ideas and words are not coming as quickly as possible. They can feel sad writing something emotionally challenging or happy when creating a more uplifting moment. Writers can also feel energized as they write, finding excitement after a particularly successful effort. What would make a fiction writer feel excitement as they write? Perhaps the execution of an exciting plot development? An emotional scene built up throughout the piece?

What about a writer creating a poem? What gets them excited? A powerful metaphor? Maybe a line that dances across the page with alliteration? A fiction writer can learn from writing poetry that the language and content of a given piece should not be independent of each other.

The Hybrid: Prose Poems

Emotional reactions are essential in poems. Except when they are not. And poems rhyme. Except when they do not. And they are always musical except for those times when they are not. And poems are always broken into lines, except when . . . well, you get it.

A prose poem is a poem that is not broken into lines and is instead a block of prose. Prose poems are a wonderful place to emphasize the relationship between these two genres. Prose poems are the specific intersection between two genres, so it should be no surprise that there is no particular formula for what a prose poem can be. In simplest terms, some prose poems are more prose than poem, and some are more poem than prose. Even simpler, some prose poems emphasize story over language, while some emphasize play with language over everything else.

Here are two prose poems by Australian writers Alison Croggon and Eileen Chong. Both poems represent a different take on the prose poem, though, obviously, no two poems could ever show us the full possibilities inherent in the form, especially a form as open to interpretation as the prose poem. Here is the first, by Alison Croggon:

The poet has no identity

The poet has no identity. She is an electrical cloud she is a swarm of bees she is a kabuki scream she is a shadow on the blind the plates in the cupboard the roar of trucks on a freeway. She is the fiery neurone and the mark on a piece of paper.

She speaks on the telephone into the ether. No one there. Maybe it is god. She writes her body with the tips of her fingers but it is no longer her body. The words are not her they belong to nobody. She writes to slough off her name. She speaks to become invisible. She desires to become what she is. When she wakes into her name it is falling asleep again. When she dreams she forgets. She is blind. She has the power of flight.

Croggon's prose poem defies the conventional expectations of prose. Not every prose poem disregards these "rules" of prose, of course, but many choose to forsake traditional sentence-level prose expectations to instead play around with the potential of language. The second sentence of this poem is a tour de force that reflects this—a collision of metaphor-driven run-on fragments that tell the larger tale of the character's plight (and, more broadly, women who write poetry). Commas or semicolons would only slow the furious momentum of the sentence—Croggon's approach propels the reader forward in an exhilarating way—before the reader is aware of the sentence's propulsion, that reader is in too deep to go back. In this way, the poem grants the same sense of overwhelm that the "poet" is feeling.

After that sentence, the poem reconfigures to more standard sentence structures. This serves to disorient the reader but never allows the reader to feel steady, even when the sentences become shorter and more conventional. Instead, the sentences become more concise and, by the end, somewhat choppy. Thinking musically, this invites a **staccato** effect (a musical term that describes notes that sharply differ from one another and create a jagged sound). Contrasting with staccato is **legato** (a musical term that emphasizes smoothness and consistency), and this poem's smoothness emerges somewhat in that second sentence (which, despite its grammatical "rule-breaking," is tonally consistent with itself) that carries to the third ("She is the fiery neurone and the mark on the piece of paper"). This third sentence eases the reader into the comforting sense of legato before jerking them back into the more erratic sentences that stagger the poem to its conclusion. This pacing fits perfectly for a poem that ambitiously depicts the many challenges and goals of poetry writers, specifically women.

Writing Practice

Metaphors are expressions that compare something in a piece of writing to something unrelated, and the unlikely comparison will give the reader a greater understanding of the first thing. Metaphors propel Croggon's poem. As in Croggon's poem, a metaphor uses the word "is"— "The book is a knife." Similarly, a **simile** uses "like" or "as"— "The book is like a knife."

Think of everyday objects and create metaphors (or similes) for them. Combine a few in a single paragraph and see what stands out to you. Does it feel cohesive? Do some stand out as more robust than others? Is there any kind of story woven through your metaphors?

Intersecting Genre

Here is another prose poem, this time by Eileen Chong:

> **Green Grief**
>
> I heard about your wedding in a Catholic church so much food and wine live jazz band how you'd lost all that weight everyone so happy. Revenge fantasies: you fell off a cliff got run over by a truck you were buried up to your neck drizzled with honey and left for the ants your plane went down over the Pacific you had a heart attack you were shot in the eyes. You see, poets have this thing for truth. The memory of crying so hard I threw up but in the shower so you wouldn't hear through there was no door on the bathroom. My therapist says I had a choice I probably was the problem I couldn't be the woman who would sit down and shut up or stand in a cupboard all day waiting until you got home and unlocked it. In my dream you were in my house and my friend who is also a poet said I have to tell you to vacate the premises because you would never ever acknowledge what you did to me. Larkin said *Last year is dead* and to *Begin afresh, afresh, afresh*. Repetition here is key.

This prose poem by Chong is more like a story than Croggon's because it is more narratively driven, but, like Croggon's, it does not follow standard punctuation guidelines. There is a story here, but the lack of commas makes it feel freer than it would otherwise. In addition to the lack of commas, there is chaotic energy driven by multiple uses of "and"—they build the prose poem upon itself, creating a frenetic energy. In most prose situations, run-on sentences qualify as punctuational rule-breaking, but in this case, it feels less like rule-breaking and more like the exploration of energetic and imaginative thought. When encountering a challenging poem (or any genre), it is wise to read it aloud. On the page, the poem is challenging; aloud, it is exhilarating.

This prose poem mentions "revenge fantasies." These chaotic sentences about these "fantasies" give us a sense of the speaker's mental state. This prose poem shows us the potential of any piece of writing—the words we use should never just be about conveying a plot or story—those words are an opportunity for a piece of writing to go deeper.

> ### Writing Practice
>
> Revenge is a theme of Chong's prose poem, with a portion of the poem describing "revenge fantasies." Typically, we do not see revenge as a noble pursuit, but creative writing can create new possibilities. For this writing exercise, write a prose poem with the title "Revenge," in which the prose poem depicts a more positive experience than the title would suggest. If the piece's content contradicts the title, that is okay. Sometimes when we write, we are looking to find those exciting places where things seem at odds but still somehow connect.

Summary

Imagining poetry and fiction on opposite ends of the creative writing spectrum is easy. But, in truth, these genres are so similar that there is much to find in common. Both genres benefit from compelling lyrical language, and writers can imitate other writers they admire in either genre. Writing is about telling and listening—striving to improve our ability to tell stories, and listening to become better writers.

A place where these genres intersect is prose poetry, and these poems are ideal places to practice our skills in poetry and fiction because they embody both genres. Rather than just being about sticking together parts of both, however, prose poems are ideal places for experimentation, including unorthodox approaches to grammar, syntax, and language.

Writing Wrap-Up

Write two short prose poems about the same moment from your childhood. In the first, write about that event as if described by someone uninvolved in it. In the second, write about the exact moment, but do it from your perspective, giving us emotional insights that would be impossible in the first prose poem.

CHAPTER 4
THE STAGE ON WHICH WE STAND
INTERSECTIONS BETWEEN CREATIVE NON-FICTION AND PLAYS

Writing plays requires a specific understanding of the **stage**, a play's physical, often literally elevated, space. A play cannot work effectively unless the writer properly considers and integrates the stage.

What exactly does this mean? The writer must acquiesce to the construct of the stage to write effectively. A play is not just about dialogue and actions. It is also about *where* the dialogue and actions take place. Anything can serve as a stage—if there is enough room in any indoor or outdoor space, it can become a stage. A play writer must create with an eye toward the stage, lest the play become a mess of unfocused words and instructions.

It might seem premature to fixate upon the eventual performance of a given piece of writing before writing it, but it is not. The stage is essential. A step in writing an effective play is being conscious that it is a play (and not some other form). When viewers watch a play, they focus on the stage and subconsciously agree that what happens on that stage is not a lie. They know a play is not a real-life event—accepting this is called suspension of disbelief. All readers and audiences suspend disbelief when they read or watch something. What you are watching (or reading) is a form of artifice—your imagination makes it real. In reality, you are reading words or watching a performance. Suppose you are watching a play that depicts a murder onstage, and you simply sit there incredulously explaining to everyone around you that it is all fake. In that case, you will not enjoy the experience, nor will anyone sitting near you. If you are watching that same play and do not realize that what you are seeing is a play, you can either slip into the lobby to call the authorities or sit there as a complicit party.

The playwright must be acutely aware of the stage and think about how the characters will move and sound on it. The writer must deeply consider the audience's expectations of theater performances in general and how best to engage that audience into their specific play. Writing plays is an active form that asks a writer to collaborate with those who stage the play and the audience who watches. We ask a play writer to consider seemingly endless factors when creating their work.

How do we ask creative non-fiction writers to write? *Just go ahead and share the experience*, the CNF writer might hear. Advice for CNF writers is often generic—write with a strong voice and be well-versed on the chosen subject. Not bad advice, but it could help anyone write anything, not just CNF writers. When advice gets more particular, it is often about factual information. This is important for the genre—the impact of what

Intersecting Genre

"truth" means is significant for CNF. It is important for other genres, too (including plays). Just telling a CNF writer that factual accuracy is crucial does not help. Play writers are given specific philosophical and practical advice before and during the writing of a play. CNF writers can get the impression what they are writing is simply fiction, just true. It is so much more than that.

Understanding how the methods and philosophies of writing original plays can apply to creative non-fiction writers will help writers see that writing good CNF is more complicated and also full of more possibilities than it might initially seem. Characters and truths populate plays and CNF, but each genre takes a different path in reaching those characters and depicting those truths. Learning how each genre achieves its goals will benefit writers in any genre.

Writing Warm-Up

Imagine a moment in your life when you proudly accomplished something. Now, imagine that moment taking place on a stage in front of others. Does that change the moment? What if you took an embarrassing or difficult moment from your life and depicted that on a stage?

Try to depict a moment from your life—great, terrible, or somewhere in-between—and write it out as a short play scene (you can keep it informal or flip over to the formatting guide for plays in Chapter 11 for some guidance). You can try for accuracy in what was said and what happened, but mostly you should try to recreate what mattered most about the moment. After you have finished, think about what is similar and different between what you wrote and how the memory plays in your mind.

The Stage

American teacher and play writer Michael Wright explains that even an empty stage is a valuable artifact because of its potential to harness imagination. In his book *Playwrighting in Process*, Wright explains, "I can sit in an empty auditorium and look at a blank stage and conjure the endless possibilities for that space." So, when writing plays, a writer should see the stage as a gift—an opportunity that will provide a clear and concise anchor for the ideas that drive a play. This stands in contrast to the concept of a writer staring at a blank screen or page, desperate for inspiration. The stage is an active space of inspiration and motivation.

The stage is not just a device. It is a clearly defined way to think about work in process and a concrete tool that can propel imagination. Even if a writer working on a play does not know who will perform it, what the stage crew will construct, or how the director will fully envision the work, the stage is grounding. No matter what else happens with an eventually performed play, it will occur on a stage.

This is no small thing. Plays have a physical and concrete reality because the stage is real. After a play, you could conceivably come to the front of a theater, touch the stage, and think, *this is where the written play came to life*. This is not possible with the other genres. You can touch a book and perhaps feel a spiritual connection, but a reader is not privy to the book's physical world as is a theatergoer. A film or TV series can trick us into thinking a fully realized screenplay is as visceral as seeing a play performed on a stage, but it is not. A film version of a stage play usually erases the stage, thus removing its theatrical artificiality and putting it into the screen's version of "realism."

The aforementioned example does not include filmed versions of stage productions. When done well, these can give viewers insight unattainable by an audience member in a theater—such as character close-ups—but the immediacy is lost. A stage is not "lesser" nor an apology—it is a promise of visceral immediacy.

So the physical stage is unique to the writing of plays. That might be true, but perhaps there are ways to share this remarkable aspect of plays with another genre.

For this to happen, the CNF writer needs to leap. We cannot fully replicate the stage for a genre that exists from early draft to complete draft to a final published version on the physical page, an ebook reader, or the internet. So the leap requires the writer to envision the CNF piece as a tangible artifact.

Writing Practice

Write a play scene set on a sparse stage—there are two chairs, but the characters do not have to sit. In this scene, you have two characters—one is you, and the other is a younger version of you. You decide how young. In this scene, have your two characters talk about anything—the younger one can ask for advice, and the other version of you can offer warnings—but make sure everything that happens in the scene is honest to the parameters of CNF.

What CNF Teaches Us about Plays

Creative writing does not work without stories, and stories do not work without characters. Studying great CNF characters (including from memoirs) and learning how to structure successful characters on the page in a CNF essay or book will lead to understanding how best to do it on the stage.

There might be reservations about using the word "character" in non-fiction. It is reasonable to think that someone might be skeptical of seeing true-life flesh and blood people reduced to being called "characters." There is some logic to this—we see characters in creative writing, not as people, but as stand-ins for people—"a person portrayed in an artistic piece," as the *American Heritage Dictionary* says. So if a character is a facsimile of a person designed to make the reader understand real people's emotional challenges and struggles, how does one address character-building in CNF? If a character is based on a real person, has it not already been "built"?

First, it is essential to acknowledge the real people who inspire characters in a memoir or other piece of CNF are *not* the characters in the memoir itself. This is obvious but important. The framed photograph of their partner a person has on their desk is not the person. The picture is a replica of the person. No one would show that picture to others and pretend the person in the photograph was their real-life partner. Instead, they would say, "here's a picture of my partner," and the person seeing the photo would unconsciously acknowledge it is a replica. Even if someone slides open their phone to show a friend a photograph and omits the phrase "a picture"— saying, "here's my partner"—no one will be confused by the photograph and think the picture is the actual person.

As innate as this understanding is, writers still have trouble with it in CNF. "That's my grandmother I'm writing about," a writer might say. "She's not a character. She's my Nana." But if the reader has not met the writer's grandmother, never sat down to chat with her over ice cream, or watched Wimbledon with her, the only way the reader will know her is as a character in the CNF work. She may be the writer's grandmother, but she becomes a character in the story.

The word "character" can get a bad reputation because of implied inauthenticity, as if a character is a lie. But a character is not a lie—a character represents someone either authentically real or inauthentically real. The writer's grandmother is real, so the character of "Nana" in a CNF piece represents a real person. As stated earlier, it is not Nana but a recreation. A fictionalized grandmother in a fiction work is inauthentically real—she is a representation of living people, even if no one specific person inspired her creation. Both CNF and fictional grandmothers are based on reality, even if only one represents an actual person.

This is important. It is easy to think that a character in a CNF piece is real, and a character in a fiction piece is fake, but calling a character "fake" is both reductive and damaging to a work's integrity. In a purely factual way, a character in a fictional play is "fake." But is this character based on something from reality? Was the writer thinking of some definite aspects of humanity while constructing this character? Of course. Whether a character exists for realistic fiction or fantasy fiction, they derive from real people and personalities. If not, the audience would not know how to respond to a character, and that character would be inauthentic. So even if a character is a strange alien in a science fiction piece, a writer who knows how to create a successful piece of creative writing will ground that strange alien with relatable characteristics. No matter how non-human a character is, it will not work unless the reader can feel something human in that character.

It is crucial to think about how CNF writers shape great characters. Writers create from their memories. If a character feels genuine, it is because the writer has given the character voice, actions, and motivations that feel valid. And they *are* valid because the person the character was based on did those things. How can a play writer constructing a made-up character benefit from the process of character-building that allows a CNF writer to achieve solid and relatable characters?

The Stage on Which We Stand

There are three main ways CNF writers develop characters:

1) A CNF writer is not pulling characters out of thin air because they do not have to. They recreate specific living people who have traits, styles, and personalities.
2) There are boundaries for a CNF character based on the real person's life.
3) CNF characters have clearly defined wants and needs because the real person does (or did). A given text might not explore every desire and need, but that information is available through memories and research (as is everything a writer might need to create a complete character).

For the play writer constructing fictional characters, reality is not essential to character-building, but the illusion of reality is necessary. CNF teaches that compelling characters are not simply about the traits that exist on the page. The CNF writer gets to pull from the full character's life when appropriate. To create fully fleshed-out characters in drama, a writer needs to know those characters as much as a CNF writer knows the real person they are developing into a character.

A writer can depict a vibrant personality in a play, but the process must begin early. A character needs to develop over time through notes and character sketches. A play writer rarely starts a serious draft without having a clear sense of the plot or story. But a writer might not have any problem jumping right into a character and assuming that they will figure out that character as they go. This is a mistake. As with plot, a writer should begin the work with a clear sense of their characters (which can evolve over a draft).

What We Know about Our Characters

In 1958, during a question-and-answer session in a graduate literature class, one of the attendees asked American writer William Faulkner about characters and how best to transfer a character from a writer's mind to the page. Faulkner's response is essential:

> I would say to get the character in your mind. Once he is in your mind, and he is right, and he's true, then he does the work himself. All you need to do then is to trot along behind him and put down what he does and what he says. It's the—the ingestion and then the gestation. You've got to know the character. You've got to believe in him. You've got to—to feel that—that what—that he is—is alive, and then, of course, you will have to do a certain amount of—of picking and choosing among the possibilities of his action, so that his actions fit the character which you believe in. After that, the—the—the business of putting him down on paper is mechanical. It's—I think, most of the—the writing has got to take place up here before you ever put the pencil to the paper. But the character's got to be true by your conception and by your experience, and that would include, as we've just said, what you've read, what you've imagined, what you've heard, all that is going

to giving you the gauge to measure this imaginary character by, and once he comes alive and true to you, and—and he's important and moving, then it's not too much trouble to put him down.

So, according to Faulkner, the first step to writing is to know your characters. Even if a character is fictional (as Faulkner's characters were), a writer must learn as much as possible to reach the point of "picking and choosing among the possibilities" of what a character can do. No person will always behave the same way in every situation, and neither will a character. The writer must understand *why* the character makes certain choices. Faulkner thinks that character-creation happens before the creative work itself is composed. Thus, instead of making up character traits and beats throughout a story, the writer already knows these things and can simply "trot along beside" the character. The writer does much more than that, but Faulkner's central idea that "the writing has got to take place up here before you ever put the pencil to the paper" is an effective way to remember how vital character-building is. It is an imaginative act that occurs early in the writing process.

So to create a character (human or otherwise) that behaves in human ways regardless of what situations occur, the writer needs to know as much about them as possible. It might seem like an impossible task to know so much about a single character, but it is not as ridiculous as it might seem. We might not know as much as we think about people we know well, yet we could still write compelling narratives about them.

Writing Practice

Start with the CNF side of character-building. For five minutes, write down as much as you can about someone you know. Maybe it should not be somebody with whom you are incredibly close (like a parent, partner, or close sibling) but someone you still know well. While writing everything you can in those five minutes, keep it to clear and direct facts, like physical features, personality, personal history, and interests. Avoid writing more detailed memories and stories. Those would be incredibly relevant in a longer essay, but this exercise is just about getting as much as possible across quickly. It might be a good idea to write this information down as a list rather than paragraphs to avoid writing too much of a narrative.

After you have finished this list, take a look. Did you come up with a lot of details? There may have been moments when you were uncertain of what to say next. This is normal. When writing about yourself, you might feel like you know too much to paint an honest picture, and it is hard to know where to begin. If you are writing about someone else, you might know less than you think. This is not a bad thing—you realize a writer can say a lot about a person they know well without knowing *everything*. A writer building a fictional character should not have to know everything either, just enough to create a full portrait.

Effective Character Sketching

Every level of writing benefits from **character sketches**, the act of writing down biographical character ideas in the developmental stage of drafting. The structure for the sketch will change depending on the writer's level, but the purpose is to construct a clear and direct backstory for a character. The word "sketch" evokes the sense of illustration and, while drawing an image (or multiple images) is often helpful for writers to figure out who their characters are, most character sketches deal less with drawing and more with text.

There is no right or wrong way to create a character sketch. A text-based character sketch could include the following:

- Physical descriptions to visualize a character's appearance
- Personality traits
- Key personal history moments
- Significant relationships with other characters

While the aforementioned categories are essential because they build the base for the character-building, the following items can also be helpful in a sketch:

- Patterns of speech and familiar verbal expressions
- Likes and dislikes
- Pop culture interests
- Less essential personal history moments
- Less crucial relationships with other characters

Personal moments could also be elaborated upon and developed so that the writer has a clearer sense of a character's defining memories. A character sketch could be bullet points, a series of vignettes, or journal entries—what matters is that a writer builds a solid working knowledge of their characters.

Going Further

There should never be an expectation that everything you write will end up in a final draft. While this is logical, writers still find themselves so attached to their writing that they do not want to let any of it go. If a writer decides to write out memories from a character's perspective to help flesh that character out, that is not something they will automatically need to include in the text. They could, but they do not have to.

Writers must write a lot. When we see a full-length play or even a ten-minute play, it is easy to forget that for every word in the play, potentially a dozen other words were written in service of that word. Some of these cut words and phrases could result from revision and editing, but much of it will be because of character sketching and establishing background information.

What Plays Teach us About CNF

If the stage is a physical entity that frames a play, then sets and settings propel it forward. Sets and settings are similar but different enough to warrant distinction. A **set** is the collection of physical objects (both large and small) that establish a scene on stage. The **setting** is broader than that—it is the time and place in which a play (or another piece of writing) occurs. The set is specific and tangible—items indicating a location can include a couch, a bookshelf, and a rocking chair. The setting, however, defines everything. If the play takes place in London in 1632, the couch, bookshelf, and rocking chair will look a lot different than if it happens in Detroit in 1978. Still, if the setting of a play explains the action is taking place in a family home today, that tells us very little. What is the family's economic class? Are they a retired couple or a young family with kids? The setting determines the set.

This is valuable in other forms of creative writing because prose and poetry writers often consider setting intentionally and set decoratively, meaning the setting is well thought out, but very little is *shown* of the set. In other cases, the writer provides too much set and not enough setting—the details of a specific scene are exact and plentiful, but the reader is unsure what those details mean. Good writing embraces both. Here is a paragraph that embraces setting and not set:

> It was 2002 as I walked home from school, desperate to escape my day's struggles. I was bullied, again, for being new, small, and quiet, though I knew they would find some other reason to bully me if I wasn't so new, small, and quiet. Even though both cities were in Minnesota, Minneapolis was such a bigger city than my hometown of Hastings. Everything was bigger and more complex than what we had left behind.

The basics of the speaker's situation are present—that is the setting. We know where it takes place (Minneapolis, Minnesota), when (2002), and a little about the circumstance (the speaker is in school and bullied). But the setting does not add set, and the background information ends before the writer provides details. Here, the essay continues with an emphasis on setting replaced by an overabundance of set:

> When I got home to my family's three-bedroom suburban home, I placed my hand on the silver doorknob, and opened the blue door slowly. I walked inside

and was immediately greeted by family photos adorning the walls. Then I took off my red backpack and hung it on the cherry wood coat rack near the entryway. Turning to my left, I entered the kitchen. Everything was painted white with a bit of blue trimming around the cabinets. The white stools in front of the kitchen island called to me, and I took my faded blue jean jacket and tossed it on top of the smooth white stool and thought about my day.

We have now erred in the other direction. The reader has details—set descriptions—but they do not add up to anything. This paragraph would benefit significantly from additional character insight and perspective, but there is so much detail that it might overwhelm even that much-desired character insight.

In a play, a writer can provide a very detailed set of directions. Alternatively, a writer can provide sparse guidance and let the director figure things out. It matters little because the play's text is not something a play audience will see. It is a tool. The director reads the stage directions and understands what the setting and set can be, but the audience can only see the final set as the director and stage manager (among others) interpret it. This means a writer needs to be clear in regard to setting and set—whatever the writer sees as essential needs to be present. Otherwise, the collaborators who follow the screenplay might not realize the writer's vision and do something the writer would not have wanted.

But in CNF, the reader reads what the writer writes. Nothing more, nothing less. If a play writer provides an incredibly detailed description of a particular set, it will not feel tedious to an audience because the audience does not read the set description. There needs to be a proper balance of setting and set.

Writing Practice

Think further about the difference between "set" and "setting." For this exercise, write about a character's childhood bedroom. It can be yours or an invented room. First, write a paragraph focused on "set"—describe the physical things in the space. Then, write another paragraph about "setting." Instead of identifying specific items, think about the room's location in the world and how it fits within its time and place.

What about the "set" depends on the "setting?" What specific details of the room would differ if it was in the present day rather than where it was initially. What would remain the same? Which of the two paragraphs was easier to write?

The Hybrid: Live Performance Storytelling

CNF and plays intersect whenever someone tells a story about a personal experience. Like CNF, the story depends upon what the storyteller saw and did, and like plays, an audience hears it. A person telling their partner about their day does not feel like an intersection between creative writing genres, but it is the personal experience of CNF combined with a restrained version of stage performance. "Performance" might seem inaccurate because the storyteller is sharing a story and not performing as one would from the stage, but the storyteller is engaging in the tools of performance—using pauses and inflections to build intrigue in the story and perhaps using physical cues (such as hand gestures) to emphasize different points. This intersection is exciting (and differs from both genres) because even if a storyteller knows what needs to be said, it will still be unscripted. The intersection between CNF and writing plays manifests into a unique form of storytelling.

Stand-up comedians will often discuss aspects of their personal lives from a stage, perhaps altering some details for laughs. In this way, some comedians are CNF storytellers who perform in front of audiences, but their sets (timed comedic stand-up routines) are never spontaneous, even if not formally scripted. "Unscripted" does not mean spontaneous. No successful stand-up comedian would ever get on stage wholly unprepared, but a stand-up who follows a script too tightly could run the risk of appearing unnatural and unrelatable. While there are occasions when a comedian will want a tight set that is highly polished (perhaps for a recorded special), there will also be times that if a comic's set is too rigid, it might be harder to improvise or feel natural, especially in front of a lively crowd. This is a benefit of live storytelling.

Not all comedians are CNF performers. While not always looking for laughs, live performance storytellers look for truths. An example of navigating at this intersection is The Moth. The Moth is a non-profit group that encourages people to tell stories through live events and podcasts, among other efforts. *The Moth Radio Hour* is an American public radio show that originated in 2009 and has featured a wide range of storytellers, typically in front of live audiences. These stories are autobiographical explorations of personal history performed in front of an audience and delivered with a theatrical flair that transcends the page. Notably, the stories told are live, and, while assuredly practiced, the live aspect creates an intimacy that does not exist in a polished reading. Stories told this way allow them to exist with imperfections, and that creates an emotional connection with the listener that is more difficult to earn than with something highly polished.

Live performance storytellers use various techniques to share their stories—humor, empathy, and suspense, among them. They take the stage prepared but with risk. Even if they know what they want to say, they typically have no memorized script and are emotionally vulnerable, especially considering the personal material these storytellers often share. That risk makes this hybrid so compelling—a storyteller tells a sensitive, unscripted story, and the audience feels empathy and connection.

Writing Practice

First, consider this prompt: "Think about a time when life forced you out of your comfort zone." Take a few minutes to mentally come up with ideas. After you have an idea of what to write, set a three-minute timer. During that time, write down as many ideas as you can. These ideas could be in the form of a list or paragraphs. After you have finished, briefly look over what you have written. Then close (or put away) these notes.

Now, tell your story. If possible, make a video recording. If not, stand in front of a mirror. Either way, spend a few minutes telling your story.

If you can, watch the video of yourself. Did anything you say surprise you? Did you repeat mostly what you remembered from your notes, or did you improvise? How different would your story have been if you had formally written it down?

Summary

In an interview with Richard H. Goldstone of *The Paris Review* in 1956, American play writer Thorton Wilder said, "A dramatist is one who believes that the pure event, an action involving human beings, is more arresting than any comment that can be made upon it." Even though plays contain action and movement, the human element matters most. This is why CNF and plays are so logically connected—both are concerned with the human experience in ways that define the works of both genres, and both require compelling characters.

What connects both genres as much as the shared desire to show the human condition is that both are havens for experimentation. Writers of these genres know the rules and conventions of their forms, but great works come from rebelling against those traditions. Stage conventions are restricting, but they provide paths to creativity—play writers and CNF writers find ways to push back on conventional expectations. These are two genres that reward a rebellious spirit.

Writing Wrap-Up

In either CNF or play format, write about some moment you regret. Regardless of the format you choose, depict the moment (or moments) of this regret and convey to the reader why this regret has weighed upon you.

CHAPTER 5
STRUCTURE OF ACTION/ ACTION OF STRUCTURE
INTERSECTIONS BETWEEN SCREENPLAYS AND FICTION

The movie term "action" is so familiar, even someone uninvolved in film knows the word's context. "Action" on a film set is a call to movement—filming is about to begin. It is a battle cry for forward movement.

"Action" is a call for preparedness and active collaboration on a film set. While no writer would yell the term aloud before writing, thinking of "action" as a cue for movement is a valuable tool. Fiction writers can learn from "action." Writers in fiction and screenplay writing need to keep moving forward, and it can be easy to forget. If a fiction writer begins to halt the forward movement of a story because of an overly long description, or if a screenplay writer gets lost in dialogue between two characters that does not progress the script forward, the energy so vital to a successful piece of writing will be lost. "Action" in writing is not about making sure something exciting happens at every moment—not even a screenplay from the "action movie" genre can only live within action sequences.

The key to "action" in creative writing is forward movement. If a scene or moment—whether it is full of activity or not—does not progress some aspect of the story you are attempting to tell, it should not be part of that creative work. Everything in a given piece of creative writing needs to further forward momentum. If some passages or scenes stop that forward movement, they work against the writer's efforts.

The great strength of fiction as a creative genre is its ability to show and do anything. Screenplays are, by necessity, more limited in what they can show and do than fiction. A viewer may be skeptical of a film that relies too much on voiceovers to indicate what a character is thinking or feeling, but a reader would likely not be bothered by that in a work of fiction. However, that freedom to leap within a character's head and a narrator's potentially limitless scope can create problems for a writer—the ability to do *anything* can lead a writer to provide background information or meditative introspection that does not progress the work forward. A screenplay may value the necessity of movement and progression but not emphasize story structure as would a compelling piece of fiction.

But screenplays and fiction are, unquestionably, different genres with different needs. According to American film director and screenplay writer Stanley Kubrick, "A film is—or should be—more like music than fiction. It should be a progression of moods and feelings. The theme, what's behind the emotion, the meaning, all that comes later." Kubrick implies that fiction is written with theme and meaning in mind immediately. To him, fiction writers *tell* their readers what to feel, and he thinks films should let viewers reach individual conclusions. While it is debatable that all fiction writers begin with theme and meaning in the forefront of their minds (or that screenwriters do not), it is important to acknowledge what Kubrick is valuing: a great work of art does not need to tell the audience precisely how to feel—it simply needs that audience to feel *something*. To eventually reach an audience emotionally, all writers need action, and active movement is a way to engage the reader.

> ### Writing Warm-Up
>
> Using prose, write a brief story in which one character chases another. Keep the story moving constantly, never letting up the chase until the end. Make sure you provide insight into the mindset of at least one of the characters.
>
> Then, taking the same scenario you created in prose, write it again as a brief screenplay scene (keep it informal or consult with Chapter 11 for guidelines on screenplay format). What changes between the two formats? You can get more introspective in fiction, but maybe the physical action becomes harder to convey. Writing the same scene in these two formats helps us understand the difference between them and gives us a sense of the potential inherent in both.

Action!

"Action" in screenplays and fiction can make us think of fast-paced chases and high-stakes battles, but action does not have to be a chase or fight scene. Action is about consistent and deliberate movement.

Here is the beginning of "Audition," a short story by American writer Denne Michele Norris:

> It was crazy for the Reverend Doctor Preston McKinsey to think there was something sinister in the wind that day, but he felt it in the way it stung his cheeks—like a miniature slap to the face—and he saw it in the hardened pellets of sleet bouncing down the stairs as he entered the subway station. He walked behind his son, watching carefully as Davis negotiated the stairs and the turnstile with his cello. A memory arose: the long-held image of Davis at seven years old, marching through the tempestuous lake-effect snow on his way to grade school in Chagrin Falls, Ohio, his cello strapped to his back and his green Wellington boots almost reaching his knees. The Reverend wondered why he hadn't driven Davis to school that day, though it was a mere two blocks from the house, a ten-minute walk even in the most inclement weather.

"Are you warm enough, Davis? It's pretty windy and that jacket is thin."

The Reverend unzipped his coat, unwrapped his scarf from around his neck, and presented it to his son. Davis ignored him. He moved away from his father, closer to the edge of the platform, his feet only steps from the yellow rubber that served as a warning to stay back.

"Davis," the Reverend said. He was careful not to raise his voice.

As more people transferred from other trains, the platform became crowded. Instead of moving closer to Davis, the Reverend kept his eye on his son's cello case, its outer shell the color of a ripe cherry. He watched as Davis peered down the tunnel looking for the lights that would signal the train's arrival.

These paragraphs pop with action and movement. It is not all physical activity, because there are also actions involving characters who talk and remember things. A director's call for "action" is about switching from the normal world into the world depicted on the screen, but action is emotional and physical. This is why Norris's paragraphs work so well; they take up the call to action in immediate and diverse ways.

This story does not hesitate at the beginning, and the long first sentence snaps the reader into action like a spring. The sentence evokes both the internal thoughts of a character and the external world he is walking into: "It was crazy for the Reverend Doctor Preston McKinsey to think there was something sinister in the wind that day, but he felt it in the way it stung his cheeks—like a miniature slap to the face—and he saw it in the hardened pellets of sleet bouncing down the stairs as he entered the subway station." As mentioned in Chapter 1, we should never bore our readers or confuse them. Two ways to avoid boredom are movement and surprise. Norris uses both in this sentence. The sentence is a quickly moving marble that bounces off things and keeps moving; we shift from the character's thoughts to the wind to his physical discomfort caused by the wind to the weather and surroundings he is witnessing. This is all in one sentence. We do not expect all sentences to move this way, but it is exhilarating when they do (and do it well). While it is not surprising that he is walking toward a goal (after all, he is outside in inclement weather), the rapid and clear movement of the sentence distracts the reader from the objectives. Surprising writing is not just about unexpected plot twists—language creates surprise. The sentence that follows unfolds more information—the character is with someone else, his son. They are walking to school. If a piece of writing provides information without forwarding movement, it stalls. Even surprising active language (like Norris's first sentence) would slow if it did not shift. An example of this would be fiction that stops its action to describe what happened earlier or tries to explain a character's backstory in excessive detail. Be wary of **infodumps** (saying too much too quickly); embrace **infodrizzles**—not as much information revealed as once, but that information is focused and detailed.

Norris uses the infodrizzle. She shows the reader what is necessary for understanding the scene gradually. The infodrizzle continues as we learn a bit about the dynamic between characters—the father attempts to present his scarf to his son to protect the boy from coldness. The boy "ignore[s]" him. The boy also moves further away from his

Intersecting Genre

father, nearly into danger. The father says his son's name but does so quietly, clearly trying to avoid conflict. The action continues in a way that effectively insinuates information about the relationship. Norris does not need to tell us the relationship is strained—the action clarifies that.

This section of the story concludes with the characters waiting for the train. They stand apart, the father noticing his son's cello case. The father's observation of the case almost feels like he is trying to understand his son from afar, maybe after too much distance. The boy remains literally and emotionally distant, waiting for the train that will take him away.

Norris creates a lively and vibrant landscape in just a few paragraphs, complete with emotional turmoil and crises. The key to successful writing in fiction, screenwriting, and any genre is a constant, controlled, and deliberate moving forward of action and emotional stakes.

Writing Practice

Writers strive for exact language. We never say, "this is sad," "she is nice," or "that tree is interesting." These phrases are empty—a writer should never tell a reader what emotion they are supposed to feel and then magically expect them to feel it. We must earn these emotional reactions. Do not tell a reader your character is sad—show the sadness.

Write a paragraph that shows an abstract feeling—sadness, love, or resentment, for example—without stating the intended emotion. Instead, use dialogue, action, and description to show the emotion. This use of detail and action will lead toward more meaningful emotional resonance than simply telling the reader what they are supposed to feel.

What Screenplays Teach Us about Fiction

Screenplays value progression. Every moment in a screenplay needs to lead to the next moment, whatever it is. A crisp screenplay can rarely linger or it risks stagnation. Fiction does not have the same expectations—fiction can be meditative and exploratory in ways that screenplays and films resist. But just because fiction can deviate from its central point does not mean it should. Fiction writers often suffer from **shiny thing syndrome**, where a writer loses track of clearly defined plot and characters in favor of a "shiny thing" that steals their attention. Instead of focusing on the story's needs, the shiny thing can take the reader down a different path—including excessive description, unnecessary subplots, or unfocused dialogue. That does not mean that an unexpected path is not worth exploring, but a tightly written screenplay is a fantastic guide for showing fiction writers the importance of staying focused and keeping shiny thing syndrome away.

Structure of Action/Action of Structure

The Eleven O'Clock is a 2016 Australian short film directed by Derin Seale and written by Josh Lawson (who also stars). The film focuses on a therapy session between a psychiatrist and his patient. The patient is a man who thinks he is the psychiatrist (and believes that the actual psychiatrist is his patient). Josh Lawson's character begins the scene in the office and is ostensibly the psychiatrist. Damon Herriman's character enters at the time of the appointment, thus insinuating he is the patient. The film moves quickly and consciously, planting seeds for a twist in the audience's expectations and building upon virtually everything introduced in the film. There is nothing accidental in this film, as should be the case with all good storytelling—especially short fiction (where things must be especially compact). Everything of note brought up in the film is revisited with extra meaning. This is a formula for good storytelling—nothing is extraneous.

The script's pacing allows the film to constantly progress with forward-moving action. It begins with Josh Lawson's suit-wearing character (named Terry Phillips) entering the office to seemingly start his workday. He briefly (and silently) looks around the office before sitting in the chair behind the desk. He fiddles with the desk's drawers but cannot open them. This is an example of the script establishing beats that will matter as the film progresses. While the viewer initially believes this man is the psychiatrist, a detail like Phillips's inability to open a drawer casts doubt during a subsequent viewing. It is an example of deliberate and relevant action that works to build character but turns out to mean more.

As he sits at the desk, a woman enters. He is agitated and asks her brusquely who she is. She identifies herself as Linda, a temporary office worker replacing the administrative assistant for the day. While the first minute seems to be simply setting up the basics for the rest of the film, it effectively pushes the story and characters forward. Some of that forward-moving action is character based: when Linda asks if there is anything she needs to know (having, as she says, "never worked for a psychiatrist before"), Phillips's answer is odd and unexpected—he merely tells her to call him "doctor . . . not sir, not mister . . . just doctor." What feels like a power move by an awkward character ultimately takes on a different resonance. Linda's line about not working with a psychiatrist before is effective because it accomplishes the primary goal of establishing the setting and characters' professions, and it does so in an organic way. Linda's line is not just about informing the audience or reader—it also reveals her insecurities to this new acquaintance. Again, nothing is unnecessary, even if some details initially seem trivial. Everything introduced in a story must matter.

Next, a professional-looking man (dressed in a suit and carrying a briefcase) enters the building. The audience does not know who this is, but he is literally progressing forward, walking upstairs. The scene cuts to Phillips, still sitting at the desk and looking agitated, unable to find the things he needs. Again, it progresses character beats (showing us that he is irritable and tense), but the film's ending eventually reveals more about the character's confusion. Phillips contacts Linda and asks her who his next patient is—she tells him it is a new patient who "suffers from grandiose illusions, occupational and referential . . . he thinks he's a psychiatrist." As this information is shared (and it is forward-moving information that pushes the film's primary plot),

Klein, the man we just saw entering the building, walks into the office. The film leads us to believe this man is the patient. He speaks to himself as he walks to emphasize a perceived mental disturbance (or at least an eccentricity). In the first two minutes, the film introduces the principal characters in a way that shows how the film wants them to be perceived while also providing actions and dialogue that will pay off by the conclusion.

After these introductory scenes, the film almost exclusively takes place in the office, but movement does not stop. Extensive movement defines Klein's entrance. The film shows him walking up several flights of stairs and down hallways. This physical activity sets up the dialogue-driven action of the rest of the film. Good screenplays keep things moving—sometimes that movement is through physicality, as in the first minutes of *The Eleven O'Clock*, and sometimes it is movement through dialogue interplay (as is seen elsewhere in the film)—but things always need to move. This creates action and progress. Fiction works in the same way—good fiction needs progression and movement. There is a difference between watching a man enter an office while a voiceover explains his perceived purpose and *writing* about a man walking into an office, but the screenplay's emphasis on action helps a writer's success in prose. Good prose needs to keep the reader thinking of and emphasizing the importance of action.

Klein enters the office (still mumbling to himself) and places his briefcase on the table. The strangeness of the man's physicality and demeanor (emphasized by Phillips's incredulous look at Klein) strikes the audience. On a later viewing, the audience notices Klein (unlike Phillips) is confident with where things are in the office (he pours a glass of water and stands purposefully at the window). Forward-moving action does not need big and broad gestures. Small detail-oriented actions carry significant weight.

Mumbling to himself, Klein wonders where his glasses are. Sitting at the desk, Phillips tells him they are in his top pocket. They both introduce themselves, each insisting they are the actual psychiatrist. The lines from Linda explaining the patient's delusions are apparent in the viewer's mind as the situation unfolds. Every moment provides movement and action—some of that progression is not recognized until the film resolves itself and reveals the characters' actual identities. Both characters insist they are the doctor, and both express frustrations over the other's unwillingness to admit they are not the doctor. Verbal movement replaces the physical movement of Klein's walk into the building as the action shifts to a fast-moving dialogue-driven conflict. Both characters continue to insist on who is the patient and who is the doctor—Klein is initially calm about the disagreement, while Phillips shows frustration and impatience (a character trait shown almost immediately upon his introduction). Klein is quick to calm Phillips—at one point, he politely tells Phillips, "not to worry—we'll sort this out." He is confused but kindly. Phillips is agitated. Physicality and dialogue reveal these essential character traits.

The film wants the viewer to see Klein as confused but good-natured. He insists that his administrative assistant is named Donna (though the film has already introduced a woman named Linda in that role). Of course, the screenplay and film planted an essential seed by establishing that Linda was a temp replacing the actual assistant, but the film (almost as a magician refocuses an audience by emphasizing other focal points) diverts the audience with the tension between Phillips and Klein.

The film also disorients the viewer through humor. Quick-paced dialogue emphasizes the absurdity of the circumstance. After agreeing to sit down and talk, both characters attempt to sit in the same chair. Klein ultimately decides to let Phillips sit in the doctor's chair and tells him he will "concede for the purposes of this session that [Phillips is] indeed the doctor." When Phillips then insists that he also concedes that Klein is the patient, Klein argues, "well, I don't think it's healthy for a doctor to pretend to be a patient for a patient who thinks they're a doctor, wouldn't you agree?" The dialogue emphasizes the absurdity, but it ups that absurdity with Phillip's retort: "I would except you're not a doctor talking to his patient, you're my patient who thinks he's a doctor talking to a patient who happens to be a doctor indulging the delusions of a patient who thinks he is a doctor. Is that clear?" The dialogue creates verbal action. It uses humor to keep the viewer engaged in the battle of wits between the two characters. Action can come from various places in a creative work, but wherever it comes from (physical movement or dialogue or anything else), the key is that it progresses either the story or the characters.

This film shows that action is not just about car chases and fast-paced sequences. Action is about a progression of story and character elements. If a screenplay or work of fiction shows character movement to explore and understand characters, that is action. This is crucial and often misunderstood in fiction. In a screenplay, a writer creates dialogue that a performer will eventually interpret with their voice and physicality. When people talk, they never simply stand or sit perfectly still as words exit their mouths.

On the contrary, characters can do many things as they talk—they can gesture wildly, fidget, or walk toward (or away) from another character. For instance, in *The Eleven O'Clock*, the performers constantly use physicality to add dimension and interest to the dialogue. During a moment in the film when both primary characters are arguing over who is the actual doctor, Klein jumps out of a chair and moves toward Phillips. As Klein speaks ("Good. Become the thing that's angering you. Whatever it is that's frustrating you. If it had a voice, what would it say?"), he leans into Phillips (on the other side of the desk), and his voice slows to indicate care and concern. He gestures with his left hand as he says the word "whatever" to visualize the word's vastness. He then touches his thumb and index finger together to make a very loose fist as he asks the question that ends the dialogue, visually asking Phillips to narrow everything to something smaller.

This is something that happens in good fiction dialogue as well. Writers often worry more about how to covey dialogue than render it. For example, a student may focus more on what dialogue tags to use (such as "they said" or "they asked") than the physicality that can accompany such dialogue. Dialogue exists to help readers understand how characters talk and further the plot, but good dialogue can do more. Beyond letting readers *hear* characters, dialogue is a chance to add physicality to define a character. Effectively conveyed dialogue is an opportunity to take a piece of good writing further.

Writing Practice

The Eleven 'O Clock finds humor from mistaken identity and confusion. This concept has a long tradition in comedic literature, including several occurrences in Shakespeare (*The Comedy of Errors* and *Twelfth Night*, among others). Write a brief scene (in either prose or screenplay format) about two characters where the first character thinks the second is someone other than who they are.

There is a reason why this scenario has endured through Shakespeare to television sitcoms and beyond—it creates a situation with evident tension but also with a clear potential for comedy (though you do not have to play your scene for laughs if you would rather not). Play with this "mistaken identity" trope and see what scenarios you can create with your version of it.

What Fiction Teaches Us about Screenplays

Dialogue in fiction can cue a reader to what a speaker intends, and physical gestures can cement that intention. Screenplay writers cannot assume dialogue will be sufficient for meaning—just because a character says something does not mean the reader will fully understand what the writer is trying to convey. It is also essential to consider **subtext**, or what the characters mean but do not explicitly say. Understanding how best to structure dialogue in fiction also helps with screenplays (or plays). While a screenplay writer can simply present the lines for the characters to say, a fiction writer must use the tools available—emboldening dialogue with action and physicality. Screenplay writers need to use their available tools to do the same.

First, here is why dialogue is vital in fiction (and CNF) storytelling.

- Dialogue allows the reader to *hear* the speaker and thus better understand that character as a whole.
- The things a character says reveal their personality.
- Dialogue exchanges between two or more characters can help the writer establish the relationship between those characters.
- Dialogue can provide information to further the story—this information must be valuable for both the reader *and* the characters (and never solely for the reader).

Before discussing these four points in detail, it is helpful to acknowledge what this list implies. If overly generic dialogue does not add anything to the story or characters (or is merely filler), it does not belong. Dialogue should not be about capturing speech as it authentically happens in the world. Instead, it is a recreation of speech that gets to the heart of what truly matters. If dialogue in fiction or a screenplay were only about being "authentic," dialogue would be filled with the "ums" and "ers" of everyday speech. There is a reason why characters in films and plays do not necessarily overload the audiences with these vocalisms (as common as they are in real life)—writing should capture the truth of humanity and, as authentic as these vocalisms may be, they would get in the way of what the characters are saying and how they are connecting. That is not to say that including these vocalisms is always bad—sometimes a character will hesitate, and the writer needs tools to depict this effectively—but using them excessively throughout limits the writer's ability to make an impact when needed.

Going Further

Take a look at this brief dialogue exchange:

> "Have you heard anything from the hospital?" she inquired.
> "Not yet," he murmured.
> "I'm getting worried," she cried.
> "You and me both," he agreed.

The writer in this example is overthinking **dialogue tags**, the phrases that follow, precede, or interrupt dialogue to inform the reader of the speaker's identity. In this example, the dialogue tags take attention away from the actual content of the conversation (which should be the focus) and give us very little information about the people having the conversation. Instead of desperately trying to find ways not to say, "he said," "she said," or "they said," writers should instead focus on how to make characters come to life. Do not worry about using "he said," "she said," or "they said"—the reader sees this type of dialogue tag as a tool and mostly ignores it. Using simple dialogue tags encourages a writer to include actions, improving the overall scene.

Here is the previous dialogue exchange without the obtrusive dialogue tags (and some additional character actions):

> "Have you heard anything from the hospital?" she asked as she fidgeted with her car keys.
> "Not yet," he said quietly, unable to look at her fully.
> "I'm getting worried." Her voice cracked as she spoke.
> "You and me both," he said, almost a whisper.

Writers need to focus on building characters and creating compelling scenarios. Overly focusing on synonyms for dialogue tags will not lead to success.

Dialogue as a Tool for "Hearing"

Character-creation is a multisensory experience, and dialogue allows readers to hear a character's voice. In fiction, a reader cannot *hear* (while a produced screenplay will enable a performer to voice a given part), so the fiction writer must create the illusion of voice through compelling dialogue and description. Each character in a given work should have a unique way of talking and communicating. This is true in all genres. For example, suppose a fan receives an unproduced screenplay of their favorite television show that features all of the fan's favorite characters with character-accurate dialogue. In this case, the fan can tell who is speaking without character identification. The fan can do this because one character's voice is unique from the others. Each character—like all people—has different conversational approaches. Some characters and people are wordy, and some are terse. Some folks use complicated words, and others keep things simple and direct.

Writers can add detail to the description around dialogue to give a further understanding of things like volume and speed. The more attention a writer gives to unique vocal patterns and quirks, the more this aspect of a character can come to life. And screenplay writers (and play writers) should never rely on a performer alone to provide voice—compelling dialogue differs from character to character in a screenplay or play. Dialogue does immense work establishing voice, regardless of what a performer may add.

Dialogue as a Tool for Revealing Personality

Characters should not simply *sound* different from one another—they should fundamentally *be* different. One of the most effective ways to reveal personality is through things characters say (and, as discussed earlier, *how* they say it). This works through dialogue that *shows* personality instead of a conversation that simply *tells* the reader how to view a character. In other words, do not have a character tell the other characters (and the reader), "Oh, am I eccentric or what?" or "I am curmudgeonly!" Instead, present dialogue (and physicality) that makes the reader reach that conclusion.

The things people say are the quickest avenue to understanding who they are. A writer must take advantage of this by presenting dialogue that gets directly to a character's heart. Do not let dialogue simply be informative on a plot level—instead, dialogue needs to be a consciously considered aspect of character-building. Writers often build personality based on how characters look or act, and dialogue is equally—and maybe even more—important.

Dialogue for Relationship Building

People talk differently to different people. How one person talks to their mother differs from how they speak to their best friend or communicate with their boss. We are aware that how we talk to one person is not necessarily going to be the same way we talk to another—this is something we do so often that we may not even switch consciously—it is just an innate thing people do.

And if humans do it, characters can too. No matter how effectively a writer has structured a voice for a character, that character will speak and react differently in different situations. By being clear with these distinctions, readers can understand the relationships between characters, and dialogue is crucial for allowing readers to understand the dynamics of varying character combinations.

Dialogue for Story Progression

In an episodic television show where individual episodes connect to tell a larger story, it is not uncommon for characters to discuss things that happened in a previous episode, not to catch the characters up on what happened before but to inform the audience. While an audience might accept the conceit of such a conversation as a tool to recap information and remind viewers (or inform those who missed a previous episode), it is a horrible use of dialogue because it is insincere and not believable. Dialogue between characters should always be about things these characters would legitimately tell each other and never simply to give the reader (or viewer) information. When actual people have conversations, they do not typically inform each other of things they would already know. Neither should your characters.

Character dialogue should always look forward. If characters discuss something from the past (as they assuredly could), there needs to be an apparent reason why the conversation must happen. Dialogue should never exist to simply inform the reader—that just makes for dull and implausible conversations that stall out the larger work.

> ### Writing Practice
>
> Write a conversation between two characters, but each line of dialogue spoken by the characters cannot be longer than four words. You can use as many words as you like for everything that is not dialogue. Since your dialogue word count is low, you will need to carefully consider subtext and physical descriptions. Let the subtext push its way to the front. Additionally, be unafraid to describe what the characters are doing as they speak.

The Hybrid: Comics and Graphic Novels

The popularity of superhero comic book movies really should be no surprise. After all, besides plays, there is no creative writing style more adaptable to film form than comic books and graphic novels. A comic book is a visual screenplay bursting with illustrated snapshots and dialogue presented as speech bubbles. A comic book is a movie storyboard complete with dialogue, narration, and thoughts. While a screenplay can feature voiceovers or narration to guide the audience, fiction often gets a reader deeper into a character's thoughts through first-person narration or close third-person point of view. Fiction also can move quickly from one character's perspective to another. This is challenging in a screenplay but simple in a comic book or graphic novel. Like films, comics and graphic novels are active, with panels frequently depicting dynamic movement and action. Comic writers and artists must think as cinematically as a screenplay writer while also having the fiction writer's sense of detail and introspection.

One such comic creator was Mark Gruenwald. Gruenwald was an American comic book writer who, among other accolades, was the writer for Marvel Comic's *Captain America* from 1985 to 1995. Before his death of a heart attack at age forty-three, Gruenwald actively explored the world of screenplays and attended several screenwriting workshops (and encouraged fellow Marvel employees to do the same). Gruenwald knew the intersection between comic writing and screenplays. Considering that, in the mid-1990s, the comic industry was amid a dramatic decline, he also knew that screenwriting was a logical pivot point for those in the comic industry looking (or needing) to try other creative avenues.

His understanding of a comic book's place at the intersection between fiction and screenplays was evident in his advice for writers. Gruenwald once shared his advice for aspiring comic writers, and much of it is relevant for writers in all genres, specifically screenplays and fiction—he encouraged character-driven, action-forward storytelling that was visually appealing and ultimately optimistic. The emphasis on optimism is the writer's choice, but comic books and graphic novels are a fascinating place to see how these two genres intertwine.

Writing Practice

Regardless of your artistic ability, take a scene from an earlier work you have written and illustrate it in comic form. It is okay if your drawings are rudimentary—what is most important is how you adapt the screenplay or fiction version of the story into this more visual form. You do not have to consider this comic adaptation to be the work's final form—this is an experiment to see what more you can learn about a work in progress.

What felt most essential to transfer into the comic book form? What did not feel essential? What new things did you learn about your story and characters as a result of this prose to graphic novel adaptation?

Summary

Characters are the heart of story-based creative writing, and screenplay and fiction writing approach character-shaping differently. Screenplays and films show characters through dialogue and physicality; fiction depicts characters through physical description and internal and literal dialogue, and screenplays depend on movement and dialogue.

These two genres are indispensable guides for character-building because of these disparate approaches. Both value action and movement, but screenplays lead to films that depict the action literally, while fiction can paint emotional and descriptive depictions of movement. Considering the character-driven nature of both genres, the stories in both are very much "told" by characters. This is true of fiction (even when a writer does not definitively state a narrator's identity). Ultimately, screenplays and fiction are successful when the writer guides the reader through active movement and dialogue.

Writing Wrap-Up

Take a character you have either created before this exercise or are creating now, and write a screenplay scene that depicts a key moment from that character's past (that would not necessarily appear in a creative writing piece that features the character).

Think about how the events you depict in this scene affect the character later in life. In what ways does this formative event shape this character? How does addressing this event help you understand the older version of the character you are writing?

CHAPTER 6
THE UNINVENTED
INTERSECTIONS BETWEEN POEMS AND PLAYS

The relationship between poetry and plays stands apart in our exploration of intersections because both genres are formally unique. Both are much older than fiction, CNF, and screenwriting. Classic oral tradition defines these genres—the urgency of voice is crucial to both. Both plays and poetry emerge from verbal artistry, and poetry and plays are *organic* in ways the other genres are not.

On the surface, this is ridiculous. Is poetry a natural and organic occurrence? The universe just randomly spits out poetry? Not exactly. The *craft* of poetry is a significant part of its existence, and people do not typically speak in rhyming iambic pentameter. Accordingly, do we believe that plays are found randomly in nature? Maybe we should. In his book *The Playwright's Guidebook*, American teacher and play writer Stuart Spencer argues,

> The idea of theater arises spontaneously in all of us. In the dawn of humanity, men and women began to perform for others around the fire, at the mouth of the cave, in the shadow of a tree. These performances may have taken the form of singing, dancing, or storytelling. They might have served as religious ritual, or as a celebration of the hunt, or were perhaps merely a means of telling a story for enjoyment.

Theater is instinctual. People constantly perform for each other. Theater is more than performances on a literal stage because the stage can take myriad forms—it can be the courtroom where the defense attorney delivers impassioned final remarks. It can be a child in the store aisle pleading for the purchase of a desired toy. It can be the table at a crowded restaurant as someone proposes marriage (knowing that both the recipient of the proposal and those nearby will serve as audience). Theater is naturally occurring. A play is a created artifact that harnesses the naturally occurring world of theater. In this way, a play makes art out of natural occurrences.

Art is a difficult concept to define. A quick internet search of "definition of art" leads to several results, but it also recommends more pointed questions asked by other users, such as "What is the true definition of art?" Few words compel people to seek a "true definition" because most other words are relatively straightforward and a standard "definition" is sufficient. Art is more complicated. As far as defining art, we can start by saying that human skill creates art. There is reason and deliberation behind it. We would label a painting of a sunset art but would be less likely to use the term to describe the sunset itself.

Intersecting Genre

Art cannot be naturally occurring—there has to be craft involved. We can see a mountain as breathtaking or, if feeling dramatic, **sublime** (an emotional reaction to art or nature that inspires awe and respect), but calling it *art* is a reach. Artists create art deliberately. Does art have to be a tangible artifact (like a painting, poem, or screenplay)? Not at all—ballet is unquestionably an art form, as is the staged play emerging from a written play.

There is also an emotional component to art. Art must make us feel something. We would be apt to call a child's drawing of a beloved pet art, but not a completed page from a coloring book (even if the child made creative color choices and stayed within the lines). This is because the drawing is both unique to its creator and more likely to elicit an emotional reaction. An emotional response cannot solely define art—being punched in the face by a stranger will create an emotional response, but it would not be art. Also, the *type* of emotional reaction from a viewer or reader determines how they view the value of that piece. Art can obviously—and often does—offend. An audience that cannot recognize art's capacity to provoke may dismiss such a challenging piece as art altogether.

Even beyond offense, there are a lot of practiced performances, drawings, and writings that most would not consider art. All would view Shakespeare's plays as art, and most would accept stage plays in general, but what about a television comedy series? A sketch comedy series? Are these art? There is undeniably a subjective element. Most would never consider professional wrestling art, but it is highly scripted and practiced. The definition can be narrow or broad depending on the individual deciding what art is and what it is not.

But the writer cannot worry about these perceptions when writing a play or poem (or anything else). They should only focus on what they can create. What is most important at the early stage of creation is that the writer controls what happens next. Even if theater is a naturally occurring phenomenon, plays do not happen by accident, and it is up to the writer to determine the direction of the play.

Writing Warm-Up

Create a conversation between two characters in which they debate the definition of art. You do not have to consciously convey your perspective in either character (though you could)—basically, just use the two characters to think of how to reason out this conversation about defining art.

When you review this conversation, do you see your perspective in either character? If you intentionally included your view, do you find that character's argument as compelling as you would have expected?

"The Very Language"

Like theater, poetry is also an art form that emerged into the world without pretension or artifice. Some may see poetry as the most pretentious of the creative writing genres, seemingly contrived and artificial. While writers can add whatever levels of artifice they choose, organic explorations of speech define poetry in classical terms. Poetry is a more musical way of conveying natural speech.

While poetic metrics can be confusing, the different metrical tools of poetry (like identifying stressed syllables) are primarily about creating natural and pleasing sounds. **Iambic pentameter**, as an example, can feel remarkably contrived. Describing it does little to make it sound less affected: an iambic pentameter line is a line of poetry that contains five iambic feet. A **metrical foot** in this context is a **stressed** syllable (meaning it is more emphasized when read aloud, in contrast to an unstressed syllable the reader will not accentuate as much). An iamb is a foot that contains an unstressed syllable followed by a stressed one. Reading the definition can be enough for a writer to be done with poetry forever.

But in reality, it is not that complicated. Meter is about sounds and, for writers, sounds are among the most valuable tools available. For example, the word "define" is an iamb—when it is said aloud, the "fine" sound is much more present—de-FINE. The stress is on the second syllable (capitalized in the example for clarity). One of the most effective ways of understanding what syllables are stressed or unstressed is to do it the opposite way: de-FINE sounds normal; DE-fine does not. So, iambic pentameter is a line of poetry with five (petameter indicates five) iambic feet: To-DAY's the DAY you WILL de-CIDE to GO. Rereading this sentence with the stresses reversed (hitting the lower case syllables harder than the upper case ones) will show you how natural iambs actually are.

The iambic pentameter line's popularity comes from a genuine desire to replicate human speech. In the preface to *Lyrical Ballads* from 1802, English poetry writer William Wordsworth discusses his use of language:

> I have proposed to myself to imitate, and, as far as is possible, to adopt the very language of men; and assuredly such personifications do not make any natural or regular part of that language. They are, indeed, a figure of speech occasionally prompted by passion, and I have made use of them as such; but I have endeavoured utterly to reject them as a mechanical device of style, or as a family language which Writers in metre seem to lay claim to by prescription. I have wished to keep my Reader in the company of flesh and blood, persuaded that by so doing I shall interest him.

Wordsworth's poems in *Lyrical Ballads* are not exclusively iambic pentameter, though it is often present (frequently in the form of **blank verse**, iambic pentameter that does not rhyme). But even the poems not in blank verse are typically structured around iambs. Why does this matter? Because Wordsworth was adamant that the poems in this collection be written "in the very language of men," and by this, he meant that he wanted to capture the way "regular" people spoke. In the previous passage, he explains that the poems are actively working to maintain "the company of flesh and blood," meaning that these poems were striving to sound honest, raw, and visceral. In our current age, well over 200 years since Wordsworth's, our impression of raw and visceral works would differ from his, but to Wordsworth, that dedication needed to begin within the structure of the poetic line. For Wordsworth, iambs and iambic pentameter punctuated the language of humanity, and this is the metrical approach that most closely parallels everyday speech.

Plays and poems may be fabrications, but they are reproductions determined to recreate something accurately. Creative writing can never, in execution, *be* the thing it attempts to be—it is always a reproduction. But plays and poems matter because the roots of the two genres emerge from replicating something authentic and organic. Writers in these genres should be unafraid to engage in artifice to follow that thread of honesty inherent within their origins.

Writing Practice

Look around you and find an inanimate object. Now, using extremely conversational language, write a stanza or two that describes this thing literally. Then add to the poem by writing a stanza about how the object makes you feel. Remember to use plain and conversational language.

After completing this poem, write another poem about the same object. However, this time, write it in the most elevated and dramatic way you can imagine. Use the same structure you used in the first poem by starting with a literal description and then moving to emotional detail.

What strikes you as the most significant difference between these two poems? Besides the subject matter, what do they have in common? Which of the two poems do you prefer and why?

What Poems Teach Us about Plays

Poems and plays are language-driven genres that can tell stories and be meditative and introspective but also must *sound* compelling. Writers know that absorbing sound patterns are integral to writing successful poems, but a poem cannot simply sound good—an effective poem has value that derives from both the meaning of the words and the *sound* of those words.

This is relevant in plays, too. When we think about people who are effective oral communicators, what they say and how they say it matters equally. Like effective writing, effective communication combines what is said and how elegantly it is said. A good poem is interesting and compellingly written. A poem needs both sound and meaning—an intellectually compelling poem that is clunky and static is ineffective, as is a poem with elegant sounds that do not resonate emotionally with a reader.

That is why poetry can be an influential teacher, not just for play writers but also for writers in all genres. Looking at poems that move with musicality and rhythm can show a writer the possibility of exquisite language in all forms. Here is a poem by British poetry writer Fiona Sampson that models varied musical techniques:

Take, Eat

Kissing and praying? Not the same.
Though each jaw, if it moves,
mumbles at a catch to prove
feeling. Capitalised Name

or nipple raised to Upper Case—
that taps your palate, jinks a toast
in soft communion—the boast
you mouth's the same in either case.

I'm yours alone. Nothing else
could mar my devotion. Self,
ambition, fall away here. See,
my praying mouth vouches for me—

Over and over. The lips part.
In shy darkness they lie, they gasp.

Sampson's poem makes its music in various ways, including rhyme, alliteration, assonance, and caesura. The poem also uses some less expected musical techniques to give it tension.

Rhyme: This poem's use of rhyme is perhaps more overt than most contemporary poems, but it is in no way a poem that exists as a prisoner of rhyme. Instead, Sampson controls the rhyme, never letting the poem feel like the preservation of the rhyme is more important than that rhyme's *effect*. The effect here is a flowing musicality that guides the reader. While the rhymes are primarily end-rhymes that occur at the end of lines, the rhyme does not feel as overwhelming as one might expect (nor do these rhymes force the reader to engage in a "sing-song" style that overly anticipates the rhyme). She accomplishes this through two main methods: Near-rhyme and enjambment.

Near rhyme is a pair of words that almost rhyme. The words *cat* and *bat* are perfect rhymes. *Cat* and *black* are near rhymes because they are two similar sounding words that don't match up in a perfect rhyme. The same can be said for *cat* and *bats*—again, the words almost rhyme but ultimately merely sound similar. Sampson's poem does this with the near-rhyme pairings of *moves* and *prove*, and *else* and *self*. The poem indeed uses perfect rhyme more often, but these examples of near rhyme (and the repeated *case* and *case* in the fifth and eighth line that replicates a rhyme) vary things and create a break for the reader, allowing the reader to realize that the poem's construct is not inflexible. It gives the poem freedom while still adhering to the rhyme scheme.

Another tool used in this poem is **enjambment**, when a sentence continues through several lines and does not end on a given line. The presence of a line in poetry is unique in that it forces the reader to approach poems in a way inherently different from how they would approach prose. Instead of reading sentences as full entities, the poetry reader must stop at the end of a line because the writer has dictated this pause through the inclusion of a line break. In the first two lines of this poem, that is not an issue—the first line ends with a period ("Not the same.") and the second ends with a comma ("if it moves,"). In both cases, the line break appears where punctuation would instruct the reader to pause anyway. But the third line uses enjambment: "mumbles at a catch to prove/feel." This forces the reader's hesitation after reading "prove" (the word before the line break) to be minimal. Instead, the reader glides through the break, only hesitating before settling on the abrupt landing of "feel" at the start of the fourth line. Near rhyme and enjambment disrupt—but do not eliminate—the rhyme, giving the reader the pleasure of rhyme without the overbearing presence oppressive rhyming can create.

Caesura: A **caesura** is a pause in the middle of a line, caused either by punctuation (like the question mark in the first line or the comma after "palate" in line 6) or a natural pause created by the language. For example, even without a punctuation guide, the reader may naturally linger after the word "catch" in line three because the "ch" sound at the end of the word makes it difficult for a reader to transition quickly to the next word. Also, complicated structures may cause a natural pause—in lines 7-8, the phrase "the boast/you mouth's the same in either case" forces the reader to hesitate on "mouth's" because of both the unexpected contraction in the word (combining "mouth" and "is") and the complexity of the phrase. Caesura is crucial because it offers opportunities to breathe and, through those breaths, moments of silence. Those small breaths are necessary for poems to find their musicality and to provide readers with brief moments of tension and potential reflection.

Going Further

While Sampson's poem shows the great potential of rhyme in poetry, it is still something that can be difficult to control. Suppose a writer is more concerned with maintaining a rhyme scheme than creating a compelling work that moves in emotionally effective and unexpected ways. In that case, we can consider that poem "a prisoner of the rhyme scheme." A poem suffers if a writer chooses a lesser word to end a line simply because the rhyme scheme dictates it. A poem cannot reach its potential if phrases are awkwardly strung together to maintain a rhythm that will lead to a rhyme.

Using rhyme in a poem can lead to appealing musicality and create unexpected joys for reader and writer both, but there is also a great responsibility in choosing to use a formal rhyme scheme. If rhyme ever overwhelms a poem and starts to be the sole reason behind a writer's decisions in writing the poem, the rhyme scheme is causing more harm than good.

Alliteration and assonance: **Alliteration** is the repetition of consonant sounds in a poem. Like rhyme, this is used to create a musical effect that can drive a poem. It is a technique used frequently in this poem—the repeated "N" sounds of "Name" and "nipple" in lines 4 and 5 create a bridge that connects the stanza on either side of the line break between the lines. Line 6 contains the phrase "taps your palate, jinks a toast," which features repeating "T" and "P" sounds that create a rhythm within the line.

Assonance is the repetition of vowel sounds in a poem. While the phrase "taps your palate, jinks a toast" is an obvious example of alliteration, those "A" sounds of "taps," palate," and "a toast" are doing just as much to make music. The similar vowel sounds created by the "A" in "part" and "darkness" help to move the poem into its final line. These musical moves (in addition to the poem's intensity and emotional weight) bring Sampson's poem to life and good writing should feel vibrant and alive.

Great art is not meant merely to be admired from afar or studied. Good writing is never an elegant and fragile vase that sits on a high shelf simply to be admired. To truly create something, a writer can never overly sentimentalize art, even great art. We should never treat poetry and plays—even the classics taught in schools for centuries with no signs of being taken off the curriculum—as something we simply point to on that shelf and ask, "isn't it lovely?" As writers, we must climb up to that top shelf and carry that vase down to see how it functions. And if we break that vase to create something new, that is just part of creating art.

Explorations

- Look at the third stanza of this poem, and think about Sampson's choice to italicize it in its entirety. What is gained from this move? What do you think the italics represent here?

- As discussed earlier, enjambment is when a line ends within a sentence (causing that sentence to carry over to two or more lines, unstopped by a period). These "end words" are important because of the weight the poems places on them. Consider the words Sampson chooses to end her lines—aside from just thinking about rhyme, why are these words important? Again, out of breaking the rhyme scheme, how would the poem work differently if she chose different words?

Creative Response

This poem is a sonnet, a poem with fourteen lines that usually (though not always) has a consistent rhyme scheme and contains a *turn* (either around the middle of the poem in the closing lines) that *turns* a reader's expectations of the poem. Write a sonnet following whatever "rules" of the form you choose to follow.

Emphasizing musicality in poems does not mean that poems should never sound like speech. Think of musicality as a more musical and energetic version of speech. Some

Intersecting Genre

poems can sound very conversational and some less so, but they should not actively work to sound archaic or difficult to understand (though they can appear that way to readers). This is relevant to writing plays because a play's approach to language is not as different from a poem's as we might think. A play should never try to emulate exact human speech—instead, it should idealize speech. A good play's dialogue moves like music. A play striving for realism will see its authenticity suffer if the dialogue is too musical, but it should still have an eye toward precision and resonance.

Writing Practice

There are many ways to create sounds in poetry, including alliteration and assonance. Other strategies could involve rhyme or repeated words or phrases.

Using any strategies you like (including ones you may have learned from elsewhere or conceived on your own), write a poem that pays close attention to sound and music. You may end up with a poem driven throughout by musicality or with something more subtle. Listen to where this poem will take you.

What Plays Teach Us about Poems

Like Wordsworth's vision of poetry from 1802, plays often use relatable language that draws in a reader or audience through familiarity. Of course, there are moments when the tools of the craft (he cites "figures of speech" that seem "mechanical") can overwhelm a relatable, naturalistic approach. Contemporary plays provide a modern playground where approachable language and theatrical artifice coexist. As explained in Chapter 2, a performed play begins with an agreement between the audience and the creators of the play that the audience will not question whether or not a work is actually real (this is called "suspension of disbelief"). Knowing that an audience unconsciously agrees to these terms allows a play to take chances that other genres would not allow.

But those chances should never dissuade the writer from finding resonating language for a piece of writing. Nick Makoha is a Uganda-born, London-based writer, and his short play *The Dark* is based on Makoha's personal experiences and shows the intersection between poetry and plays through his dramatic structure and poetic language. Among other characters, the play contains multiple variations of "Nick," theatrically representing the writer at various points in his life and experience. One of those characters is "Narrator Nick," who appears early in the play to establish the tone, story, and structure. The character's first monologue is compelling because it directly addresses the audience in an informative and casual way (at least at first) that incorporates a variety of poetic and dramatic language strategies. The speech moves from a direct, comfortable address to the audience to something more personal, more metaphorical, before losing the sense of the audience in favor of the character's emotional journey.

The Uninvented

Narrator Nick's speech moves in so many unexpected directions in terms of tone, metaphor, audience awareness, linguistic construct, and musicality, it is necessary first to read the speech as a complete piece before discussing it. Various moves in this speech will be broken down in the analysis to follow, but experiencing it as an entire speech as Makoha intends, emphasizes both its ambition and accessibility:

> NARRATOR NICK: Hi, How was your journey? You could be anywhere in the world, but your journey brought you here. Thanks for coming, I'm Nick . . . and I want to tell you a story. My story. My journey. Stories are so important. They are fragments of memory and imagination that help us find out who we are and how we got to where we are. It is what separates us from The Dark. Sorry, that's a bit deep to start with. Well . . . you knew it wasn't gonna be a rom-com, youknowwhatImean, so . . . Anyways . . . I want you to do me a favour. I want you to close your eyes. You are me! The Nile is sleeping, a bus is waiting on the escarpment. The runway is tired. The trees, the earth, the sky have become houses for the dead. Bodies are skinned trees. Vehicles have no number plates houses have no doors. What name do you give me? Am I made of clouds, or of feathers? The air's murmuring, see how it argues with the sky? Night is not the only darkness. It keeps pouring onto the landscape. In this liquid heat the guards ignore you, and there are the watchmen, playing cards, drinking gin, eating banana figs. A girl my age is a ghost. My uncle has thrown his life in a lake. Is ghost another word for stranger? I have the eyes of a bird. The strangers are asking me to join them. Prisoners bring news. *If a stranger or anyone you do not know offers you the song, sing of everywhere.* On the edge of every day, an unnamed mountain sleeps.

The beginning feels warm but exhibits more distance than may seem to be present at first glance. The speaker is directly addressing the audience with a question—"How was your journey?" Starting a piece with an attempt to draw in the reader is an intelligent strategy. While an audience could reasonably answer this question, the conceit of the theater would not allow that—the audience hears the question, feels seen by it, but cannot respond. This also occurs in poems—many poems are structured around questions the author knows the reader cannot answer. The point is to hook the reader. In Makoha's case, his question is not rhetorical but simply unanswerable due to the polite restraints of the theater.

The opening sentences are inviting and instructive—Narrator Nick establishes a bond with the audience and presents an offering of storytelling. The offer is made more impactful with the proclamation about the importance of stories. Here, a story's value begins as currency—the audience has decided to spend their evening in the theater, and the exchange for their presence is a story.

Things turn intimate—this is not just any story. Nick emphasizes, "My story. My journey." There is a promise of intimacy. Nick quickly questions the familiarity forced onto the audience but then rationalizes that the audience knew the risks of attending. It lets the audience know that, while the writer is aware that the audience expects detachment (and offers suspension of disbelief in exchange), this will be darker, deeper, and more personal than they might have expected. An invitation becomes a warning. It is writing that is innately aware of audience perceptions.

So Nick asks the audience for something—for the audience to assimilate with the character: "I want you to close your eyes. You are me!" There is no audience—there are only characters, and the audience becomes part of the speaker's psyche.

This is a strategy frequently incorporated in poetry. Whenever a poem uses "you" to directly address someone, the reader must consider who that "you" is. Sometimes it is a clearly defined "you"—either the audience or another character. But often, the "you" is a way for the writer to explore themselves without taking on the vulnerability of "I." Not always, of course, but often "you" means "I" (and the speaker is talking about themselves in the second person). This is a way to merge writer and reader. The monologue creates an intimacy that deliberately draws in the audience. In poems, the writer often uses "you" without thinking of who "you" actually is. Decisions to involve a "you" must always be considered and thoughtfully planned.

Narrator Nick is very much a fourth wall-breaking character. In plays (and less often in screenplays), breaking the **fourth wall**—where characters acknowledge and directly address the audience—is standard practice. Here, Narrator Nick not only addresses the audience but recognizes the reality and genre of the play in which he appears ("Well . . . you knew it wasn't gonna be a rom-com, youknowwhatImean"). This awareness of a character's role within the work is also valuable in poetry—the speaker in a poem should be conscious of who they are addressing and why. Ultimately, the identity of a specific "you" is less important than the writer (and speaker) knowing who it is.

Going Further

Even in poetry and CNF, where the writer and speaker may seem to go hand-in-hand, they are always two different entities. The writer creates the text, and the character—even if it is ostensibly a stand-in for the writer—is an entity who exists exclusively within a given text. This distinction is crucial. A speaker is a creation, an artifice. Even in a deeply personal work, there is a distinction between writer and speaker.

This distinction allows the writer to fabricate whatever is needed. Even in a work of memoir, the reader knows that there is likely some modification from literal truth. Also, assuming the speaker and the writer are the same is problematic for a writer creating personas in poetry. To respect creativity in writing, do not assume the speaker is always the writer. Even in autobiographical work, the speaker is never exactly the writer, but in poetry there is even more of a distinction.

While the Makoha monologue begins in a conversational tone, it does not end that way, moving from casual conversation to something more abstract. His language becomes more fragmented, with declarative sentences followed by phrases less literal but haunting. Take these mostly short seven sentences: "Night is not the only darkness. It keeps pouring onto the landscape. In this liquid heat the guards ignore you, and there are the watchmen, playing cards, drinking gin, eating banana figs. A girl my age is a ghost. My uncle has thrown his life in a lake. Is ghost another word for stranger? I have the eyes of a bird." These sentences drip with metaphor, even if some feel less obscure than others. These short sentences build and leave the reader potentially uneasy yet emotionally invested.

In Makoha's writing, we know what "my uncle has thrown his life in a lake" means, even if we do not take the sentiment literally (though we could). Phrases like "liquid heat" and night "pouring onto the landscape" are examples of provocative poetic language for the stage. But while Makoha's monologue shows the value of adding metaphor in plays, it is an essential lesson on continuity to poetry writers. It is easy to get caught up in the joy of a metaphor well-rendered and lose track of the message a poem can convey. Makoha's work uses metaphorical language but does so in a way that connects the monologue's ideas. These metaphors do not exist for mere language play—they are there to control a narrative. And good poetic language, whether in a play or a poem, needs to contain images and moments that power the ideas surrounding it.

Writing Practice

Metaphors are closely related to **idioms**. Idioms are popular expressions that mean something to people familiar with them, even if the words themselves do not literally express the sentiment. Popular idioms include "bite the bullet" and "kick the bucket." To a person outside a culture, these phrases would make no literal sense.

For this exercise, take an idiom with which you are familiar and write about it (in either play or poem form) in a way that makes it literal. So, if you were to use the expression "it's raining cats and dogs," you would create a world where that is actually happening.

The Hybrid: Plays in Verse

Plays in verse are nothing new. The idea of plays relying on poetic language is quite old. Shakespeare's plays, for instance, are often structured around iambic pentameter lines and, with a few exceptions, are almost always written in poetic lines (occasionally even in rhymed verse). This was true of Shakespeare's contemporaries. Plays were oratorical experiences, and poetic language was a logical way to create that necessary oration. By the twentieth century, play writers rarely used such formal poetic language. Instead, the language became more realistic and choppier. Long poetic monologues were less fashionable; characters often spoke in more back-and-forth bursts.

Intersecting Genre

The basic definition of a **verse play** (or dramatic verse) is a play that uses poetry to convey action and dialogue. If a play writer uses musical language, this approach can undoubtedly create lyric energy that can lighten and soften words spoken by the characters. While audiences can find comedies written in this fashion, verse plays can get more serious. So, yes, Shakespeare's comedies and romances are dramatic verse, but so are the tragedies. Does the effect of the verse language in *As You Like It* differ from the verse language of *Othello*? Absolutely. While the language works to merge the romantic pairings of the former play, the opposite occurs in the latter. There is a tension between characters with opposing viewpoints heightened by the lyrical nature of the language. In the case of Iago, the duplicitous antagonist of *Othello*, there is also the fact that he speaks differently depending on who he is addressing (or when he is alone). Even though some writers might incorrectly think that verse plays are a relic of the past, the possible tension within the form makes it an essential contemporary form.

In scholar Kasia Lech's book *Dramaturgy of Form: Performing Verse in Contemporary Theatre*, she writes that plays in verse are growing in popularity for a variety of reasons, including verse's ability to deconstruct prescriptive patriarchal tropes (because of its traditional approach to dialogue), its dedication to patterns, and its innate ability to force the audience to know that the performer is reading a script (because of the less-conversational nature of lyric language). Overall, Lech explains that verse plays are uniquely appropriate today because verse plays traditionally emerge from different or conflicting voices within the work. In this way, verse plays reflect critical global issues like multiculturalism and conflicting viewpoints.

Reclaiming a genre thought obsolete or, at the very least, less relevant than in previous generations creates a remarkable opportunity to adapt it for new audiences. Writing a play where characters speak in lines of poetry may seem unusual, but once a writer accepts the challenge and dives in, it becomes an opportunity to try something new. Using old methods to say new things gives power to poetry and plays.

Writing Practice

Think about something that happened to you in the last week and write a short poem about it. Do not overthink—just write. You will likely write it in the first person, but that is not required. Just write.

Then, think of a character and give that character a name. In play format, attribute the lines in the poem you wrote above to that character. Do not change anything about the poem. It is now simply dialogue.

Next, create another character and have them respond to the first character with another poem as dialogue. Keep it going. Did this approach to combining poetry and plays change how you wrote the second (and subsequent) parts? What do you think of the verse play you have created?

Summary

Despite their differences, poetry and plays are historically and artistically connected. While both genres have unique approaches to language, both depend upon careful attention to language for success. Both are old forms, rich with tradition, but the experimentation inherent in both makes them full of contemporary potential.

We think of poetic language as being musical and metaphor-filled, and, while it can be, it can also benefit from clear and direct language that connects with the reader. While plays use concise language to give their characters a voice, there are plenty of opportunities to use poetic language to enliven and enhance plays (including relying solely on verse throughout a play).

Writing Wrap-Up

Write a play scene featuring two people in a car. You decide who they are and where they are going. Regardless of those details, imagine they are listening to Vivaldi's *The Four Seasons* (you should listen to it as you write, if you can). How does the music affect their dialogue? Weave in musicality throughout their conversation.

CHAPTER 7
THE SELF AND THE SCREEN
INTERSECTIONS BETWEEN SCREENPLAYS AND CREATIVE NON-FICTION

A screenplay is for the screen; creative non-fiction is for the page. Both may begin as individually created projects, but a screenplay needs collaborative involvement to become a film, while CNF is usually a solo effort. Screenplay writers think of an audience of potentially many, so a writer for a screenplay generally considers various audiences (the eventual film's audience, the film's producers and directors, and the performers who will portray the characters, among many others). The inspiration for a given screenplay could come from countless places—the writer's personal experience, history, mythology, or a preexisting intellectual property. For a CNF writer, the inspiration is usually (but not always) personal and local—the writer's experiences drive the narrative.

This does not mean personal experiences never influence screenplays. A screenplay directly inspired by the writer's life is an obvious example, but even one less directly inspired by the writer's life could evolve from experience. For a screenplay to lead to an effective film, the characters must be convincing. This is true if a writer is penning a screenplay about historical figures, superheroes, space aliens, or the family next door. The characters—and the circumstances—need to feel as authentic as possible. If a character thinks and acts in disingenuous ways, an audience will not believe in the character, and the screenplay will fail.

In a way, this may seem silly. Screenplays (like many types of genre fiction, like science fiction and fantasy) often do not occur in worlds with the exact rules and species as our own. If a writer's screenplay is about an alien race in space, why should that writer make those characters human and relatable? They are not human. If a screenplay in the fantasy genre focuses on a quest through fantastical lands to retrieve an unrealistic object, why should that writer be concerned with reality? Do relatability and humanity need to be present in non-realistic genre-specific screenplays?

Absolutely. Suppose the screenplay is about an alien, a talking shark, or sentient pineapple. In each case, the writer needs to instill relatable traits and desires into the characters, or the reader simply will not engage with the story. Storytelling needs humanity. Aliens, superheroes, dinosaurs, and talking lions dominate the list of top-grossing films in the United States in the 2010s. The closest to a "realistic" film in that top ten has a scene where a car drives through multiple skyscrapers. Audiences are not always concerned with realistic scenarios, but the emotional stakes in these films ring differently. Those stakes involve relatable feelings—love, friendships, family, and loss. It does not matter if a character flies or shoots lasers; if an audience or reader can forge an emotional connection with that character, any work can succeed.

This is not to say all screenplays are fantasy. There are plenty of biographical, dramatic, and comedic films with more plausible situations than superhero movies or animated fantasy tales. But what drives all successful screenplays is the same—relatable characters making understandable decisions and feeling relatable emotions. This is true for a fantasy blockbuster and a memoir about substance use disorder. Whether your characters are werewolves or accountants, they must be relatable to an audience.

> ### Writing Warm-Up
>
> Think of your favorite movie. Now, write down the names of three main characters from that movie. Under each name, write down that character's primary wants or needs. What exactly drives these characters? There are likely multiple wants and needs for most complex main characters, so write down as many as possible. These are likely not all equal wants and needs, so it may be helpful to number them in order of priority.
>
> Finally, write down what the character does to fulfill those wants and needs. Are those actions plausible? Are they what you would do? And if they are not, is it still believable that the character would act this way?

. . . Based on a True Story

It is not hard to find movies based on true stories, but the gap between the "true story" and the movie based on it is often vast. It is not uncommon for someone to watch a biographical film about a historical figure, become interested in that historical figure, and then decide to look up more information. After a few minutes of internet investigation, our researcher is suddenly jaded because so many things the film purported to be accurate turn out not to be. Maybe the movie left out key details of the subject's life, or perhaps it changed major points altogether. Whatever the change, the film that purports to be true is often less accurate than an audience would think.

Movies set us up for this. The phrase "Based on a True Story" is not promising a true story. In a way, the phrase is a misdirection—promising something not exactly fulfilled. The word "based" is an alibi, making it clear that 100 percent accuracy is not the goal. Even if an audience expects a "based on a true story" movie to be historically or personally accurate, the film might not have those intentions. This hypothetical (but all too real movie) is not calling itself a "true story"—it is merely saying that actual events *inspired* the story on-screen. This technicality gives the screenplay writers and filmmakers the flexibility to adapt their source material into what they feel will make the most entertaining or thought-provoking (or profitable) film possible. If a screenplay writer wants everything in a screenplay to be accurate, they may believe it will make it harder to tell a compelling story. There is a freedom to *based on a true story* that the *true story* part resists. Besides, when watching a movie based on a historical figure, the audience already knows the film is not 100 percent historically accurate. After all, the audience knows the person playing the historical figure is a performer. No matter how convincing a performer is in a role, the audience is always aware of that level of remove, especially when the historical figure is incredibly renowned (or the performer playing the part is extremely famous). And since someone is pretending to be the character, the audience accepts that things in the film will not be entirely true. After all, we are already aware that people are playing the real-life characters depicted in the film. But even if the audience knows that the film is a reproduction of history, it can still feel like a betrayal if the film violates historical facts. Likely, "annoying" is as harsh as the criticisms will get (assuming audiences recognize the changes). If the film is good, that may be enough for most audiences to forgive the changes. In some cases, audiences and critics might even applaud changes that, while untrue, enhance the film's drama.

CNF is different. The reader is less likely to accept what they see as historical inconsistencies. They might be bothered if they see something that seems inaccurate in a film. If they spot inconsistencies in a CNF work, the reader's trust in the writer may break. A reader's expectation for CNF is that they are getting the absolute truth—it is not seen as a "reproduction" of the truth as a screenplay and film would be (though it is precisely that)—an audience could see anything that deviates from that truth as a violation of trust.

This is not to say that a reader will be angry about any deviation. As discussed in Chapter Two, no writer can (or should) recreate every conversation in a memoir verbatim. But when these factual inconsistencies are not minor, they can feel like betrayal. While audiences often overlook fictionalized history in film, falsified memoirs are less forgivable. For widespread audiences, the expectations for film value entertainment over absolute accuracy, while expectations for CNF seem to value honesty over all else. This is unfair to both forms—CNF writers deserve freedom, and screenplay writers deserve scrutiny. Instead of violating a reader's trust, CNF writers must find creative ways to engage audiences, and screenplay writers benefit from honest storytelling.

Writing Warm-Up

Screenplays and CNF are versatile. Screenplays can adapt to many different film genres (comedies, dramas, horror, and romance, to name just a few), and CNF can take the form of memoir, literary journalism, autobiography, and travel-writing, among many others. Both of these genres house almost limitless numbers of subgenres. A major difference between the two is formatting and overall presentation.

Try to think of a recent conversation that dealt with a subject matter that is important to you. While you do not need to use formal screenplay formatting, recreate this conversation, not in prose, but in scene form (complete with dialogue).

After you have written it, look it over. Is there a subgenre categorization in which you would put this (is it comedy, mystery, or something else)?

Now rewrite the conversation back into prose (still relying heavily on dialogue) but tweak the scene's reality a bit to make it fit into a subgenre. What would you do to make this scene a western, science fiction, horror, or something else? For the first part of the exercise, maintaining "truth" is unimportant—now you will see how your real-life conversation can play as subgenre fiction.

What Screenplays Teach Us about CNF

A screenplay writer must know how time functions in and affects their screenplays. It affects things in prose, but a prose writer may find more flexibility with length (including writing a shorter work if what they wish to write does not warrant novel-length). The screenplay writer will have to keep the script to a specific length to accommodate the directors and producers who will eventually be integral to putting the screenplay on-screen. This may sound like it could compromise the writer (and that could certainly be the case). Instead, see it as a call to focus.

All writers should strive for economic language. Regardless of genre, writers should be exact and concise. It is vital in poetry, emphasizing individual words and lines, but it is also crucial in CNF and fiction, where the writer should provide precise language. Good CNF and fiction contain compelling **scenes**—a scene is a creation of a moment, showing characters, dialogue, setting, and as many sensory details as fit within the context to make the reader feel immersed. Scenes are essential aspects of prose writing but are not the only tool available. Besides depicting literal scenes, prose writers can provide introspective moments of characters' thinking and remembering. The scene, however, is necessary to a CNF or fiction story's vibrancy and relatability.

The "scene" is a clear commodity for screenwriters, and it is crucial to analyze how scene construction impacts a screenplay to show how it benefits CNF writing. While screenplays can include voiceover narration, flashbacks, and other devices, the scene in a screenplay is always central. For example, while a flashback in a work of CNF serves as a general remembrance, it will be depicted as a scene in a screenplay. So the screenwriter tells a story for the screen that is a series of strung-together scenes. Not every screenplay is this easily described, but we can think of most screenplays as a sequence of scenes. If the screenplay is a sequenced series of scenes designed to tell a larger story, we must consider why the screenplay writer has chosen to depict the included scenes (and omitted other implied scenes).

Some viewers may see scenes in a finished film and think, "Ah yes, there was no other way to tell the story that movie wanted to tell without those scenes." Maybe sometimes an audience may think one scene is less necessary than another and that the writer should have cut some scenes completely. Regardless, there is always a recognition of the integrity of the basic structure. Importantly, scenes are in a clear and direct order—the first scene in a screenplay is the first scene for a reason, the second scene is deliberately the second scene, and so on until the last. This may seem obvious, but it leads to a crucial question. *Why* was the first scene chosen to be first? More specifically, why was *this scene* selected as the starting point of the screenplay? A screenplay should be a self-contained story. But the story represented within that screenplay is a moment in a character's overall life. The film is choosing what particular aspects of that life are most worthy of focus. It is not an unconscious matter—the writer needs to decide where and when within a larger story to focus.

There is a story that begins before a screenplay's action starts, and there is a story that continues after the point at which it ends. The plot is the part of the story the writer has chosen to cover in a specific work. Maybe the writer does not care or know what happens after the plot, but it is worth remembering *something* happens—a screenplay represents a blip in a character's (or multiple characters') timeline. Knowing this helps us structure the part of their lives we need to write about. A writer must consider why they have chosen to start a given screenplay where they have started it and why the scenes that follow are there. Often, writers think this is instinctual—the screenplay begins at a particular point because it has to. They will explain that the opening scene is where some specific event occurs—or it is directly before a certain event occurs—and, therefore, the action needs to begin there.

However, what feels obvious or instinctual might not be the right choice. When starting a screenplay, a writer needs to stop and ask what it is about this particular scene—and even more specifically, this moment—that makes it the ideal starting point. What if the screenplay began an hour earlier? An hour later? What if we started two weeks earlier? What changes? A writer must understand *why* they have made the choices they have made. A writer is always in control, and that control includes where every scene begins.

Multigenre Advice

If screenplays require a thoughtful approach as to where to begin, so do all other genres. It is just as important to consider why specific moments are the appropriate starting and ending points in fiction and play writing as it is in screenplay and CNF writing. These are all story-driven genres where the writer needs to consider how various options might work (and whether a given beginning or ending is the best choice).

This consideration is also crucial for effective poetry writing. Often, a poem might be better if the writer cut the first several lines (or the last several lines) and began (or ended) elsewhere. A writer can improve a poem by adding a few lines to the beginning or ending (or taking several lines away). Even though poems are not always as narratively driven as other genres, it is always essential for writers to question their choices and reconsider what is best for a particular piece.

Intersecting Genre

If a screenplay is merely a snapshot of a larger universe from which a writer can draw, then this is even more true of a CNF work. The CNF writer's memories and research build that larger universe. To start, CNF writers must ask the same critical question as screenplay writers—why is this the essential place to begin? While good writers of fiction or screenplays need to know the world of the characters and universe beyond what the screenplay depicts, there is an excellent chance that the CNF writer already knows this universe. Plenty of CNF can be written about events only tangentially connected to the author (or even unconnected), but something closely related to the writer often inspires the work. Even if the writer is composing a creative profile of a person, for example, they will have done plenty of research. The writer is aware of a larger universe because they have already experienced (or researched) it.

Remember, a first draft of a screenplay (or any genre) will create a different piece of writing than the second, third, or fourth draft. It is common to begin writing from the "beginning," including where the idea started when it first came into the writer's head. Many first drafts begin in a different place than the final draft ends up. A writer writes a piece into existence, which often means "overwriting," or adding more than is necessary. When writing early drafts, it is wise to try several things (including beginnings and endings that might not make the final draft) and then rely on the revision and editing stages to change things. Just because a writer chooses a sentence or line as the beginning does not mean that sentence or line has to stay there.

An interesting film to discuss is *Me and My Moulton*, written and directed by Canadian-Norwegian writer and filmmaker Torill Kove. The animated film takes a memory from Kove's childhood and builds around it. It is a film from a screenplay based on a personal experience. As with many CNF essays, the topic is personal and, while the topic may not necessarily seem remarkable to an audience, it is significant to the speaker's growth and development as a person. The film follows the narrator (voiced by Andrea Bræin Hovig, who also provides the voices of all other characters) as she and her two sisters are gifted a bicycle by their parents. While the children just want a bicycle like those owned by other kids in their neighborhood, their parents decide on a unique bicycle they feel better suits them as a family. Throughout the film, details show that the narrator's family differs from the other neighboring families because of their values and philosophies. The film captures this through humor and attention to small details.

Despite being an animated film, the narration and approach allow it to have much in common with prose CNF. For example, the film's ending enables the narrator to make a significant emotional statement about what the events depicted in the screenplay (and final film) mean on a personal level. Here is a quote from the narrator reflecting upon her (and her sisters') feelings on receiving the bike:

> Our parents have bought the bike they wanted for us. . . .We remember one Christmas when our parents gave all three of us new skis. We were so surprised and happy. We threw ourselves into their arms and were swept up in the success of the moment, a perfect balance of giving and receiving. This is what we want again. So we jump, grateful and needy, into our parents' arms.

A lot is happening here that, even if it is typically the stuff of CNF, works well in its context as an animated short film because it balances cute and lively animation with dramatic coming-of-age themes. She starts by explaining the reality of the bike. Specifically, it is the bike their parents wanted, not the children's choice. They had different expectations for their eventual bike, but the parents chose something else. Is the narrator upset by this? The first sentence makes this seem likely, but the audience is not entirely sure. While the audience thinks perhaps the second sentence in the narration will explain her feelings, the next sentence moves in a different direction—instead of further discussing the bike, the narrator talks about a joyful Christmas memory where she and her sisters received a gift they truly loved. Instead of moving forward, the screenplay narrative steps back to give the audience greater context for what is happening. Ultimately, the narrator explains that she and her sisters were so happy receiving skis as a Christmas present sometime earlier in their lives that they wanted to recapture that feeling and, therefore, thanked their parents the same way. Is the narrator (and her sisters) as happy with the bike as they could have been? It does not seem that way, but it is more complicated than simply saying, "she and her sisters didn't like the bike." The film uses narrative tools such as memory-recalling and self-reflection to paint a more complex picture that makes the reader feel more emotional resonance. Had Kove presented these actions without context or feelings, the viewer's emotional reaction would be limited.

Writing Practice

Write a screenplay for a short film about some event from your childhood. As you write, consider that this will not be a live-action film but instead be animated. How does knowing the final film would be animated affect how you present the particulars of the event you wish to show? Think about the potential of two genres to tell a personal story: screenplay and animation. How do these genres change the story more than if told as a prose CNF?

What CNF Teaches Us about Screenplays

Any writer is free to deviate from traditional approaches to story structure. Still, the basic expectations help keep the reader's focus on the character and story. It is beneficial to begin with thinking about what constitutes a story or plot. While there are different definitions, the simplest way to think about a story and plot is that the plot is what happens within the individual work you create. In contrast, the story is the more extensive information that does not completely fit into the particular plot (as discussed in Chapter 3). For example, a CNF short essay might involve a writer reflecting on the first day of his first job at a store. The plot is about the writer's experience with an angry customer who gets mad at a simple mistake made while the writer was trying to help the customer find something. The story is larger—it involves the writer's life before and

Intersecting Genre

after that plot, including experiences in that same store and whatever job experience the writer had before and after. Some of that story will get into the plot, but most will not. As a writer, it is valuable to know the larger story to understand what the plot needs.

In CNF, this awareness of the larger "story" is organic. After all, if the writer is crafting a memoir, they already know the story because it is constructed from lived material. For a screenplay writer, this is less organic—the story in a screenplay could undoubtedly come from lived material, but it does not have to. CNF needs to begin with experience. Screenplays create experiences but do not always showcase the writer's personal story. It is beneficial to look at a CNF work to understand how a story can be made and conveyed. This is a CNF piece entitled "Bee Man" by American writer Scott Loring Sanders:

> *"Loneliness is the poverty of self; solitude is the richness of self."*—May Sarton
>
> Mid-April, brutal hot, spring in the Blue Ridge. I'd pedaled twenty miles already, absorbing the pastel colors of emerging redbuds, dogwoods, and tulip poplars. The formidable hill was scorching my quads when the man—white-haired, overalls, rounded belly—called out, "Hey, buddy, want a cold drink?"
>
> I stopped, dismounted, shook my water bottles like maracas. "Think I could grab a refill?"
>
> "Sure. And I'll get you a so-dee pop, too."
>
> I relinquished the bottles, declined the soda, and he vanished through the screen door.
>
> The homestead was typical of Appalachia in southwest Virginia: shotgun house, backyard abutting a hardwood forest, clothesline, garden plot strategically angled for maximum sunlight in those unforgiving hollows.
>
> After he disappeared, I noticed a strange movement near a solitary porch chair. The floor appeared to be flowing, lava-like, in a trippy, psychedelic manner. Clambering over the wooden slats and surrounding the chair were hundreds—perhaps thousands—of honey bees.
>
> "Here's your water," he said upon his return. "And a cold drink." He'd either misheard (or simply ignored) my earlier refusal. But in that heat, I must admit, the knockoff Sprite was perfect. The sweetness, the cold. Ambrosia. He continued, "I see you discovered my buddies."
>
> "Yes, sir," I said, venturing closer to the bee horde. "What're they doing, exactly?"
>
> He approached the perimeter, tipped his own soda, wiggled his wrist. "Keeping me company." Droplets splattered the floorboards, momentarily dispersing the insects. "I first did it to attract raccoons. Sit out here in the evenings, watch them rascals waddle up like they own the place."
>
> Perplexed, I said, "For what reason? You try to pet them?"
>
> "Lord, no," he chuckled. "They'd bite the daylights out of me. I just watch."
>
> I nodded. "That must be nice. It's so peaceful out here."
>
> "Me and my wife lived here nearly sixty years. After she died a little while back, it got kind of lonesome. So, sure, it's nice. I enjoy their company."

A beautiful and heartbreaking image. This lonely old man tucked in the mountains, missing his wife, fabricating companionship. I imagined dusk in that hollow, spring peepers peeping, masked creatures venturing from their oak den each night, the man gently bouncing in his chair . . . waiting. Did he converse with them? Name them? Recognize specific personality traits, like an Appalachian Jane Goodall? How long did they stay? How long did he?

Until the last ringtail had scurried off, I bet.

"So what about the bees?" I asked. "You ever get stung?"

"Naw, they don't bother me none. They're so gentle," he said with grandfatherly admiration. "Tickle your skin when they crawl on you. Sometimes I lure one to my hand, raise it to my face, say, 'Hey, Mr. Honey Bee, you got the purtiest little eyes.' He never pays me no mind, just uses his teensy tongue to lap that sweetness from my wrist."

I finished my drink, thanked him, found myself smiling. His affection, his demeanor, it was contagious.

"You come back and see me," he said, raising his can in salute.

* * *

I crushed the final ten miles, preoccupied with a fantasy from adolescence: of becoming a hermit, living in an isolated cabin, vanishing from society to be alone. No, not to be alone—to find solitude. Because solitude, I now realized, was far different than loneliness. Loneliness was sad; solitude was contentment.

Loneliness breaks the spirit, so goes a Jewish proverb. But the bee man had concocted a method to defy that maxim, to rectify his loneliness. Or at least keep it at bay. And I admired that.

What form might my future loneliness take? Sitting on my own porch in the mountains? Writing if my fingers still worked? If my mind still did? I envisioned not just sprinkling soda at my feet but pouring it all over my body, longing for the bees to fully envelop me.

I imagined it as pleasant, peaceful: fuzzy insect legs tickling my skin; little "tongues" lapping nectar from my arm hairs; "purty little eyes" paying me no mind.

Absolute solitude . . . and yet, companionship. Something odd to strive for, perhaps, but the entire time I pedaled home, my smile never wavered.

Sanders creates the plot from experience, and it moves logically and chronologically. If we think of the story as the more extensive series of events that lead to the plot (the specific events within a text), the story has already begun when "Bee Man" starts. The narrator has already been biking for twenty miles. That is relevant to the plot, but it is not essential to show those twenty miles. Here, a quick explanation of the distance (rather than a detailed several-page account) is sufficient. What happened in those 20 miles is not specifically relevant, so that journey is condensed and summarized. We know what is essential—20 miles is a long distance, and someone cycling that far will be tired. The plot of this story is what happens when he sees the man who offers him water.

The speaker gets off his bike and looks around the stranger's "homestead" while the stranger goes inside the home to collect water and cold sodas. The narrator then sees the bees (numbering in either hundreds or thousands). It is important to note that, at this moment, the narrator does not think or speculate about the bees. Almost everything in this section of the story happens on a literal level—virtually everything is what any observer would conclude without needing to know what anyone is thinking. Eventually, the narrator asks about the bees, and the man says that his wife has recently died and the bees are pleasant company for him. The narrator then explains that this is a "beautiful and heartbreaking image." While that is a moment of the narrator telling the reader what he is thinking, it is hardly a unique way of seeing the situation—an observer watching the exchange would likely also see the beauty and heartbreak of the man's story. The "Bee Man" then explains that the bees are gentle and never hurt him. Our narrator rides off with minimal interior commentary.

The essay does an interesting thing here—this part of "Bee Man" ends with a visual break in the form of a few asterisks. Often in prose writing, these asterisks would mean a change in time or location, but here it indicates a shift in perspective. The "plot" part of the essay is over. During that portion of the story, the narrator is primarily neutral, reporting the events that transpired (and the commentary included is fairly inarguable). After the asterisks, the story goes internal, and the narrator discusses his emotional reaction to the encounter with the man. This is crucial for multiple reasons (and instructive for writers in all genres). The meeting described in the first part of the story is unique and interesting—it is not every day you meet a person who has thousands of bees for company. But the essay does not rely on that unexpected encounter for its emotional impact—it pivots to a meditation on loneliness and coping. The ending of "Bee Man" is not based on the action depicted in the plot. Instead, the ending reflects the events recounted in the plot and why they mattered to the speaker.

Writing Practice

Using Sanders's "Bee Man" as a guide, write a CNF piece in which the first two-thirds of the essay recount the events of something interesting (but perhaps *not too interesting*) that happened to you. In the last third of the story, discuss how you felt after the event, what you took from it, and how that affected the long-term course of your life afterward.

"Expands in the Mind"

American writer Flannery O'Connor explains that a piece of writing "really isn't any good unless it successfully resists paraphrase until it hangs on and expands in the mind."

For O'Connor, what matters is that the creative writing work "hangs on and expands in the mind." If someone can paraphrase (to use O'Connor's word) a CNF piece (or any type of creative writing) and successfully capture everything that matters about that piece, the piece likely lacks merit in the first place. Here is a paraphrase of Sanders's "Bee Man":

> a cyclist is biking a long distance in hilly terrain when offered water by a stranger. This stranger has a horde of bees, and he briefly tells the tired cyclist about his gentle relationship with them. The cyclist leaves and thinks happily about the bees and what he learned from the man about loneliness.

Does that capture the essence of the story? It captures the plot but little else—it informs us about what happened in "Bee Man," but the plot is less important than the emotional resonance the speaker achieves at the end. Just explaining the literal events does not convey the emotion of the CNF essay. In this way, "Bee Man" resists paraphrase and, much like it does for the narrator himself, it does not reach its complete form until the reader thinks about the events, allowing their significance to expand "in the mind."

Going Further

While similar, summary and paraphrase are two different concepts. Both involve rephrasing something into new and original words, but the amount of detail differs. A **summary** only recounts the key moments of something. If you summarize a work, you are not telling your reader (or listener) everything that happens in the original—just the most important aspects. A **paraphrase** is different—a paraphrase is more detailed and longer than a summary. We could condense a summary of a movie into a sentence or two. A paraphrase of the same movie would be much longer.

Beginning-Middle-End

All works of writing need a beginning, a middle, and an ending. We will refer to this as the **BME** structure, or just BME. This is simple and self-explanatory, and it is also too important to introduce without elaboration. Even if the BME structure is instinctive and intuitive, thinking consciously of it leads to intelligent and well-plotted creative works.

- Writers must deliberately consider the beginning, middle, and ending of a piece of writing.
- Just because all creative works have a beginning, a middle, and an ending does not mean that each part of this structure functions the same in all pieces of writing.
- There are rarely clear definitions between sections.

Intersecting Genre

So there must be a beginning, middle, and ending, but the writer can dictate what constitutes each. Sanders' "Bee Man" begins when the cyclist arrives at the stranger's house and the owner offers him something to drink. The middle is the conversation with the stranger about the bees, and the ending is the cyclist reflecting on the interaction as he rides away. In this case, the "ending" is after the "action" of the story has stopped. If Sanders wanted to begin the story by talking about his views on loneliness before meeting the stranger, that would be the beginning. If that case, maybe the ending of the cyclist reflecting on the conversation would be reduced simply to explaining how he could not stop smiling, thus asking the reader to reach the necessary conclusion on how the speaker was affected. The writer decides what part of the story will be used for plot and in what order it will be structured.

Also, chronology is not always relevant in this structure—what matters most is what the writer prioritizes (which may be emotional resolution rather than chronological consistency). The beginning of a plot could be its chronological middle or end, while the rest of the story explains what happened prior. Even if this would not fit the convenient explanation of BME, it fits into a narrative explanation. We need to tell our stories in the way that best accomplishes our goals, whether logic or precedent fit at all.

> ### Going Further
>
> To further think about the BME structure and how it can work in and around chronology, choose a favorite movie and, numbering between one and twenty, list twenty important events from the film in the order in which they occur (go ahead and reduce the number of moments if you need to).
>
> After you complete this list, ask yourself a few questions. Does anything happen out of chronological order? Is there anything that challenges the traditional BME structure? Even if there are no chronological shifts, significant time jumps might occur. As you look at your list, think about this: you have dissected one of your favorite movies on a plot level. What does this dissection tell you about the movie itself?

The Hybrid: Documentary Podcasts

While there are many types of podcasts—including interviews and conversations about specific topics—one of the most popular podcast genres is documentary. The documentary podcast will typically spend multiple episodes investigating a particular topic, perhaps a murder or crime. It certainly could be less nefarious, but this type of podcast often involves a crime (and "True Crime Podcast" can be a more specific form of this genre). These podcasts are scripted and in series form (in which a more extensive story unfolds episode-to-episode).

While the word "cinematic" may feel inappropriate for an audio genre, for a non-video form, documentary podcasts are quite cinematic. That quality emerges through a typically polished and highly edited approach. While most conversation-based podcasts will sound casual and unrehearsed, documentary podcasts are different—they are not recorded and then published with minimal editing (as would be the case with a conversational podcast). Instead, creators carefully and thoughtfully edit these types of podcasts. Even in a podcast series with an overarching theme, individual episodes typically have themes unique to the episode (while still developing the overall series' larger story). Adding to the cinematic quality is the often professional use of sound, including background music and sound effects to enhance the podcast's believability (and, when appropriate, suspense).

Unlike most podcasts, the documentary approach emphasizes long-form storytelling. This long-form documentary approach is well established in film, with examples of long-form multipart documentary series examining a broad topic (like a war, musical genre, or sport) being quite common. But these series differ from a documentary podcast in crucial ways—the audio media (with video removed) encourages intimacy. A film documentary uses video and images to tell the story, but with a documentary podcast, there is only the voice of the host and those interviewed (when applicable). While there can still be music and audio effects, these enhance the experience, not overwhelm it. In a documentary podcast, everything must be in service of storytelling.

Audiences typically listen to these podcasts alone, often on commutes or in solitary moments. There is only the podcast and the listener. And the podcast itself is narrowly focused on a topic. This is genuine intimacy. The documentary podcast uses that intimacy to whisk the listener away.

Writing Practice

Go to a news site and find an article that interests you, preferably about something that is not a top news story but still compelling. Do not settle for the first thing you see—dig deeper for something interesting.

Once you have found a topic, spend some time researching to learn more about it. Write down some ideas about how you would present this news story to others. Write down two paragraphs in which you summarize your news story.

Look at those two paragraphs and find sentences with the potential to be expanded. How would you develop these ideas? What would you like to know more about regarding the topic? How would you develop these ideas? Those ideas are a jumping-off point toward a documentary podcast about the subject.

Once you have found a topic, spend some time researching and perhaps learn more about the topic. At that point, write down some ideas about how you would present this news story to others. Write down two paragraphs in which you summarize your story.

Intersecting Genre

> Look at those two paragraphs and find sentences with potential to be expanded. How would develop these ideas? What would you like to know more about? How would you develop these ideas? Those ideas are a jumping off point toward a documentary podcast about the subject.

Summary

Creative non-fiction often explores personal experiences to understand how they affect the writer emotionally and mentally. While CNF essays can delve into complex and painful moments in one's life, they do not have to—sometimes, CNF explorations are about events that can seem mundane from the outside but manage to usher in some kind of change. Compelling CNF depends less on the subject than the overall meaning. Readers connect with all types of writing—the subject matters, but it is not the only thing that matters. CNF writers—and writers in all genres—need to consider structure. A good essay needs structure.

The best screenplays do too. They also avoid generalization and instead go for interesting details and particulars. When we think about our personal experiences, we often think about big moments, even those dotted with minor details. When we tell our stories—by providing the plots that guide our experiences and characters that matter—we want to reach an audience emotionally, and structure help make that happen. Structure can lead to emotional resonance.

> ### Writing Wrap-Up
>
> Whether it was a high-stakes situation or something relatively minor, think of a time in your life when someone betrayed you. Spend five minutes writing down everything relevant you can remember about the moment and then depict that moment in screenplay form.
>
> Retelling an event to others makes it easy to stay general and non-specific. When writing a screenplay, that is not an option. Be detailed, be specific, and remain scene-oriented.

CHAPTER 8
WANTS AND PERSPECTIVES
INTERSECTIONS BETWEEN PLAYS AND FICTION

Successful plays and great fiction stories have a lot in common—compelling characters who strive for specific goals (that are clear to an audience) and use convincing dialogue that shapes the characters and drives the creative work forward. The easiest way for a play or work of fiction to fail is through poorly rendered characters. The importance of great character-building is beyond debate. A compelling work of fiction or an effective play begins with characters in whom readers can become invested. A play or piece of fiction can have a great plot with twists and turns and a wildly satisfying conclusion, but if the audience does not care about the characters experiencing those twists and turns, nothing else matters. If a story or play lacks good characters, it is probably not going to be successful. Therefore, the first step to writing compelling plays and fiction is understanding how to create compelling characters.

When a work features a prominent setting or even crucial objects, audiences and readers might argue that those things are characters. Think about a novel set in a rugged desert landscape with a plot that follows a handful of characters as they navigate the terrain. That terrain is causing problems for our characters and establishes itself as a significant element of tension, thus elevating its presence. And there is nothing more important in a novel or play than characters. If a reader sees a setting as a character, the writer should know that this is high praise.

So if good characterizations are the key to successful storytelling, the obvious question is: *What makes for a good character?* The first step is creating characters to whom readers can relate. On the surface, a lot of successful characters are not particularly relatable. Science fiction is full of sentient robots, and fantasy gives us dragon-tamers and wizards. Even realistic fiction and plays can provide us with characters whose experiences are unrelatable. So how does a writer create a robot that makes a reader or audience member think, "I understand what that character is experiencing?" How can an audience member in the twenty-first century watch a play about a fourteenth-century Danish Prince (written in the sixteenth century) and feel connected?

While it is tempting to assume a secret formula is behind all this, there is nothing mysterious at work. Great works contain great characters, and compelling desires motivate great characters. Successful writing begins with understanding what every character wants.

Writing Warm-Up

A character arrives at a restaurant to meet someone they have connected with online. Their date has not yet arrived, so our character has decided to wait on a bench outside the restaurant. You can fill in the blanks about what type of restaurant we are in and the character's expectations about the person they are meeting.

Now, write three things this character wants. The first want should be something modest, the second should be something bigger, and the third should be something other characters in this universe would not realize.

Then, write a brief monologue from this character's point of view as they wait. How does knowing those three wants affect your writing? Did all three wants directly make it into your writing? If not, is the emotional resonance of an unmentioned want still present?

What a Character Wants

Every character must want or need something. It is that simple. If a character wants something, then the character is easier to write and understand. If the character's desire is shallow or too superficial, it might not lead to a compelling conclusion. Engaging a reader or audience might be challenging if a character simply wants to eat some cake. But a simple want is still better than an abstract one because a specific want will always motivate a character directly. It will also be easier for a reader or audience member to comprehend. If a character wants something abstract, like happiness, creating a concrete manifestation of that need is essential. If the character's want is love without any concrete manifestation, the character may end up seeming naïve or too implausible. The want needs to be present, but it helps to have something that can ground a character.

If a character has a primary and clear-cut *want*, it is much easier for the reader/audience to become invested. For example, two similar characters exist in two separate short stories. Both characters are jugglers who perform at kids' birthday parties. In the first story, the protagonist juggles for fun simply because she loves doing it. If she can be said to have one, her want is vague. She *wants* to juggle because she enjoys it. In the second story, the protagonist's *want* is more defined. She enjoys juggling, but she wants to be a more serious performer. She wants to afford to go to acting school with the dream of someday being in a play on London's West End. Maybe kids' birthday parties are beneath her a bit, but her *want* (the desire to go to an acting school) drives her motivation. The second story is more compelling because there is something at stake.

This need for want is not only relevant to main characters. Even secondary and minor characters should have something they are chasing. Characters who meander with no focus are not typically characters that earn our attention. Characters who wander about for specific reasons? That is something else entirely.

Defining what a character wants allows a writer to explore other dramatic elements. If Character A wants something and Character B does not want Character A to have that thing, we have created a story with **conflict** and **tension**. Conflict is a struggle that informs a creative writing work. Tension is uncertainty about what will happen (with a concern that things will not turn out well). All successful work has some sort of tension (if a novel has no tension and no characters seeking something, it will be very dull). Conflict and tension keep things interesting.

Going Further

It is often easy to find inappropriate inspiration when it comes to conflict. For example, the type of conflict that will suit a realistic fiction novel or a play about a family's inner drama will be different than the conflict at the heart of a big-budget action movie. In that kind of movie, the central tension could be, for example, between two secret agents (one good and one evil), both trying to obtain a priceless relic and willing to kill the other if necessary (the good secret agent only seeing such a solution as a last defense). While this might make logical sense for that particular movie, a somber family drama will have quieter conflicts. Even though the word "conflict" makes us think of life-or-death confrontations that is not always the case, especially if the genre pushes back against such fireworks.

It is helpful to think of conflict as a volume dial. The higher we turn up the dial, the more intense the conflict. Does a character want a cookie? That level of conflict and tension is pretty low. This exact conflict is potentially appropriate in a children's book because that should not have a particularly "loud" conflict. A character wants the nuclear codes to start WW3? That is a loud conflict. A mother telling her child the truth about her father? Well, the volume here depends on the reveal. If he is a ne'er do well who left mother and daughter because he did not love them, that is a lower volume than if that father wants to obtain the nuclear codes to start WW3. The volume level does not mean a "loud" conflict is better than a quieter type (or vice-versa)—it simply means readers and audiences will respond to varying volume levels differently. The lower the volume, the more intimate and personal the struggle. The higher? It is more bombastic and action oriented.

An essential aspect of conflict building is ensuring that the type of conflict introduced is at the appropriate "volume level" for your project. Remember, a moderate volume level does not ruin a play or novel. Not only does every possible volume level has a place, but a single piece may contain many different volumes.

These volumes reflect the conflict, but character wants and needs dictate that conflict. While crucial, wanting something is only the beginning of shaping character needs. When developing short stories, novels, or plays, writers need to consider character motivations, especially for significant characters. To properly convey information to the reader, a writer must know *what* a character wants and *why* they want it so badly—a writer needs to show the *what* and the *why* directly. *What* without *why* is incomplete.

Both *what* and *why* must be convincing. For a writer to fully immerse themselves in a work, the reader must believe that a character would be motivated in the way depicted. If the reader does not accept the writer's explanation for the character's wants, the reader will likely disengage. A successful character is a believable one, and believability starts with motivation.

But it cannot end with that same motivation. Characters build from wants, but they grow through dialogue, descriptions, and actions. Characters take shape by how they interact with other characters and their environments. There is no one way to create a character, but motivation is a prime place to start. If want drives a character, the character will feel more alive—they will talk about their wants and needs and act accordingly. Their interactions with characters and environments will be affected by that want, even their choices of *who* they interact with and *where* they go. If a character has a specific want, that will affect how they present themselves to the world (so if a character wants someone else to fall in love with them, they better dress and groom accordingly). There are several ways to establish and build characters, but motivation is where best to begin.

Writing Practice

Imagine yourself as a character. Now, think of your day yesterday. What were five *wants* you had over the day? They can be big or small. Now, come up with why you wanted each of those five things.

This list may seem mundane. Compelling writing can begin with the ordinary.

Now, write a short scene (either in prose or play format) in which you create a fictionalized character using some of the wants and reasons you wrote out earlier. Remember, this is not you—you are crafting a fictionalized character who might eventually have nothing to do with you. Structure this piece in the first person (literally in prose, or with this character as a constant presence if in a play). These wants will help drive the first-person narration through the quest to fulfill those wants.

What Plays Teach Us about Fiction

Plays and fiction use characters to tell compelling stories with a plot that has a clearly defined beginning, middle, and end. Those characters have wants and needs, and audiences can become emotionally invested. While the formatting and final delivery of the two genres are different, there is more that separates the two, including aspects we might not initially consider. Here is an excerpt early from a piece of writing titled "Before" by Penny Jackson:

Josh, you freaked me out today and I need to record what the hell is happening because the facts are still messed up in my mind. My mom's always checking my computer, but I can hide this camera. So it's just you and me, dude.

When you texted me, "Hey bro, I have the answer to your problem," I thought you were coming over to help me with my college essay. But when you slammed the door and said, "We need to go down to the basement, like *now*," I thought what the fuck? I mean, you're the cool one, Josh, the one who never breaks a sweat, and here you were, acting all CIA with me.

So where were we? Right. Down in my basement. You're checking it all out, as if you need to be sure no one is down there, like someone's really going to be hiding in the washing machine. "What's up?" I asked. You just shook your head and grinned.

"I got a present for you, Scottie. A present you'll find really useful."

You were carrying a shopping bag, Josh. A shopping bag from Abercrombie and Fitch and I thought you were going to give me a T-shirt. But you took out a Keds shoe box. Like, what the fuck are you doing with a Keds shoe box? Then you placed it on the Ping-Pong table and opened it and it's a gun.

Here is another excerpt from a different piece of writing titled "Before" by Penny Jackson. Like in the first example, this comes from the piece's beginning. While these two excerpts are similar (with the same title) there are significant differences between the two:

It's too easy. That's the problem. Or that's part of the problem. I mean Robin's the problem. My problem. But my buddy Josh told me he had the answers.

Josh just left in his new red BMW, an early graduation present from his dad. At first, when Josh phoned to say he was stopping by, I thought he was just coming by to brag about the new wheels. But when he showed up at my door and said we needed to go down to the basement, like NOW, I didn't know what the hell he was talking about.

So when we went down to the basement and Josh dug deep inside the bottom of his backpack and took out this shoebox, a shoebox from Keds, I sure as fuck didn't expect a gun. I think I even laughed.

While we will discuss the differences, the similarities between the two are apparent. These are two versions of the same piece but are not two separate drafts. Instead, they are both explorations of the same story and characters that vary in one overarching way. More than two different versions of the same basic concept, these are written in two different *genres* based on the same idea. One of these excerpts is from a short story written in the first person, and the other is a short play with one character who delivers monologues throughout three scenes. As shown in these two excerpts, Jackson does not use the exact phrasing in both circumstances because the two genres have different expectations. The decisions Jackson makes in both versions derive from genre-specific needs.

Intersecting Genre

> **Going Further**
>
> Before reading any further, think about the two versions of "Before" and choose which you believe is the excerpt from a short story and which is the excerpt from a play? Why did you choose each of your answers?

In the first version, the speaker addresses "Josh" directly (in the second, the speaker discusses Josh but does not address him directly). The second-person address in the first "Before" also creates more of an intimacy with the "you" (Josh). The first version also explains that the speaker is recording his words, making sure they are not found by just anyone.

In contrast, the second version takes some of the emphasis (at least in this excerpt) off Josh by mentioning him along with other characters. Both excerpts are conversational, and while the point of view difference (from first- and second-person POV to just first) is crucial, it is not the only distinction. The first excerpt is a bit chattier, more willing to include minor details. Both feel ominous, especially at the end of each passage when Josh reveals the gun. Josh is more sly in the first version about going to the basement; in the second, there is an urgency in his shouted "NOW." The first is conversational and comparatively meandering, as if a story told by an uneasy speaker. The second is urgent and far more direct.

The first "Before" excerpt is the beginning of a one-act play. The second version is the beginning of a short story. Now that you know this, reread them both. Do you see anything you missed before? Does the first seem more performative? Does Scottie's act of recording the speech feel theatrical? Think of how this monologue would work in front of an audience. Scottie is directly addressing Josh, but it is clear Scottie is not sure Josh will (or can) respond. The chattiness feels a bit anxious, as if the speaker is nervous. While Josh is not a literal presence, the audience in the theater would be. So they serve as a proxy for Josh. That makes Scottie more personal and colloquial because his friend is the implied audience. Would this same intimate, direct-address approach work in a short story?

It could. But expectations are different. There is no expectation of reading a work of fiction aloud, so it can be difficult for a reader to get into the oratorical mindset. So fiction reliant on performance is a difficult sell. With a play, however, even before the eventual performance, a reader will *listen* to what they read in a way that differs from prose. So the first version is livelier to the ear and possesses an aural energy the second is less interested in reaching.

But the second excerpt is doing something else—crafting a story. The second version immediately introduces "Robin," a character implied but not mentioned in the first. The prose allows the scope to widen. The first version builds suspense through conversational energy, through the dynamic between the speaker and the implied listener. The second version builds tension through story. There is a narrative pull in the second that is not in the first. The narrative goals of each piece are the same, but their processes are different. The world in the fiction excerpt feels larger by mentioning Robin and the BMW. The play version focuses very much on the dynamic between the speaker and the audience. Seeing where things merge and subsequently diverge is a crucial part of genre intersections, and we need to spend time in those divergences and find out why they matter.

Writing Practice

A **monologue** is a solo speech in a play, typically read aloud to the audience with no other characters as an audience (and, typically, no other characters on stage). While monologues are not a realistic device (and require suspension of disbelief from the audience), they are valuable in that they allow the audience to get a sense of what a character is thinking.

Write a play scene that features a character, alone on stage, speaking a monologue to another character who is not present in the scene (and the speaking character is aware the other character is not present). Your monologue should be about something (whether literal or metaphorical) that the other character has taken from the speaker and that the speaker wants back. Perhaps the speaker is aware that they likely will not get this thing back. Even if that is true, it does not change the speaker's desire to get whatever it is back.

What Fiction Teaches Us about Plays

Play writers can introduce and develop characters through the words and actions those characters say and perform. Fiction is a less visual form than plays, relying on written description rather than performance, but what fiction can do with character and point of view is a crucial teaching tool for a play writer. Fiction writing always conveys a point of view (even if a writer can complicate that point of view for literary purposes). Somebody is telling the story; there is either a clear limit to what that narrator knows or no limit. A play's point of view is simply less defined than in fiction. Understanding how point of view works in fiction can help screenplay writers explore perspective in their plays.

Point of view is simply a way of telling a story. While there are layers of complexity to each point of view (POV), there are three basic types:

- First person—the story is told by a speaker who identifies as "I."
- Second person—the story is addressed to "you."
- Third person—the story does not have an identified "I" and instead a narrator simply identifies the characters as "he," "she," and "they."

First-person and third-person POV are the most employed perspectives in fiction, but these POVs are more than simply using "I" or "they." There is nuance to each POV.

In first-person POV, the writer must think carefully about who is telling the story, what that narrator thinks about what is happening, why they are telling the story, and what they know and do not know. It is helpful to think of POV as a sliding scale—does the narrator know everything, or do they know very little? In first-person POV, we must consider whether the narrator is the **protagonist** (the main character), a **deuteragonist** (the secondary protagonist—not the main character, but the second most important), or someone else. This is crucial. If the speaker is the main character, they can tell the reader everything they are thinking—including backstory and motivation. If the narrator is a secondary character, they can observe the actions from a distance (and maybe have objectivity the main character cannot have), but they cannot tell the reader what the protagonist is thinking. They can only speculate on another character's thoughts (or discuss their own). If a writer wants to keep the protagonist mysterious, it is beneficial to use another POV. Unless a first-person narrator knows every character and situation, we call them "limited."

Going Further

In POV, **limited** simply means there is a limit to what the narrator knows (which is true for all of us in real life). A limited third-person POV involves a narrator who only knows and sees what a particular character knows and sees. While the limited third-person narrator stands at the opposite end of an **unlimited** narrator (where the narrator knows everything every character knows—and beyond that), these are two extremes of a line, not the only options. Any narrator who is not entirely **omniscient** (all-knowing) is somewhat limited, but that does not mean they only know what one character knows—they just do not know everything. Before delving too deeply into a draft, a writer should know what type of narrator will be best for their story. And, once the writing begins, that narrator must be consistent.

Understanding your narrator is not just about what they know—you also must consider the context of their narration. *When* is the narrator telling their tale? Is it while the action is taking place? Many years later? If it takes place many years later, the narrator can have a perspective that could not have existed at the earlier moment—no character would see things the same after so many years. English writer Emily Bronte's *Jane Eyre* is written this way, with the protagonist reflecting on what occurred a decade earlier. American writer F. Scott Fitzgerald's *The Great Gatsby* is often used to discuss POV. In that book, Nick Carraway is the narrator, and, while most readers see Jay Gatsby as the protagonist, Nick's narration and perspective drive the story. Seeing it through his eyes makes it feel like his story, even if the subject matter of his narration mainly focuses on another character.

Nick is **unreliable**, a narrator the reader cannot wholly trust. There are many reasons a first-person narrator would be unreliable:

- The narrator is deliberately dishonest
- The narrator knows less than they think they do
- The narrator is extremely limited in their knowledge of a situation and simply cannot explain much outside of that narrow awareness
- The narrator is influenced by substance use disorder
- The narrator suffers from delusions, depression, or self-aggrandizement
- The narrator is biased toward (or against) specific characters

While an unreliable narrator could be unreliable because of intentional dishonesty, that is not usually the case, and often there are multiple reasons for a narrator's unreliability. In the case of Nick in *The Great Gatsby*, for example, we can argue he is telling stories about a time in his life dominated by his struggles with substance use disorder (specifically alcohol). He suffers from depression during the retelling, and he feels loyalty toward Gatsby (which makes him incapable of seeing Gatsby unbiasedly). While the items listed above are specific reasons a narrator can be unreliable, all first-person narrators are inherently unreliable. At the very least, all speakers have limits to their knowledge, and even the most knowledgeable first-person narrator has limits to what they know. In first-person POV, this is less a problem than an opportunity. Understanding what your speaker does not know—and why they do not know it—provides a path to making that character relatable and engaging.

The choice of narrator in a work of fiction might feel obvious, but it is one of the most critical decisions a fiction writer can make. It is imperative to remember that point of view does not happen by accident. In many cases, one POV will feel more organic than another, so it may seem like an instinct more than a choice. But that does not mean the writer has not made a choice. A writer should never be afraid to revisit a POV choice while writing a piece because they can never know if something will work or not (including POV) until they try it. Sometimes things do not turn out the way we hope—that is okay. We can just try something else.

The third-person POV eschews "I" and "you" and instead tells a story using "they," "she," or "he" pronouns. So while first-person POV allows the writer to have a storyteller who is involved in the story (deeply or tangentially, depending on the author's choice), the third-person POV elects instead to include a narrator who is not explicitly a character and, if the author chooses to do so, could know whatever information is (or potentially is not) relevant to the plot.

While the third-person narrator is not a directly named character in the story, this does not mean that the third-person narrator is without characterization or potential bias. The writer has chosen a narrator and, subsequently, decides what characters and events upon which that narrator will focus. The third-person narrator is arguably a character (albeit a detached, unnamed character).

Intersecting Genre

In that case, what is the point of such a narrator? Why not just make it first person? Because even a limited third-person narration provides different options than a first person. Even if a third-person POV perspective is closely tied to a character, that POV is NOT the character, so the reader will not feel the same intimacy. With such a limited narration, the reader can still know a character but have a distance that can allow detachment.

Second-person POV, the least often used perspective in prose, has a prominent role in poetry (where the presence of a "you" is commonplace, usually an address to the reader or a stand-in for the writer) and in **epistolary** writing (creative work in the form of letters). While this form is less used in standard prose, it can convey urgency or intimacy with a reader.

Poems use second-person POV with some regularity (usually coupled with a first-person speaker addressing a "you"), but in fictional or CNF storytelling, it is less common (though assuredly used). In prose, it is often a placeholder for the speaker ("You knew what you were doing when you went out that night. . .") that makes the reader feel more involved with the action described. It can also make the reader feel more comfortable ("I'm telling you this story because I know I can trust you. . .") or uncomfortable ("I saw you through the window. . ."). When it comes to plays, it is helpful to think of second person because, in a way, most plays have the second-person POV in mind. We must always consider our audiences, and a play must decide what the reader or audience needs to know to ensure they stay invested. In this way, all plays have elements of second-person POV, whether the play acknowledges that reality or not. Typically, the viewer is an anonymous observer, simply watching from a distance, unnoticed.

Writing Practice

An epistolary novel is a work composed entirely of letters, usually written back and forth between characters. This form allows for a sense of realism (because there is an authenticity to letter writing) as well as insight into character perspectives.

Over time, this form has fallen out of favor because letter writing is not the prominent form of communication it once was and therefore contemporary readers would see less realism and urgency from the form.

But that does not mean the epistolary novel needs to disappear. Write a short story using a modern-day form of letter-writing—text messages. Try to shape an emotional narrative solely using an invented text conversation between two characters.

While the narrative structure differs in plays, the narrator concept is worth learning. Some plays have narrators (especially when characters break the fourth wall to explain the events to the audience, as discussed in Chapter 6), but a play that follows one character throughout also has a point of view. Does the play have one character that is in every (or almost every) scene? If so, we can argue that the play has a limited perspective, especially if we rarely see anything outside of what that primary character sees. Suppose the play is working with a large group of characters featured in different combinations through various scenes (without any single character appearing in every scene). That play functions with a much less limited perspective. The reader (viewer) can be wherever the play writer needs them to be, not simply attached to one character.

There are merits to both limited and unlimited POVs in plays. The unlimited perspective gives the writer much more freedom and flexibility—and gives the reader (viewer) more variety. The limited approach will allow the audience to feel much more intimacy with that single character, which could increase the audience's attachment to the play. It is another reminder of the high stakes of so many decisions we make as writers.

Writing Practice

Think about a character who is uniquely bad at something. This does not have to be anything of extreme consequence, just something they cannot do very well. Maybe they are a lousy singer or an awkward runner. Perhaps they cannot physically wink. Whatever it is, write a few paragraphs from a third-person omniscient POV about this character trying to do this thing.

After you have finished, switch to a first-person POV in which the speaker is the character you created and wrote about in the first version. Now, write a few paragraphs in which that specific character writes about trying to do the thing they cannot do very well. How do the two pieces of writing differ? What did you discover about this character by writing this in two different ways?

The Hybrid: Closet Dramas

A closet drama is a play without the intent of formal performance. If performed at all, a single individual typically reads it to a small group, or the small group simply reads it to each other. The audience is small. A closet drama is not staged or practiced, and there are no props or stagecraft. It is a writer using the play format to get ideas across without considering the stage. The words and the ideas matter most. Perhaps it is written and casually performed to entertain the writer's friends, or maybe it is a way to explore ideas that would otherwise have little chance of formal production.

Since the stage is part of what makes plays unique, a closet drama takes away that aspect to create something that feels like a drama/fiction hybrid. The closet drama finds its place primarily within its pages, even if read aloud. In other forms of drama, a writer must think carefully about the audience—after all, a play needs a live audience more than any of the genres discussed in this book. Audiences give plays a reason to exist and thrive. A closet drama is personal and intimate—the performance is less critical than the product. A closet drama is not a reading or rehearsal of a play—those typically occur in anticipation of a more formal production later. Such production is not the objective of a closet drama.

Closet dramas are not new—they date back to Elizabethan England and were prominent among eighteenth-century British Romantic writers, often as an activity for writers and poets to show off playful or personal ideas. Also, the Romantics (such as Lord Byron) felt that plays left too little to the imagination. A closet drama allowed the reader or listener to take the imaginative exploration that the British Romantic writers valued. Twentieth-century American scholar H. A. Beers explains,

> The closet drama is a quite legitimate product of literary art. The playhouse has no monopoly of the dramatic form . . . indeed, as the closet dramatist is not bound to consider the practical exigences of the theatre, to consult the prejudices of the manager or the spectators, fill the pockets of the company, or provide a role for a star performer, he has, in many ways, a freer hand than the professional playwright.. . . He does not have to consider whether a speech is too long, too ornate in diction, too deeply thoughtful for recitation by an actor. If the action lacks at certain points, let it lag. In short, as the aim of the closet-dramatist is other than the playwright's, so his methods may be independent.

Beers's concept of the writer's "aim" is vital. What is a play writer trying to accomplish? To create a play that could be compellingly performed for an audience and could evoke appropriate emotions? The closet drama writer, also interested in proper emotional responses, has eliminated the need for their words to be interpreted through performance. This is a play without "play." So, in a way, the closet drama uses the language of the stage but eliminates the stage itself, thus having the spirit of fiction while still maintaining the beating heart of a play.

While the pursuit of imagination was the reason for the closet drama to gain popularity in the Romantic era, closet dramas have merit today for their intimacy and potential for dramatic narrative. This hybrid should not be confused with live performance storytelling (introduced in Chapter 4) because that hybrid form involves performance in front of an audience (something discouraged in the closet drama), and off-the-cuff personal storytelling. The closet drama is not spontaneous, and while individual events could inspire it, it is not non-fiction. A writer seeking intimacy and valuing the sounds of speech without the structure of a traditional play could find a closet drama an ideal hybrid for their writing.

> ### Writing Practice
>
> In a previous "Writing Practice" exercise in this chapter, you wrote a monologue where one character addressed a non-present character about something that was taken away (and that the speaker would like back).

Now, thinking of closet drama, write that monologue again, but instead of thinking of a character addressing an audience and an implied other character, just write about what was lost. Keep the word "you" absent from this monologue—instead, focus only on the speaking character's personal needs. This is no longer a desperate plea to have the thing returned. What is it? That is up to you.

Summary

Characters do a lot of things. They talk, they think, they act, and they react. They want things. They *need* things. Whatever a person can do, a character can do the same. Characters do not only think and act and talk in our stories or plays, but they can also narrate and tell their stories. Even if a fictional story has an unnamed third-person narrator, that narrator is still an implied character because they (whoever they are) determine what characters we spend time with, where we go, and—crucially—what we do not see and experience.

Both fiction and plays tell stories, but the construct of the theater (and the oratorical aspect of the stage) dictates storytelling approaches for plays. Most importantly, both fiction and plays emotionally affect the audience (whether that audience encounters the stage, the page, or both).

Writing Wrap-Up

What scares you? Is it something abstract, like loneliness? Or something more concrete, like spiders? Whatever it is, write for five minutes about why it scares you.

Then, using those notes, write a fictitious scene in a play where two characters have to deal with that fear. One of the characters is as afraid of it as you are, and the other is not afraid at all. How do these two characters interact? Does the second character try to calm the first? Do they get frustrated with each other?

CHAPTER 9
THE SMALLEST BUILDING BLOCK IN THE UNIVERSE
INTERSECTIONS BETWEEN POEMS AND SCREENPLAYS

One of poetry's most significant challenges is its greatest strength—while our other genres build from stories and character, words and sounds create poems. Moments build screenplays; sounds *representing* moments build poems. A poem grabs readers through musicality and rhythm, and language patterns turn moments into worlds.

This is also potentially true in screenwriting. If a language moment can grow into something more significant in a poem, there is no reason why those small building blocks cannot assist writers in other genres. Since poems are language-based, it is fair to consider language moments as a vital component of a poem, but that cannot be at the expense of another critical building block—images. An **image** is a written description of something typically captured by the senses. While using an image in lyric poetry is discussed in more detail in Chapter 12, the image as an individual tool is relevant here. Poems and screenplays can tell stories, and the way the poem furthers its narrative—through an emphasis on image and sound—can teach how to write better screenplays. A great screenplay is typically great because of its ability to communicate intellectually and emotionally in understandable language. Poems that value accessibility (without sacrificing sentiment and musicality) can succeed in ways that aggressive obscurity denies.

Accessibly begins with images. Great poems create something the reader can visualize and feel. A compelling image connects to a poem's overall meaning. Images do not rely solely on visuals—good images contain multisensory aspects. Poems and screenplays must prioritize particulars and details when creating imagery. If a poem or screenplay merely calls a lamp a lamp, there is no way for the reader to know how to visualize it further. If a poem explains that a lamp is on a table, it informs the reader that it is not a floor lamp, but that is still not particularly specific. In a screenplay, if a writer only mentions a lamp as an element in a room and does not provide any details, they are at the mercy of whatever lamps the set designers and director decide to use. Whether in a poem or screenplay, the writer needs to intervene if a lamp needs to be a specific *kind* of lamp.

Details are where we intervene. Is the lamp a cheap desk model with a flexible neck that bends too low from overuse? Is it a stained-glass Tiffany lamp with a metal pull

Intersecting Genre

cord? A modern lamp that looks less like a lamp and more like a vertical rectangle with natural wood veneer and a hidden LED light? Each of these examples would create a different mood. If it matters, the writer has to explain it to the reader. Otherwise, the lamp you have dropped into in your writing will become something other than what you intended. Maybe that will not matter. But perhaps it will. Details can accomplish a great deal, and one of the most important things is to lead a reader to precisely the emotional response the writer is seeking.

> #### Writing Warm-Up
>
> Think of an object you may have nearby—a basketball, a spoon, or a chair, for example. Write a few lines or sentences that describe the object specifically (whether it is a literal description of an object in front of you or a description from your imagination).
>
> Now consider the same object, but in a degraded state—the basketball is deflated, the spoon rusted, the chair broken—and describe it using clear and specific descriptions as you did in the first step.
>
> Does the damage you have given to the object make it easier to describe? Harder? Did you learn anything about the object you did not know at the beginning of the exercise?

Creating an Image

When thinking of an image, it is easy to think only about pictures—visual recreations that capture the reader's attention and imagination. While an image can mean "visual description," this interpretation makes a mistake. An image does not solely need to represent something visually; it could—and perhaps *should*—include multisensory elements. Images also do not have to be static—images can feature movement and action. No image in a creative writing work is valuable simply as a recreation—the only way an image succeeds is if it creates sensory *and* emotional reactions.

Here is the poem "Change" by Australian writer Maggie Shapley:

I mourn for your breadmaking days,
that tense kneading in the dawn light:
slap down on the board,
turn over, and push, push, push,
taste the oven blast,
scorching nostrils and throat.

Today you watch croissants
skate slow around the microwave,

prod them open, and wait
for me to pass the jam.

The poem begins with an abstract description of an act (and an emotional response to the loss of said act): "I mourn for your breadmaking days." This hardly qualifies as an image, but it is a beginning—"breadmaking" can evoke an image but is not specific. Different people can have varied responses, thus giving the term multiple meanings depending on the audience. However, the speaker's act of "mourn[ing]" the "breadmaking days" provides an emotional entrance into the poem. At this stage, a reader does not know if the speaker is mourning the days themselves or the loss of those days, but the word "mourn" shows emotional severity, regardless of what caused it.

The first six lines provide the vivid imagery that makes the presence of "mourn" in the first line resonate. The following breadmaking description comes to life for three key reasons: active description, a multisensory approach, and emotional resonance.

- *Active description*: Active language ripples through these lines, making it impossible not to see the movement. Interestingly, Shapley provides little visual guidance—we do not *see* the hands or tools—but the repetition of "push" and the ferocity of "slap" immerses the reader in action.

- *Multisensory Approach*: While there are minimal specifical visual cues, the image of the breadmaking is vibrant because of how the multisensory examples create a scene so vivid the reader's mind fills in the missing visuals with aid from the other senses. There is the feel of the dough slapping against the board and the smell of the baking bread.

- *Emotional Resonance*: If this were simply a poem about making bread, the images would only be able to engage the reader for a short time. That reader might be absorbed initially by the imagery and movement, but if the poem never veers away from the act of breadmaking, the reader would eventually wonder, "what's the point?" That never happens here because Shapley immediately creates emotional context with the word "mourn" and further explains that feeling in the concluding stanza.

That second stanza also uses imagery that contrasts with the breadmaking in the first stanza. The meticulous and active craft of breadmaking in the first stanza—a clear feast for all senses—is replaced by a less active form of cooking in the second. Here, a microwave—and not the chef—does the cooking. Shapley describes the "you" as "watch[ing] croissants/ skate slow around the microwave." In the first stanza, the imagery of the baker preparing and baking the bread is vibrant and full of life. The imagery is active, and the reader feels like a participant in the creation. Here, the reader and the "you" are passive observers, seeing the bread mindlessly spin until the microwave informs of completion.

There is a poignancy here—we see that the speaker mourns the loss of the "you's" creativity and craftsmanship, replaced with the artificiality and automation of the microwave. While the poem does not inform the reader of what has caused the "you" to lose touch with their craft, the poem gives enough for the reader to theorize—but the feeling of mourning and disappointment is perhaps more critical than any particulars.

Imagery and emotional resonance must exist together. Imagery should never just be about painting a lovely picture. Sure, the descriptions may create something the reader can visualize. Still, that image will be short-lived without an emotional connection—a cloud shaped like a dragon that slowly dissipates from both the sky and the viewer's consciousness. Images should never exist solely to be "seen"—the reader must "feel" them too.

But emotional resonance is difficult to achieve without the reader (or viewer) connecting to an image. For example, readers can feel a sliver of emotion if the poem says, "this person was once a great chef, but now life is pretty busy, and they only have time to cook things in the microwave." That can elicit sympathy from the listener, but it will not be the kind of sympathy that lingers because the listener has no image on which to anchor that sympathy. It will be a quick "that's too bad" before the reader moves on. In Shapley's poem, those croissants skating "around the microwave" provide that anchor.

> **Writing Practice**
>
> Write a brief poem or paragraph in which you describe something in specific detail. It can be two people standing outside a restaurant or a child playing with a puppy. All that matters is that you create something filled with tangible images that your reader will be able to visualize. This poem or paragraph should be very image-driven.
>
> Now, provide a title for this short piece. The only rule is that your title must be one word long, and that word must be an abstract concept (love, sadness, patriotism, or faith, for example). If you connect the right title to the piece, it will create the type of emotional resonance that makes your images come to life.

What Poems Can Teach Us about Screenplays

In addition to using sound techniques that establish poems as verbal art, a **narrative poem** tells a story. Some narrative poems tell stories with clearly defined beginnings, middles, and endings, while others tell stories through less complete narrative techniques. It is important to note that all poems, whether lyric or narrative or anything else, have room within them for images. To better tell stories within poems, build a clear character or speaker, and use images to help the reader visualize moments within the poem. It helps to see examples of works that accomplish those objectives. Here is a poem by the American poetry writer Susan Blackwell Ramsey:

Sow's Ear

I paid a fortune for this horrible yarn
   years ago, this overspun, thickthin mess,

this inferior string whose grubby lumps
   alternate with thin stretches kinked to thorns.
I was young. I was seduced by color
   and by funk, the way an ugly, confident man

makes conquests through persistence, the tang of revulsion.
   This is the Diego Rivera of yarns,
pop-eyed, pus-gutted. You could spin one better.
   So could the woman who sold me this, but she knows
bad sells "because it looks handspun," especially
   when she prices it high. This is cynical yarn.

For years I wouldn't knit with it. Disgusted
   with myself, I forgot it in a closet.
So coming across it by accident last week
   was bumping into Diego in Detroit;
after three children and years of happy marriage
   it would be silly not to have a drink,

to cast it on. My technique has improved,
   and as I watch the string and slubs form fabric,
as the plums, browns, blues slide through my hands,
   intriguing, compelling, I see there's no question
of stopping now. It won't take long to finish;
   I know I'm going all the way.

This poem features a speaker telling us about themselves and how they have changed and evolved over a significant chunk of life by using the "horrible yarn" introduced in the first stanza as a guide. In a poem, a metrical event is something that establishes sounds and patterns. This poem does not seem to follow strict metric rules, but metrical events are happening. Sometimes, the poem adopts a bit of a sing-song quality (read the first lines aloud a few times, stressing every even-numbered syllable a bit more than the odd-numbered ones). Most of the poem's lines range between nine and eleven syllables, so it creates a metrical consistency.

More than this subtle musicality, however, the poem comes to life through its voice, which is charming, funny, inviting, and intimate. The speaker's voice is that of an old friend who already knows the reader is comfortably aware of the speaker's passions and interests, which conveys confidence. For example, the poem does not need to talk about the speaker's passion for needlecraft—the information provided about the yarn in the opening paragraph makes that clear, and the speaker does not need to waste breath by explaining things the reader will understand simply by being in the world of the poem.

Intersecting Genre

If one were simply to describe the concept of the poem to another, it would not sound like a work of significant emotional stakes: *a person describes some low-quality yarn they bought years ago and, after finding it unexpectedly, decides to use it.* So what brings the work to life? First, the descriptions of the yarn bubble with energy and personality: it is a "thickthin mess" filled with "grubby bumps." Even the word "horrible" in the first line, while not an unexpected descriptor for a poor quality item, is not what a reader may expect from a poem (especially when paired with the colloquial "I paid a fortune" earlier in the line). The poem's voice is built on familiarity and comfort, and this helps the reader feel at ease.

A notable moment in the poem is when, at the end of the second stanza, the speaker states directly, "This is cynical yarn." The moment is funny because a reader, while perhaps accustomed to **personification** in poems (the act of giving inanimate objects human personalities and traits), would find a quality such as cynicism is unexpected. But it is also completely earned due to the speaker's description of where and how the yarn was purchased, and its quality. This *cynicism* is also a telling description of the speaker—this is how the speaker views the yarn. So the reader is not simply learning more about the speaker—they are becoming unexpectedly comfortable and intimate with the poem's voice.

This intimacy makes the poem's concluding stanzas effective. We see an epiphany in the concluding stanzas as the speaker realizes that they have *earned* the right to use the yarn: "after three children and years of happy marriage/it would be silly not to have a drink" (and "drink" in this case is a metaphor for getting reacquainted with the yarn, continuing the poem's level of approachability and comfort). Accordingly, the poem ends with the speaker's goal in sight—regardless of what they make with it, the speaker has done enough to finally use the yarn to its completion.

Ramsey's poem accomplishes three important things: creates compelling images, the narrator's voice-driven style evokes personality, and it is effectively emotional. Ultimately, the emotional result does not come about because of simply the images or the narrator's voice—everything is tied together. In an effective work of creative writing, nothing happens in isolation. If the images are compelling, but the narrator's voice is unconvincing, the reader likely will not see the poem as a success.

If poems are typically (though not always) one writer tying all of a poem's threads together, films are profoundly different. We have all seen films where we thought, "the acting wasn't great, but the movie looked beautiful." In this case, perhaps we value the film's costumes or cinematography even if the performers were unconvincing. It is also not uncommon for the screenplay to work in some ways and not in others—for example, we may think that the story is compelling, but the characters are lacking.

Creative Response

- "Sow's Ear" builds off the concept of the speaker revisiting a regrettable purchase made in the distant past. Write a poem that starts with a recollection of something you regret buying, and write a poem that shows what that purchase represents now.

- Ramsey energizes the poem in exciting ways, such as vivid detail, description, and cultural references. The mention of Diego Rivera and her portrayal of him ("pop-eyed, pus-gutted) bring both strategies together. Try writing a few lines that describe a cultural or historical figure with vivid and unexpected language.

Screenplay writers can learn from poetry that everything needs to be in harmony. Everything in a work needs to be relevant, and it must fit together. American poetry writer Ted Kooser advises writers to leave a poem alone until "it begins to look like somebody else might have written it." Kooser continues, "then you can see it for what it is, a creation independent of you, out on its own." While Kooser's poetry-specific advice is relevant for all forms of creative writing, it is especially suitable in screenplays and plays because each character in a screenplay needs to sound and act differently. It is not a matter of a screenplay not sounding like it was written by you—in a way, it should not sound like *anybody* wrote it. It needs to feel organic. The characters must feel like they speak and act of their own accord, occasionally on impulse, and certainly not like each other.

Even if characters in a screenplay need to feel organic and independent of one another, they still need to fit the world they occupy. If the character feels incongruous with the world they inhabit, making them feel particularly real in any other way will be challenging. That world must feel complete and vibrant, just as the character's words and actions must be convincing. Details matter because they lead to emotional resonance. Effective screenplays tie details to emotions. When a screenplay writer can understand what makes for a good poem—that all of the various parts must fit together so that everything feels connected and natural—then that writer's screenplays will start feeling complete and organic.

Writing Practice

Write a short screenplay scene with three characters: a couple arguing (about anything) in a supermarket and a stranger who has decided to intervene to help them resolve their differences. When writing this scene, make sure that the characters speak in lines you would usually only use in poems. This does not mean the lines have to rhyme—the characters just need to speak in the often-not-quite-straightforward language of poetry. Do not focus only on the language—the scene should have constant movement and activity, including interactions with items on the shelves, carts, and so on.

Now, try your hand at the scene again. However, this time, you can write dialogue in a non-poetic way (so characters can speak however you like). Instead, write the *stage directions* poetically. This will help you think about how you are conveying information for settings and actions.

Intersecting Genre

What Screenplays Teach Us about Poems

Humor is often an essential aspect of film. While any genre can use humor, it is often part of films, especially within specific genres (including but not limited to comedies). Humor's roots in poetry date back to some of its earliest appearances in English, but readers rarely expect poetry to be funny. English writer Geoffrey Chaucer's *The Canterbury Tales* was written in Middle English in the late fourteenth century and contains a shocking number of fart jokes. The way screenplays can incorporate humor into their narrative is ultimately helpful in finding ways to incorporate humor into poetry (and other genres). For instance, one of the most reliable humor strategies is to surprise the reader with something unexpected. If a scene progresses so that the reader expects certain things and then something shifts from those expectations, it can result in several possibilities, including humor (although horror, for instance, could also be possible).

Some of the most widely appreciated movies are dramatic and tonally dark. Many highly lauded films are considered comedies and highly praised for witty screenplays. Plenty of films are mostly known for their drama and intensity but also have humorous scenes. In fact, with scarce exceptions, most dramatic films have some moments of levity—maybe some dramatic films do not have many (and some, indeed, do not have any), but most do. Starting in the 1980s, virtually all action movies feature a hero willing to joke through every threat.

This instinct toward humor is understandable, even in the darkest of times. Humor can be a coping mechanism, *especially* in the darkest of times. Humor helps people get through both mundane and tragic times.

Even beyond the relatability of using humor in films is its undeniable effectiveness—superhero movies became the dominant box office force of the twenty-first century because almost all the most successful films of the genre combine action, suspense, and comedy. These films have succeeded partly because of quippy characters who exchange jokes as readily as laser blasts.

Audiences expect this, and they go into many movies—even films not directly labeled as "comedies"—ready to laugh. This is not an expectation for all genres. Plays can be funny, and some fiction writers are known for their humor, and readers may enter those works with specific comedic expectations, but even then (and especially for writers the audience or reader either does not know or does not think of as "funny"), the joke must be written (or delivered on stage) in a way that lets the reader know it is a joke. Readers often need a permission structure before knowing it is okay to laugh at something. Regardless of the situation, some people are always looking for a joke.

But most people are not. A lot of readers of creative writing works do not expect humor. This may be especially true for poetry, where readers often expect (unfairly) somber or serious work. Readers who are not looking for humor will usually not find it, even if a writer is metaphorically slipping a whoopee cushion on a reader's chair. They need permission to laugh. This is not out of ignorance—often, readers lack the confidence to understand a creative work and assume most work is trying to be profound.

Here is a scene that shows this scenario (depicted in informal screenplay structure):

The Smallest Building Block in the Universe

INT. WEDDING RECEPTION—NIGHT

A crowd of people has gathered. There is dancing and laughter. The bride and groom are happy. But our focus is not on those two. In another part of the ballroom, away from the frivolity, music, and dancing, a man and a woman sit on opposite sides of a couch. They are scooted as far to their respective ends as possible.

MARCUS: *(defensive)* Look, I'm not great with names. Sorry. Just tell me yours again.

MONICA: *(dismissive)* It's fine. Monica. My name's Monica.

MARCUS: That's right. That's what you told me.

MONICA: *(looking around the reception hall)* Yep. *(getting up)* I should . . . go. My friends are probably looking for me.

MARCUS: *(getting up partway, with urgency)* Wait. I was curious. You said you were a writer, right?

MONICA: *(standing)* Yes. You remembered that.

MARCUS: I did. What do you write?

MONICA: *(shrugs)* I don't know. Lots of stuff. Short stories. Poems. Mostly poems.

MARCUS: Poems. Cool. I don't know a lot about literature. I'm in finance.

MONICA: Yeah, you've said.

MARCUS: What *kind* of poems do you write?

MONICA: I don't know. Poems that matter to me? I guess I want them to be funny too. I like funny poems.

MARCUS: *(surprised)* Funny? Poems aren't funny. Poems aren't supposed to be funny. Poets aren't funny.

Monica rolls her eyes and turns to leave. She looks back at Marcus before she walks away.

MARCUS: What? Did I say something wrong?

MONICA: I'm sure your finance classes spent valuable time discussing poetic humor.

MARCUS: Not really.

MONICA: Have a beautiful life, Marcus.

Monica walks away. Marcus looks at his glass and drinks the last of it.

MARCUS: *(to himself)* I know what's funny.

The dialogue-heavy scene captures two characters at a wedding reception and attempts to show how they view humor. While the scene is not teeming with jokes (there is no witty rapport between characters), there is a good reason. Monica, who talks about her interest in humor, is chatting with someone she perceives to have a narrow perspective on the subject. If Monica and Marcus suddenly traded witty remarks, the conversation would change dramatically (as would our perception of Marcus). As it is, Marcus immediately shuts down Monica's description of what she values in her writing. Accordingly, she leaves the conversation.

But what if Marcus was a character more willing to accept Monica's assessment of her writing? What if Marcus was funny? Being in finance does not automatically mean he

Intersecting Genre

cannot have a sense of humor. Also, it is important to remember that just because the reader does not see Marcus as funny in this scene does not mean he is not. If we saw him at other moments, maybe we would see him as quite witty. The author's choice is to depict him as we see him in this scene. Think about how different the scene would be if the author made Marcus funny and likable? How difficult would it be to adjust his character to make that possible?

> **Writing Practice**
>
> Here is a kids' joke, reduced to only a setup and punch line:
>
>> A basketball game takes place between animals and insects. The animals are far ahead after the first half, and a centipede enters the game in the second half and lifts the insects to victory. When asked why the centipede did not play in the first half, the insect team's coach explains that the centipede was busy tying his shoes.
>
> Not particularly funny, right? Well, make it funny. Keep the punch line (the last sentence). Expand the joke—write out more details and think about how it could be funnier. Think constantly about how to best wring out laughs. Does it help to depict the joke as a scene where you create animal and insect characters who have dialogue? Then do that! If it feels most natural to create a character who is telling the joke, perhaps with a specific style and delivery, then do that. Find a way to make this as funny as possible.

Easter Eggs

One of the great joys of watching a film is finding something you did not expect, not necessarily in regard to plot or characters, but in terms of details. This does not always happen with a movie or television show, and sometimes it requires multiple viewings when it does happen. Still, occasionally, perhaps in the background, we spot something we almost missed (or, if this is the third or fourth time watching, something we missed before). This can be an understated joke, a reference that did not make sense until later in the film, or a small but significant detail blended into the other props. Audiences love this sense of discovery—so much so that there is a name for it: *Easter eggs*.

An **Easter egg** is an image or message "hidden," traditionally in a film, TV show, or video game. Usually, we consider Easter eggs a feature of electronic media, but they do not have to be. The term dates back to 1979 when a programmer leaving the company left a hidden element in an Atari video game he was programming called *Adventure*. When a player found the element (the programmer's name) and contacted the company, one of the company's managers excitedly considered the possibility of planting "Easter eggs" for players to find. Another use of the term in media was to describe hidden elements on DVD releases (typically on the main menu screens), where an audience may find a feature not otherwise marked on the screen. Movies have long done this, dropping references into scenes that are not directly addressed and requiring audiences to pay thoughtful attention. The viewer or game player does not *need* to find an Easter egg to enjoy the film or game, but it enhances the overall experience by giving the viewer more ownership. The viewer or player feels they have accomplished something, even if they have merely found an inside joke.

While the phenomenon of Easter eggs is typically limited to electronic media, there is no reason that the delight of surprising details cannot make it into other forms of writing. Screenplays (and their films) provide examples of how Easter eggs can enhance an experience, but poems could include Easter eggs too. While this might sound unlikely, it is not hard to find examples. In a way, poems have been hiding Easter eggs for centuries. Poetry writers have hidden messages in poems (often through the initial letters of each line) and by crafting "shape poems" that give the work a shape that offers the words additional meaning. A writer has limitless ways to engage the reader.

Writing Practice

Try your hand at writing a poem that contains an "Easter egg." **Mesotic** poems hide messages in a poem vertically. This is also true in **acrostic** poems (where the writer hides a message vertically hidden in the opening letters of each line), but a mesotic poem hides the message in the middle:

> a poeM is most
> memorablE
>   when Someone
>   shOws you
> a secreT you
>   mIssed somehow
>   and Can't remember why.

See how the poem hides the word "mesotic" in the middle? This sample poem capitalizes the word, and that is a formatting choice that is up to the writer. It makes it easier to find the message, but the Easter egg becomes perhaps a bit too obvious.

Try your hand at writing one of these. You can connect the hidden word to the poem, or it can seem unconnected—that is up to you. What matters is that you build the rest of the poem around that word. You will also see that arranging the poem around that hidden vertical word in the middle of the lines creates a unique shape that will make your poem visually engaging.

The Hybrid: Videopoetry

The term **videopoetry** originated with Canadian writer Tom Konyves in the 1970s, who used it to describe his multimedia work. Konyves defines it as "a genre of poetry displayed on a screen, distinguished by its time-based, *poetic* juxtaposition of images with text and

Intersecting Genre

sound." He further explains that the purpose of the genre is "to demonstrate *the process of thought* and *the simultaneity of experience*—visible and/or audible—whose *meaning* is blended with, but not illustrated by, the images and the soundtrack" (Konyves's italics). The form is an opportunity to explore different avenues of a poem. As Konyves points out, this is not a form where the video "explains" the poem. There should not be an obvious literal connection, and he encourages a disconnect. Instead, the videopoem is an opportunity to see two or more seemingly independent artistic endeavors (the poem, the video, and the audio, when applicable) in the same artifact.

But why is a connection between the elements discouraged? A videopoem has no desire to be a multimedia "explanation" of a poem. It is not intended to improve one's ability to analyze a poem but is instead a way of getting more meaning from the poem *and* the seemingly incongruous video accompanying it.

While videopoetry has long had great synergistic artistic potential, smartphones' ubiquity and capacity to record videos and sounds make it a form ripe for even more exploration. The form emphasizes poetry, of course, but in a videopoem, the poem is only as important as the other elements that hold each other upright.

Videopoetry can be many things—some creators take a preexisting poem and present the poem's text against video footage that either accentuates or challenges the content within the poem. Others will use their own poems. Some videopoems contain the audio of the featured poem, and others rely solely on the visual text that appears on-screen. Heather Haley, a Canadian writer and filmmaker, explains, "I define a videopoem as a wedding of word and image . . . unlike a music video—the inevitable and ubiquitous comparison—a videopoem stars the poem rather than the poet, the voice seen as well as heard." A music video is typically a form where we see either the song performed by the artist or visuals that directly represent the song (or, most often, some combination). A videopoem is a reaction against that symmetry. It is also, as Haley states, a response against the poem's writer, instead emphasizing the art over the artist (and perhaps transforming the art into something new through the relationship with the visuals and soundtrack).

Technological advancements simplified a form writers may have once found intimidating in the late 1970s. Videopoetry is a more accessible format today. But regardless of accessibility, a vital component of the form is the synchronicity between the different elements. This is not a form that works if one element is excellent and others are lacking—there must be a collaboration between all working parts. This approach is essential, not just in videopoems, but in all forms of writing—it is at the intersections—between media, genres, or ideas—that great work occurs.

> ### Writing Practice
>
> Creating a videopoem may seem like a difficult task (and maybe it is), but it is worth considering. If you do not feel confident making a complete videopoem, think of the process in stages.

For example, write or find a poem you admire, and then think of what visuals would complement it in a videopoem. Remember, you are not looking for a perfect fit—instead, you want to find visuals that enhance (or challenge) some part of the poem. For instance, if you are using a poem about ducks, the video accompaniment should avoid ducks or water—such an accompaniment will not enhance the poem's meaning. It would just be ducks on top of ducks.

But what if the poem is about a duck found in an unexpected place—squawking in a department store parking lot? You should avoid ducks and cars, but what if you include a video of a child playing alone on a playground? Or a tumbleweed rolling down an desolate road? Suddenly, the poem has a new context based on the visuals. What type of audio would you use? Again, you do not have to create a videopoem, but plan one out. If it is interesting enough, you might have no choice but to create it into existence.

Summary

Images exist in life and writing. Our phones may be full of images of places we have been and exciting things we have done, and our minds are full of these memories. Images are not just essential building blocks in our literal lives but vital elements of our writing lives. A film is essentially a vast collection of images—most of those images move, but the images themselves are the building blocks connecting the narrative. A screenwriter cannot fully determine the images a director will employ to create a screenplay's film, but they can structure the story and plant the seeds for what will eventually appear on-screen.

And while a poem can take many forms, one of the most reliable tools in a poem is the image. If a poem carefully presents images—and then makes the image's emotional resonance clear through text or context, that poem will become much more than words on the page. Multimedia explorations are not only for screenplays and films; poems can take on new life when paired with video. The possibilities for videopoems are infinite—exciting intersections of genres and media create endless opportunities for exploration and experimentation.

Writing Wrap-Up

How would you write a poem about a movie? What about a screenplay about a poem? While this chapter has explored many intersections between these genres, they can still seem unrelated. Connecting them by writing about one in the other genre is a way to understand each further. So try one of these two prompts (or, preferably, both):

Intersecting Genre

- Write a poem about a movie or TV show you have recently seen. You can approach this in several ways—write about the characters in the film or show, about your emotional reaction to it, or about some aspect that you found interesting enough to expand.
- Write a screenplay scene about a poem. It can be a poem you have written or something by another author but write a scene that attempts to find the *story* within the poem. Try to avoid quoting lines from the poem and instead focus on the poem's story and its emotional resonance.

CHAPTER 10
VOICE AND PERSPECTIVE
INTERSECTIONS BETWEEN FICTION AND CREATIVE NON-FICTION

Understandably inspired by epic storytelling, especially in novels and films, many writers take a particular interest in **world-building**. World-building, creating a unique and detailed universe for storytelling, is ambitious and exciting. Examples of world-building include creating various fictional locations, massive historical backstories, and sometimes even making up entire religions and languages. Playing God with a universe of your own making is exhilarating, and it is easy to see why writers would get energized and caught up in the prospect.

The problem is that world-building is nothing without scene-building, and some writers jump into world-building without thinking of essential details. Without effective scene-building, a writer can accomplish nothing in plays or screenplays—and very little in fiction and non-fiction. It can be easy for writers to take scene-building for granted. But for storytelling purposes, the scene is a writer's most important commodity. A writer cannot worry about ambitious world-building if they have not spent time thinking about how to build the scenes that will make a reader care.

Everything takes place somewhere. You are reading this in a place—perhaps that place is a bedroom, library, or a car. It is happening in a specific location. If a creative work uses scenes, then there is a setting. Often, writers underthink the setting, prioritizing other aspects over successful scene-building, but a scene will not fully succeed if not for dedication to establishing place. Both CNF and fiction rely on both scene and place. It is easy in both genres to become introspective, especially in CNF and first person POV fiction. A writer in these genres must never lose track of where the action takes place.

There are several factors to consider with setting, not all of which make it into a scene. It is helpful to think cinematically—an **establishing shot** in a film can show us the exterior of a building where a scene is to take place. A shot of the interior of that same space follows the establishing shot. The film moves from a general location to a more specific one, but they are both setting. Moving from the most universal (what the characters have the least control over) to the most local (where the characters do have control), some of these factors of setting include:

- Chronological season/time of year
- Chronological time of day (including time passing within the scene itself)
- Weather/Climate

Intersecting Genre

- General location (perhaps a building or park)
- A specific location within the more general space (like an office in a building or a tree at a park)
- The elements of that specific location (including furniture and objects)

While it might feel outside the above descriptions, we can also consider the location's mood as part of the setting. The occupants' moods within a space determine that location's description.

After a championship basketball game, for example, the mood of the winning team will be joyous and triumphant, and the players and coaches around their end of the court will be jubilant. On the losing team's side? The mood will be quieter and more subdued. There may be anger, perhaps tears, but the important thing is that the mood will be different—two different groups of characters in the same space with two very different moods. Even if we see the basketball court as a single space, if we were to describe it in writing, the different moods would create the need to differentiate the space into distinct settings.

While setting is the space characters occupy, it is impossible to fully distinguish the setting (or much else in a work of fiction or CNF) from the characters. The characters determine the setting—both how it looks and feels. Setting is not solely about physical descriptions but also what can be touched, smelled, heard, and felt. If a character cannot interact with and influence a setting, the reader will never be able to immerse themselves.

> ### Writing Practice
>
> Think of a family gathering room you remember from your childhood. What are three things that immediately come to mind about that space? List those three things and spend a few minutes describing each and why they matter.
>
> After you have those three things described and firmly in your mind, write a brief scene in which you are in the gathering room you use now (it could be a living room, a common area, or anything else). However, those three things from that childhood room are in your present-day space. How do they affect your routine? How do they affect your mood?

Personality as a Path to Structure

Think of a person who tells great stories. What makes those stories so compelling? Is it the events themselves? The attention to detail? These factors help, but some people are better at it than others. Two people can tell the same story, and it can be engrossing when delivered by the first storyteller and simply dull when told by the second. A great story is often more about delivery than the story itself. Effective storytelling depends upon the storyteller pulling the audience in with details and unexpected turns.

Voice and Perspective

Regardless of how interesting the raw material of memories or fictional ideas a writer has compiled to tell a story, those basics will never reach their full potential without a compelling speaker. A great story does not become great without an effective *voice*.

The ability to tell a compelling story depends on the speaker's **voice**. In this context, voice refers to the personality and approach of the person telling the story. If the narration of a creative work is funny, that is because the story's voice uses humor and charm. A story's voice can also covey cynicism or bitterness. Think of voice as the speaker's attitude.

The voice of the story is what drives a piece of writing. It contributes to character-building because the speaker's voice allows the reader to better understand who the speaker is. It helps move a narrative by explaining and giving value to the things that occur.

The voice greatly determines the creative writing work, and that personality conveyed by the voice is a crucial component to creating the world of whatever it is you are making. But for a real or imagined world to come to life, it needs more than just personality. It also needs structure.

While a work without a compelling voice might be uninteresting, a work without structure might be incapable of standing on its own. There is no one aspect of creative writing that matters above all else—it is a matter of figuring how best to get them to work in unison.

Writing Practice

A timed free-write is an excellent idea if you are eager to write but running short of workable ideas. It involves spending a specific amount of time (say 3–5 minutes) and writing down everything you think of during that time. In a timed free-write, you should never stop—even if you cannot think of anything. Just write down something until your brain catches up. Likely, it will. It is a fantastic exercise for idea generation.

Another less-considered use for timed free-writes is voice-building. For this exercise, write about something that happened to you (exciting or not) involving a pet or other animal. What matters is that you tell this story in a way that emphasizes how you tell stories. As you write, think about how you—or if you would rather, an incredibly gifted storyteller you have met—might tell this story about the pet. Do not rely on the story alone to guide the reader—let your voice do that.

What CNF Teaches Us about Fiction

CNF is a versatile form—despite the need for truth-based storytelling, the form allows freedom (as we will see in the discussion of the lyric essay in Chapter 12). One of the reasons it allows so much variety is the organic way people tell stories. The stories we tell are defined by who we are. And, just like we tell most true stories with a straightforward BME construct, we also tell them in our personal voices. When a person tells a story about something they experienced, they might think about what details must be included (or omitted), but they do not think about *how* they will tell their story. That part is organic.

For CNF, organic storytelling is a clear strength. This does not mean that a writer does not work on their "voice" in a story—far from it—a writer must carefully consider how best to represent their "voice" by providing careful word choices and convincing language.

Considering that CNF is typically (though not always) written in first-person from the author's point of view, the speaker's voice is often easier to establish than in a fiction story with a created character. This is not to say that a writer who writes from their own perspective will automatically write in a compelling voice—it takes craft and practice to be compelling—but one advantage of CNF is that the creation of a speaker's voice begins from a more organic point. Again, this does not simply happen by accident—a writer needs to craft their way through polished and well-developed language to create that voice, but CNF is a great place to learn about voice because of how the speaker and the voice of a given piece are connected.

While voice can often manifest itself with snark and cynicism or jokes, it can often be effectively understated. No matter the piece of writing, it will always have a voice. Here is the brief first section of a lyric essay entitled "Prophecy," by American writer Eric Tran:

> A patient says his god is almighty and most of the staff agrees with salvation and devotion. He says his god will crush us underfoot and we have nothing to say in return.
>
> The next day he focuses on his healing god powers: He passes me in the hall, his hands in prayer: "Be blessed, not stressed."

On the surface, Tran is letting the memory dictate the story. After all, he is telling a straightforward narrative without bringing in words that create sentimentality or dismiss the severity of the situation. He simply presents what happens. He is working with patients (as it progresses, the essay makes clear the speaker is a doctor).

But in that presentation is an incredibly subtle voice and the choice of what *not* to include. Tran chooses the moments he wants to feature and how to describe them. Both the word choices and what he omits dictate his voice. Think about the inclusion of "his" in this section—this immediately separates the "patient" from the speaker. Usually, capitalization would not feel like voice in an essay, but Tran's decision not to capitalize "god" in the first sentence further emphasizes a disconnect between the speaker and patient. If Tran had written, "A patient says God is almighty," the reader might have been inclined to think the speaker was sympathetic to the patient's message. These incredibly small decisions reflect otherwise (and the further separation between the speaker and the rest of the staff in the second part of the sentence emphasizes this further).

The next sentence is aggressive, and the speaker's tone is, again, unsympathetic. At a glance, it feels like he is choosing to deliberately not have a clear voice (full of distinct personality), but the way he presents it—and the way it distances the speaker from himself—indicates otherwise. This is not a flashy voice that calls attention to itself, but because the moves Tran makes let the reader know the speaker's perspective, it is definitely voice.

The small details and word choices dictate how we read these paragraphs. Tran uses voice to help us understand his reaction to the encounter, even if the choices he makes are so subtle, they do not feel like choices at all.

Going Further

When revising our work (Chapter 14 will discuss revision in more detail), it is easy to feel cutting as much as possible will benefit the story. Often, this is true—maybe it is usually true. But we can also over-cut when we revise, losing words or phrases that, while not necessarily contributing to the plot, are building voice and character.

But be careful—some word choices may be essential to character-building and voice (like "his" and "most" above), but others simply slow progress (such as excessive vocalisms like "um" and "well" and unnecessary words like "very"). Make every word count.

The most apparent difference between CNF and fiction is that one is real and one is not. Ultimately, this information is not particularly useful. It does inform us of the basics of each genre, but once we begin writing either a work of CNF or a piece of fiction, the reality of this difference is irrelevant. In truth, no two genres discussed in this book have more in common than fiction and CNF. It may seem as though screenplays and plays could rival CNF and fiction, but the stage and screen are so different, the writer's technique and mindset must differ when writing one or the other. Writers often approach fiction and CNF assuming a significant difference between the two, but that is wrongheaded. Fiction writers might think they should not—or cannot—write CNF because CNF does not allow the creative freedom granted in fiction writing. A CNF writer might think fiction cannot reach the levels of relatability and emotional connection possible within non-fiction, but the reality is that both genres are capable of whatever the other can do.

So a CNF writer can take a story from their own experience, and a fiction writer can make things up out of thin air, but there comes the point at which each of those writers must put their respective stories down on the page. When that happens, those differences dissipate into the reality of prose. In that reality, the work itself is what matters, not whatever inspired it. The way the story begins and progresses—regardless of whether it is truth or fiction—is a key to its ultimate success.

And regardless of the inspiration, a good work of fiction or CNF depends on the chosen structure and shape. Stories and novels need basic structure to move effectively. While there are multiple ways of thinking about story structure, the easiest is to think of a beginning-middle-end (BME) structure (as discussed in Chapter 7). Once writers grasp this, they can move on to more nuanced storytelling. With a BME base established, a writer can begin to add nuance in the form of flashbacks, flashforwards, and non-linear storytelling. Each of these strategies gives the writer more control over both time and overall storytelling.

> *Flashbacks*: A **flashback** is a scene that takes place earlier than the rest of a work's main timeline. In CNF, flashbacks are natural and organic. If a writer can remember, they can write a flashback. Typically, a CNF piece is an extended remembrance embedded with multiple flashbacks. For example, suppose a CNF writer writes an essay about a spelling bee competition from their youth. In a way, the entire essay is a flashback—the writer is not currently participating in the spelling bee and, therefore, is required to reflect on their past to share the experience. In that same essay, the writer can employ further flashbacks. For instance, perhaps the essay is about the writer's fear of public speaking, and it benefits the essay to include other accounts of times when the speaker froze in front of a crowd. In that case, a flashback to an earlier scene can help the reader understand this writer's longstanding anxiety.
>
> One of the critical components of a flashback's success is ensuring the reader knows why each flashback matters. A writer should always know what a particular flashback will add to a larger essay. If that connection is not immediately apparent to the reader, a writer can use the first-person narrative structure of a personal essay (assuming that construct is in place) to directly tell the reader why a flashback is relevant.
>
> *Flashforwards*: A **flashforward** is a narrative technique that jumps *ahead* in the chronological structure to reveal a scene that has not yet happened. For example, many novels and films start with a snippet of an exciting scene before jumping to something that takes place at the timeline point where most of the narrative occurs. That exciting scene will appear later in the novel with more detail and context, but time shifts let the writer share it earlier to establish the long-term stakes of the novel and show the reader a glimpse of what is to happen.
>
> In some cases, that initial flashforward to the exciting scene later in the narrative is the only occurrence of flashforwards in a novel or film. Often, a flashforward comes at the conclusion of the work as a **denouement** (a scene at the end of a plot that provides final resolution) to show the long-term effects of the plot on the characters. We can compare flashforwards to **foreshadowing,** a literary technique that clues the reader (or viewer) to information that will be relevant later on in the narrative. While foreshadowing is often subtle (a slight allusion to something that later becomes relevant), flashforwards take the audience directly to a future point in the narrative.
>
> *Non-Linear Storytelling*: Instead of adhering to the BME format in chronological order, **non-linear storytelling** abandons chronology altogether, instead providing scenes that are chronologically "out of order." This structure allows

a writer to surprise the reader by unfolding an essay in an unexpected way. While non-linear storytelling can be confusing because readers might not always know where or when a scene occurs chronologically, these shifts can provide new insight and suspense. A chronologically straightforward essay may miss opportunities to find relationships between scenes that occur at different times, and jumping around a timeline gives the writer freedom to explore those relationships.

Using non-linear storytelling does not mean a writer abandons the BME structure. The essay should maintain those aspects, but the order in which they appear changes. Often, this approach can effectively present the mindset of a character who remembers things out of standard sequence, but it can also replicate chaos by rapidly jumping the reader in and out of situations. Non-linear storytelling creates suspense and intrigue by providing glimpses of characters, concepts, things, or places before they are more thoroughly introduced.

This narrative structure can be challenging to manage, so writers should plan accordingly. When engaging in non-linear narratives, it is often wise to plan out a detailed BME structure in advance to know how to properly manage those chronological scenes in a non-linear way.

Writing Practice

Take a CNF essay or fiction story you have already written that adheres to a traditional chronological style (and does not jump around in time). Cut and paste that essay or story into a new file and rewrite it with a non-linear narrative. This will involve moving scenes around and shifting things, likely dramatically. You might not change many of your words, at least not immediately; you are just changing *when* the scenes happen.

As you are doing this, think carefully about how much these changes affect the original piece of writing. Do you suddenly see new relationships between characters and events? Does it increase intrigue and suspense? Non-linear storytelling is a challenging, but rewarding narrative tool.

What Fiction Teaches Us about CNF

A story needs to move forward. Good fiction builds from narrative movement and storytelling, and good CNF should move in a similarly forward-moving style. Here is a short story entitled "Lobster" by American writer Rachel Reeher. It uses a first-person POV and absurdism to tell an emotional story (involving fictional characters). The first-person POV is worth pointing out because it is the POV most clearly associated with CNF (and that connection helps pull the reader into this short story). This is indeed fiction, something evident through its strangeness:

My father creeps down the hall in his lobster costume, big red tail ssss-ing as it drags across the carpet. It's been this way since my mother left two Junes ago, piling her things into the back of a cab, headed for Hollywood or Vegas, somewhere bright and impatient.

"I never did get to do the exciting things," she said, tying a pink kerchief around her crepe-skinned neck. She squeezed me to her chest like I was sending her off, blew a thespian kiss to my father, a cruise-ship sayonara. We stood in the yard after the taillights disappeared, thinking maybe she didn't mean this. Thinking, how could we go inside, how could we make this real? My father tucked himself away behind the locked door of their bedroom for a week and I left plates of food that only attracted ants.

I was in the kitchen early the morning he came through the door carrying the monstrous plush lobster suit like a child from a burning building. He smelled of dumpster and spilled scotch.

"Look here, look here, tossed on the side of I-90, what a treasure, yes?" he said, eyes blitzing, and it was the first time I'd seen his face for a cold week so "yes," I said, a treasure. He hoisted the suit in both arms and disappeared, and I imagined my mother as a tiny canary, black velvet hiding her from a world of light.

Soon he started wearing the suit for every meal. He'd scoop forkfuls of shepherd's pie through the little breathing hole, spoons of butterscotch pudding. Then it was while he watched soaps in the afternoons. Then it was always.

I came into the living room one evening, a home video muted on the TV, every curtain drawn, my father rocking his knees to his chest. On the screen, my mother had her back to the camera and she was swinging my three-year-old body in her arms, dipping me like a tea kettle as I laughed. She put me down and I toppled past the camera, out of view. Inside his lobster shell, my father leaned toward the screen, a grandiose shadow cast on every wall. We both waited for my mother to turn around, waited and waited until the video cut to a recording of the Macy's Day Parade.

Her belongings started to go missing. I bought pistachios and her hummingbird nutcracker was nowhere to be found. Then her Sonny and Cher memorabilia plate was gone from the kitchen wall, her knitting needles pulled from a ball of powder pink yarn. When I grew too curious, I crept into his room while he napped on the couch, half-expecting a shrine of her things or a mound to curl up against. But nothing. Even her jewelry box was wiped clean.

That night, I made his favorite brand of frozen lasagna and planned to ask about the disappearances. When my father got up from the table to wipe lasagna off his claw, a pearl earring dropped from the nostril of the crustaceous getup.

"Mom's?" I asked. He bent to pinch it up and looked at me from somewhere inside that dark hole before he tottered toward the hall.

Tonight, I listen to him lug past my bedroom door. It's late, but I hear him turn the coffee pot on. Too many times he dumped scalding coffee through the breathing hole and down the inside of his shell before he started using a turkey baster to suck it from the pot and squeeze it into his mouth.

In the living room, a pincer clicks the record player on, moving the arm into place on my mother's favorite violin concerto. This is new. I move to the doorway and in the flicker of a dying bulb I see my father waltzing, claws raised, holding the air in the shape of my mother, pulling her close, dipping and twirling and spinning together on the wool rug.

"Dad." I step into the light and he turns, the black hole where his face must be reaches straight through me. "Isn't it time?" I ask. His claws are still raised. I cross the room and when we're face to face I reach for him, lifting the suit up and over his head. Coffee dribbles have dried on his chin and he stares at me through teary eyes, worlds and worlds away. I slide the suit down over my own body.

Inside, a galaxy of my mother, glittering bracelets, balls of yarn that smell of her perfume, nail clippers with crescent clippings still between the teeth, a wad of hair woven into her comb, a toothpick smudged with lipstick, the nutcracker. My mother dangles and dances on the walls of this shell home, nestled into the structure's frame, whispering into my ear as the concerto rolls. I see my father's face through the hole in the suit. He wraps his arms around me and we sway and sway.

Reeher's story benefits from action and plot forward movement. "Lobster" covers at least several days of action in a concise story (barely over 800 words), yet it never feels like a summary of events. It is short but also vivid and cinematic. It moves briskly but not frantically.

It is also appealingly weird. Not every story has to be strange, of course, but this piece is strange in a specific way. It is not, by definition, surreal. While the father finding and then wearing (and hoarding his estranged wife's belongings in) a lobster suit is weird, it is not surreal. **Surrealism** is dreamlike literature, blending fantastical images into reality in such a way as to obscure the truth. If this story were surreal, perhaps the lobster suit would merge with the father, turning him into a lobster man. That does not happen. The scenario is unusual but grounded in reality. The ending is emotional and affecting because we grow sympathetic to the father and his sadness. Had the story taken more fantastical turns, earning that emotional investment might have been more challenging. That does not mean the story would be inherently worse if it were surreal, just different. Again, we constantly make choices about our work's directions, sometimes without even knowing we are making those choices.

The story progresses with scenes (always in the "present moment" though reflecting on the departed mother). There is little to no summarizing of events in the story—it is all scenes and details. The details are vivid because they are focused and unexpected—like the missing nutcracker and the father's challenges in drinking through the suit's tiny hole. Good details build authenticity, bringing a story to life, whether fiction or CNF. If a

Intersecting Genre

writer provides details that "prove" the plausibility of a world—invented or otherwise—the reader is likelier to take the journey with that writer.

> ### Explorations
>
> - Why do you think Reheer chooses a lobster suit in this story? When answering this question, do not think about "literary analysis," but instead think practically. What does putting the character in that suit allow the writer to accomplish?
> - Why do you think the writer uses the first-person point of view from the child's perspective for this particular story? Why does this POV benefit the story more than another POV?
>
> ### Creative Response
>
> - Write a brief story that is sad and emotional but involves a character who is (or is wearing) something inherently silly. How do you create emotion when the reader expects not to take things seriously?
> - One of the defining aspects of "Lobster" is its final reveal—the mother's vanished items inside the lobster suit's "shell." While the ending is surprising, Reeher earns it by discussing the things that have gone missing and by describing the suit throughout. Write a story with a similarly well-earned and surprising ending.

Proper Pacing

Pacing is the speed at which a piece of writing moves. Something that is slow-paced moves methodically and deliberately. Instead of providing quick action and development, a slowly paced work is patient. If it is too slow, it can bore a reader by not satisfyingly advancing the work. A fast-paced piece of writing is quick, jumping rapidly from one scene or idea to the next. A fast-paced work can be exciting but shorter in details and development. A story that moves too quickly can make the reader unsure and confused.

It may seem like the solution to proper pacing is to land somewhere in the middle—not too quick, but not too slow. It is not that simple. No pace will be appropriate for every work of creative writing. While a breakneck pace might doom a work of reflective and serious fiction, a quick pace could benefit an action story. But a slow-paced adventure story (perhaps lingering too long on description) will likely fail—while a slower pace will suit a historical romantic drama.

Ultimately, it is best to avoid pacing extremes. While a fast pace will benefit many works, it is likely less successful if the writer moves too quickly. Regardless of a fiction subgenre, pacing that does not allow for development and breathing will try a reader's patience. While such a hyper pace could succeed somewhat in a shorter form (like a short story), it is a lot to ask of a novel reader. Over time, the pacing for fiction stories has sped up—it is less common today than it was 200 years ago to read a story that spends more time with description and philosophical asides than forward-moving action.

One of the challenges to effective pacing is film and television. Most films (especially blockbuster movies) move incredibly quickly—an action movie screenplay typically sets up its conflict in the first few pages and then moves from crisis to crisis (typically with very little time for introspection).

Going Further

Another obstacle created by popular fiction, film, and television is the prevalence of death. Many movies feature deaths, some meaningful and others flippant. Some television shows feature a death each episode—an opening scene murder that propels the show's protagonists into action.

Some writers are more affected by this trope than they realize and incorporate death in too liberal a fashion. These developing writers might use killing characters as a tool in the way they use metaphor and point of view. In this way, death becomes a crutch—if a writer is not sure what to do with a particular character, they can just kill that character off. Problem solved.

Except nothing is solved at all. Unless it is integral to the plot or the development of another character (or characters), it is best to avoid excess character killing. Whenever you are about to kill a character, it is essential to step back and think of the following questions:

1. Why does this character need to die?
2. How will this death forward the plot?
3. How will the other characters grow because of this death?

People die, both in life and in stories, and there will be times death is necessary. But all writers should know how such an event will affect a creative work and its characters.

The Hybrid: Surreal Memoir

A memoir is an extended look at a period or theme in the writer's life. Perhaps the subject is the writer's struggle with mental illness, or maybe it is the writer's relationship with their mother. Regardless of the subject, we know a memoir will use personal experiences to tell the story, complete with memories depicted as scenes to invite the reader into the moment. We also know what a memoir is not—it is not a retelling of the author's entire life (that is an autobiography), and it will not fictionalize important details.

But what if a memoir broke that second rule and decided to wreak havoc on the laws of reality? What if, instead of steadfast dedication to truth-telling, the memoir told the truth through a dreamlike lens? The fundamental truths of a personal story can remain unchanged, but a surreal memoir can add dreamlike aspects that, while not possible in the actual world, provide personality and tension to a memoir that would not be otherwise possible.

In literary terms, surrealism is an artistic tool that bends reality in non-realistic ways. The movement was defined by French writer André Breton in 1924, who emphasized the merging of dreams and reality. He also advocated resistance to rational and moral values, thus unloosening societal restraints. For Breton, there were both literary and societal impacts of surrealism. The literary value is that writers could explore any avenues without rational resistance. If the moon is accompanied in the sky by a frying pan, there is no room for rational thought to argue. By choosing to disregard factual and logical norms, surrealist writers possess more control over their aesthetics and art. For Breton, surrealism is an act of defiance and artistic power.

Surrealism has long influenced literature and still does so today. **Magical realism** is a popular contemporary fictional approach that combines real and fantasy by employing realistic worlds that unexpectedly contain magical elements. Notably, the worlds in magical realism are typically mundane, and the "magical" elements do not overwhelm the world with magic but instead highlight a world's possibilities. This allows magical realism to stand apart from fantasy, where the fantastical elements dominate the story, plot, setting, and characters.

A surreal memoir is a memoir that takes moments and themes from the writer's life (like a traditional memoir) but mixes surrealist elements in the memoir. Often, the purpose of this is to emphasize the writer's mental and emotional states. While surrealism (and its related styles) makes sense in fiction, it opposes CNF's dedication to truth. However, including surrealism in a personal story does not violate CNF as much as expand it into something new. For one, it embraces the dreamlike qualities long valued in surrealism—if a writer evokes the visions of their dream-state, it is not a lie as much as an invitation to a different state of the writer's consciousness.

American writer Tobias Carroll discusses the benefits of the surreal memoir by emphasizing the power of unpredictability in crafting personality for both the author and the memoir essay itself:

> The means by which certain authors utilize surreal or otherwise experimental narrative elements in their memoirs can turn certain familiar narratives into something unpredictable. But more than that, they also create a way for the authorial voice to be magnified, and for certain distinctive motifs to emerge. The surreal can be a valuable tool for some writers, and it can help take the memoir into new territory along the way.

So much of genre intersection is about finding methods for writers to say what they need to say. We have all had experiences where our words have been insufficient for explaining our feelings. Children often find themselves unable to express difficult emotions and end up frustrated and upset at their limitations. Adults have more words and language tools available, but complicated feelings are often impossible to describe. Neither language nor reality is always enough. Surrealism offers an opportunity to convey the impossible—when reason and structure are insufficient, a writer can—and should—turn to the surreal.

Writing Practice

Think of a moment where you felt less in control of your emotions than usual. It does not have to be a significant moment; perhaps it was a quick panic over misplacing your keys or a conversation that left you feeling insecure. Write a few paragraphs about this moment—do so quickly without considering extensive detail or elaboration. Get the basic information of the moment and your emotions across as best as possible.

After you are satisfied with your paragraphs, reread them with an eye toward surrealism. What can you include in this brief memoir to convey your feelings to the reader? In the first version, you could not include anything that was not factual, but in this surrealist rewrite, you have no such burden. See where surrealism can take you.

Summary

Fiction and CNF are thoroughly intertwined—both are prose-driven narratives that tell stories involving characters who go places, interact with others, and change. While both can derive from facts and history, CNF is generally more accurate, while fiction has more opportunity to play loose with facts. But ultimately, the two genres are more connected than not—a story is a story, whether it is true or not, and knowing how to tell that story is what matters.

Once a writer understands the basics of storytelling—including *who* tells the story and *why* they have decided to tell it—fiction and CNF become approachable. It is important to remember that even though works of CNF and fiction might have different inspirations, they might not. It is possible that a single personal experience could inspire both a fact-based personal essay and a fictionalized version. The two versions of that event might not even be recognizable as coming from the same inspiration. What ultimately matters is our inspirations and what we choose to do with them. CNF and fiction provide two incredibly different and valuable paths.

Writing Wrap-Up

One of the most significant challenges of writing is vulnerability. When writing anything, you open yourself to scrutiny and potential criticism. When writing about your experiences (and the people who shaped those experiences), that challenge grows exponentially.

Think of a personal story you are afraid to write. Your reasons for not wanting to write this story are yours and yours alone, but whatever it is, you do not want to put it on the page.

Write about this experience or theme, but do it as fiction. Shifting a personal story into fiction can be as simple as changing the names or locations, but it can be more. You can change anything you want—as long as you leave intact the emotional center of that experience that made you so reluctant to share it.

CHAPTER 11
KNOW YOUR AUDIENCE
INTERSECTIONS BETWEEN PLAYS AND SCREENPLAYS

Plays and screenplays both use a formal style that is not exactly prose or verse. Writers can—and should—read all genres in their written forms to best understand the approaches taken by all writers, but the vast majority of audiences see a play or a film without first (or later) reading the play or screenplay itself. The reader encounters a fiction or CNF work in its original written form. When a writer pens a screenplay or play, what most of their audience will experience is something different than the actual play or script—they will see an imagining of the original text (most often by people who are not the writer)—that moves the words off the page onto either the stage or screen.

Despite their similarities, there are many crucial differences between screenplays and plays—one of the most significant is how each of the final forms of these genres interacts with audiences. When a screenplay becomes a movie, every audience that watches it sees the same artifact, and the film itself never changes. With a play, the onstage action can differ from performance to performance based on many factors. A performer might do something different than rehearsed—big or small. Perhaps a prop—or part of the set itself—could malfunction, and the performers must improvise. A play audience's reactions might influence a performance. A film is a static artifact. A play is fluid. Having a live audience is a critical difference between the two genres.

A performer in a film does not have to worry about immediate audience reactions. If a character in a movie says a funny line, the film continues, regardless of the audience's laughter. A character in a film cannot reasonably respond to an audience—the movie wrapped long before the audience sees it. The film is available for viewings in the future—if the audience misses something in their first viewing, they can watch it again.

The relationship between a play's performers and its audience is more intimate. Performers are aware that an audience is present. Using the example above, if a joke causes the audience to laugh during a film, the performers cannot respond. In a play, they can and *must* respond. If a joke causes the audience to fall into uproarious laughter, it is a bad idea for the performer to keep proceeding with their lines as if nothing has happened. The audience might not hear the next few lines. If that occurs, the audience might have to relearn how to react. If the audience laughs at a joke—and the laughter lingers—and the performers do not pause to let that laughter breathe, the audience may unconsciously decide that they need to curb their reactions. This would change the audience's relationship with the play.

Intersecting Genre

Writing Warm-Up

This book is primarily about understanding connections between genres, but the similarities inherent in screenplay and play writing make the differences a bit more provocative than with the other genre dynamics in this book. To get further into the mindset of understanding these two genres, spend a few minutes writing down as many things that set them apart from each other as you can.

After you have compiled the list, think about what these differences mean. Are some more about the final product? Which ones affect the writing processes of both genres?

Be Your Audience

To properly reach an audience, a screenplay or play writer must address the first most crucial audience—themselves. During the writing process, the type of audience—and how to reach it—changes. At the earliest stages, the audience the writer needs to listen to is themselves. After all, you know your personal wants and needs better than anybody else's. You should always understand why you are writing and what you hope to accomplish.

To write is to write for a reason. Everything written—regardless of how big or small—is written for a reason. Writers write grocery lists to remember to buy celery and olive oil. Writers write letters to companies to complain about policies. Writers write blog posts about political issues. Writers write text messages about when they need a friend to pick them up for dinner. These are examples of writing with purpose—we write *celery* and *olive oil* on a grocery list because we need them and do not want to forget when we go to the store. We post product reviews to convince other consumers of an item's quality (or warn others about its lack of quality); we write political posts on social media to convince others of our opinions. We text our friends when to pick us up for dinner.

But none of these examples are necessarily creative writing (though, as we know, it would not take much to make anything more creative). So, where does creative writing fit into this idea of "writing for a reason"? Does creative writing need to have a reason to exist? Do plays and screenplays have a reason for being? Do they need a reason?

The short answer to all of these questions is yes. Each work of creative writing comes with a purpose. The writer might be conscious of that purpose or, perhaps, they are mostly unaware. But there is a reason every creative writing work in the world exists. Some of those reasons could be cynical—writing to get a good grade or composing a screenplay or novel because a writer thinks the idea (likely similar to popular preexisting works in media) can make money. This is not to say that money and success are not legitimate goals in creative writing, but an idea that begins out of hope for commercial success is likely an idea that has less to do with a writer's vision than it should. What matters most for a work's success is that the writer's reason behind a particular piece comes from a place that values the creative integrity of the work itself. If the work matters personally, it can succeed on a more significant level.

Readers read for a reason, too—because they have to, because they want to, because they want to learn something, feel something, or simply want to escape. Readers read countless things in a single day—some to survive (road signs or prescription bottles) and some to enjoy life. Unless a reader has an academic or professional obligation to read a given book or creative work, they have the right to stop whenever the thing they are reading no longer earns their attention. Every line or sentence in a piece of writing should work to compel the reader to the next line or sentence. It is valuable to think of each part of a given piece of creative writing as a sort of argument—the title tries to compel the reader to read the first sentence (or line or dialogue exchange), and the first sentence drives the reader to the second and so forth. Ideally, there comes the point in a piece of writing where the reader is simply too hooked to stop, but that does not usually happen immediately. The writer's job is to get the reader invested quickly—and keep them invested.

If a writer feels a particular creative writing piece is not working or if they simply lose interest, that writer can stop writing. It would be nice to say this happens without shame, but regret often follows when a project does not work out how it is "supposed to." There should be no shame in that—some projects do not go as expected, which is okay.

Writers must know why they are writing, but they must also consider why a reader (or audience) would be interested in what they are creating. Writing for an audience is a critical part of successful writing. If a writer can think of an ideal audience and write so that this idealized audience would be interested in the content, they are well on their way to creating something that matters to others.

> ### Going Further
>
> Have you ever finished watching a movie and thought, *it's like this movie was made specifically for me*? This is not true, of course, but there was just something about the film that spoke to you and appealed to your interests. In this way, you were the idealized audience for the film—you are a person who embodies the audience that the filmmakers were most hoping to reach. This does not mean anyone consulted with you before making the film—the filmmakers were thinking of you without knowing who you were.
>
> When we think of idealized audiences, we imagine the group of people who would most want to interact with whatever we are creating. It can be helpful to think about that audience because it will help you know how best to draw them into your work. You do not always have to keep your idealized audience happy, but you should know what will engage them.

And while writing something that matters to others is an important goal, it should not be the only goal. What is the likelihood that a group of strangers will be deeply invested in a particular creative work if the author themselves does not care? The first

Intersecting Genre

audience a writer should consider is themselves. Creative writers should never write *solely* for themselves—in the same way that, outside perhaps of a personal letter or note (or something similar), a writer would never write with just an audience of one person in mind. A writer should begin by writing something that would bring pleasure (or poignancy or some desired emotional outcome) to them if they were to read it. This is truly a pivotal place to begin. Think of it this way—if a writer personally does not enjoy their work, what is the likelihood that others will find joy within it? It could happen, of course, but the level of engagement a writer puts into something they love eclipses how they will feel about a piece they are simply going through the motions to complete.

The idealized audience begins with the writer. A writer should never write *only* for themselves, but they should always know their personal reasons for writing (and enjoying) a work they have created.

> **Writing Practice**
>
> To truly know yourself as an audience, you must spend some time thinking about yourself as a writer. You do not need to share these answers with anyone else—just answer them and keep them as a reminder of what you are feeling at this moment. Your reasons for writing might change in the future, of course, but these answers can be a chronicle of where you are right now.
>
> - In a general sense, why do you like creative writing?
> - What is your purpose in creative writing? What do you hope to accomplish?
> - What are your personal and professional goals in creative writing?

What Plays Teach Us about Screenplays

An audience enters every work of art with expectations, whether they are consciously aware they are doing so or not. These expectations can change throughout a reader's engagement with a text—a reader gains a greater understanding of what an author is attempting as they read a given piece of creative work and will be more aware of what to expect as they progress. They start with a certain set of expectations and then, based on the material, those expectations evolve as they continue reading. While a reader or audience can engage with a play for entertainment, that audience is just as likely to be emotionally moved by a play as wholly entertained by it. Here is the beginning of a ten-minute short play entitled "Choices" by American play writer James McLindon:

> *A modest living room (think poor graduate student), the present. The PROSPECTIVE CLIENT sits at his/his coffee (or dining room) table across from the DEBT COUNSELOR, who has the calmness and patience of a funeral home director for the most part, there to help and alert to steer clear of any heaviness with a ready*

euphemism. All of that is underlaid with an enthusiastic love of his/her product. The PROSPECTIVE CLIENT is a little anxious, really needing this to work. The DEBT COUNSELOR has been waiting for the PROSPECTIVE CLIENT to finish reading a pamphlet. The PROSPECTIVE CLIENT now looks up, perplexed.

PROSPECTIVE CLIENT: I'm sorry. I just don't get it.

DEBT COUNSELOR: It's pretty simple. It's just . . . disruptive.

PROSPECTIVE CLIENT: No, I know, it sounds simple.. . .

DEBT COUNSELOR: Think of it as a choice. We're all about choices. You can choose this. Or not.

PROSPECTIVE CLIENT: No, no, I want to choose this, believe me. I feel like I'm on a hamster wheel just trying to keep up with the payments, but . . . this just seems too good to be true.

DEBT COUNSELOR: That's often what disruption looks like. Remember all of the things you used to have to pay to read, like newspapers, magazines? Now you get them on-line for free. We're disrupting the entire dept consolidation industry, sort of like that.

PROSPECTIVE CLIENT: Okay, but . . . I still don't get it.

The Counselor and Client's conversation occurs within a barely defined setting—"a modest living room." It is quickly apparent that the characters—not the setting—are the guiding force of the scene. The setting is established, but the character interactions (and these are the only two characters in the play) are the focus. It would be possible to stage a detailed and realistic set of a poor student's living room for a performed play, but this play does not rely on an audience's immersion into a setting. This play is about these characters—what they say and how they interact. In a screenplay, the audience would expect a realistic setting—here, McLindon knows that audience will likely be satisfied by minimal set pieces and props because the characters are the focal point, not the setting. Therefore, he provides the bare minimum for setting description while emphasizing dialogue and character interaction. The characters—and their dialogue and actions—propel the play forward.

In these opening moments of this short play, the Client (like the audience) is unsure of the Counselor's plan, even after reading more about it. The Counselor, like a salesperson, is trying to be patient, hands-off, and persistent at the same time. The audience and readers think of the play's title—"Choices"—as the Counselor talks to the Client (the Counselor's second lines of dialogue contain three versions of the word "choices" in three consecutive lines) but remain unsure as to what they are discussing. That is clearly by design—the dialogue intrigues the reader or viewer because of the unmistakable sense of mystery behind the lines.

A good writer needs to know the tools available to them but also must consider the power of how dialogue can engage the audience. In this case, McLindon leaves the audience to play a crucial role in understanding what the Counselor is presenting. The audience knows that a significant part of the equation is lacking at this point, but the play is interested in unfurling its premise, not revealing everything at once. A dialogue-

Intersecting Genre

heavy play must let the dialogue lead the way. That means letting information and intrigue unfold through the characters' words and how the other character responds to them.

> DEBT COUNSELOR Tell me what you don't get.
> PROSPECTIVE CLIENT: So, you pay off my student loans.. . .
> DEBT COUNSELOR: Your crushing student loans.
> PROSPECTIVE CLIENT: Yes, thank you, my 247,000 dollars in student loans, and all I have to do is pay you seventy-two dollars a month?
> DEBT COUNSELOR: Yes.
> PROSPECTIVE CLIENT: For twenty years.
> DEBT COUNSELOR: Yes.
> PROSPECTIVE CLIENT: And that's it. That's all I ever have to pay you.
> DEBT COUNSELOR: That's all you ever have to pay us.
> *(The PROSPECTIVE CLIENT calculates in his/her head.)*
> PROSPECTIVE CLIENT: Okay, so I'm not really great at math, but I think that's only, like, $170,000?
> DEBT COUNSELOR: It's actually about $17,000.
> PROSPECTIVE CLIENT: Only 17,000 dollars?! Okay, now I don't get this even more.

As the scene continues, the audience receives just enough information to remain as uncertain about the offer as is the Client. This very-much "too good to be true" offer enfolding in the scene makes the Client's skepticism understandable. The audience is very much in the Client's mindset at their inability to grasp the Counselor's plan but also sympathetic to the Client's debts ($247,000 in student loan debt) that make their willingness to take on a potentially shady arrangement plausible. Interestingly, McLindon does something at the end of this excerpt that causes the audience to reevaluate the situation. The reader knows that the Client is desperate, but their hesitancy toward the offer is understandable and wise. But then the Client's inability to do relatively simple math makes an audience question their ability to properly "keep up" with the conversation (thus allowing the Counselor to take advantage). This, and everything else in this play, is created entirely by dialogue. Not every play uses dialogue quite this way, but the power of dialogue is a crucial lesson to learn.

Dialogue works differently in plays than it often does in screenplays—while both need compelling dialogue, the audience for a play will have more patience for extended dialogue. Screenplays build ground up from character and dialogue, but the film's eventual audience may tire more quickly of dialogue in want of seeing movement and action.

As the play continues, the Counselor's proposal becomes more precise—the Counselor explains that the company is paid through a client's life insurance and, after encouraging the Client to read the fine print in the contract, the arrangement becomes clear. Here is the moment in the play immediately after the Client reads the fine print:

PROSPECTIVE CLIENT: Oh my God!

DEBT COUNSELOR: *(Excited for the first time.)* I know, right!? The first time I read it, I was like, Whaaaaaat!? But the more you think about it, the more genius it is. Dis! Effing! Ruption! Amiright!? *(Catching himself, quieting).* Sorry. I just love this product so much.

PROSPECTIVE CLIENT: I'm not going to agree to this! Does anyone agree to this?

DEBT COUNSELOR: No. *(Pause.)* Not at first. But they think about it. And they think, well, when I took out my crushing student loans, I knew that they would impact my life. Severely impact my life. For a whole lot of my life. Decades and decades. And see, that's all this is really. You just assumed that the impact would be frontloaded. And all we do is . . . backload it for you.

PROSPECTIVE CLIENT: Me dying at *(whatever age is twenty years older than actor)* in twenty years, that's what you call "severely impacting" my life?

DEBT COUNSELOR: Well, it seems severe to me.

PROSPECTIVE CLIENT: No, it's severe, it's very severe!

DEBT COUNSELOR: Yes. But. What a much better life it will have been. These next twenty years anyway. Which, after all, is your prime.

With this revelation (the Client would be signing away their life in twenty years in exchange for debt relief), the tension rises, as does character development. The Counselor, whose lines have been mostly rigid and informational to this point, gets lines that show enthusiasm (guided by exclamation points, the expressiveness of the expanded spelling ("Whaaaaaat!?"), and general enthusiasm ("Dis! Effing! ruption! Amilright!?"). While the performer playing the role will emphasize this enthusiasm on the stage, the dialogue dictates everything. Stage directions are minimal in this play. Instead, McLindon uses dialogue to carry the action, almost exclusively. The play is successful because the natural and engaging dialogue is coupled with content based on relatable topics, with thought-provoking absurdities that accentuate that relatable topic. The things the characters say dictates everything else, especially who they are as characters.

This is something that plays can teach screenplays: dialogue is essential because it elucidates characters. Characters are what they say and how they act, but one of the most important ways a writer can convey a character to an audience is by showing how that character interacts with others. This short play vividly demonstrates this—the tensions evolve through dialogue interaction. The tension at the onset is about what the Counselor is offering and then, once that offer is clear to both the Client and the audience, the tension is about the morality of the offer (and if the Client will accept it).

It can be easy to overlook character interactions in a screenplay in favor of things that are harder to do on stage. For example, suppose we discuss the different types of conflict in literature (most commonly expressed as character vs. character, character vs. self, and character vs. nature). In that case, all could be effectively depicted on stage. However, character vs. character and character vs. self are easier to show on the stage than character vs. nature. If character vs. character is a psychological battle—or even a physical battle—between two characters, dialogue exchanges and stage combat can depict those struggles. Character vs. self generally refers to an internal war waged within a character—that might be easier to depict on stage than on-screen because of a theater audience's comfort with stage monologues and more self-reflective work in general.

But character vs. nature—a character battling the outside world, perhaps an unruly landscape, a vicious animal, or a dramatic weather event like a typhoon—is more complicated to depict via stagecraft. While a stage performance has to find creative ways to show such conflict, a screenplay can rely on visual effects. This could end up as a crutch—for one, a screenplay writer cannot always assume the film version of that screenplay will have an exorbitant budget, but more importantly, a writer might rely on potential effects over emphasizing a character's humanity. A play must find ways to highlight conflict through dialogue and character development, and a screenplay should always try to find ways to do the same.

Going Further

The three conflicts listed earlier deserve further explanation.

- **Character vs. character** is a conflict between two characters with opposing needs or viewpoints. One of these characters is likely a protagonist and the other is the **antagonist** (the primary adversary to the protagonist). A standard structure would be a protagonist who pursues a specific need or goal, opposed by an antagonist who has clear reasons (greed, vengeance, or law enforcement, for example) to stop them (though certainly a conflict involving a protagonist who needs to stop an antagonist's goal is common too).
- **Character vs. self** affects a character internally. A character debates whether they are willing to change to fulfill personal goals. The conflict is about a choice this character will or will not make.
- **Character vs. nature** is a conflict that instead of being challenged by another character, features non-human elements that confront the protagonist. The conflict can manifest with a character stranded alone on in unforgiving landscape or facing the challenge of an untamable beast.

While these are three common conflicts, they are not the only possibilities. For example, rather than a character challenged by nature, **character vs. technology** could create conflict (this is especially prevalent in science fiction, but our increasingly digital world makes such conflict more grounded than it would have in the past). **Character vs. society**, where a character stands up against unjust laws, policies, and governmental structures, is also a conflict worth exploring.

What Screenplays Teach Us about Plays

A writer should not only like their work but also be aware of *why* they like it and what it is doing that makes it appealing to them personally. It is also valuable to remember that writing can be helpful to the writer even beyond the transactional value of writing something successful. Sometimes *successful* writing is about a particularly effective scene or dialogue exchange, but often writing works simply because it has value to the writer. American screenwriter and director Paul Thomas Anderson explains,

> I write pretty selfishly, feeling like I'm writing for me, for myself, not to direct but just to write. . . . I didn't get a chance to write today and I don't feel "right." You know, I mean, I feel fine. It's been an okay day but it's not as good a day as—at the very least—if I had had 15 minutes this morning to write.

As Anderson explains, the idea of 'selfishness' is a writer's need for time and environment to write. This is valuable regardless of a writer's preferred genre—if a writer can be selfish with their opportunities to write, it will significantly benefit their creative output. So a writer's connection to their work is both about *process* (as Anderson describes) and *product* (what they create).

But what does a writer do with that creative output? What should a screenplay be *about*? This is a loaded question. It has been repeatedly established in this book that, as with all things in creative writing, the subject of a creative writing piece is a choice that begins and ends with the writer. If someone decides to write about a particular topic or thing, they should 100 percent write about that thing. Writing should be process-oriented—the main goal of writing is to write. And if a writer wants to write about a violent and seemingly endless war or a marble they found in the back of a kitchen drawer, it does not matter. Writing is not just about the products we create but also how we make those things. *It is about the process of writing.* Everything we write is only as important as whatever we write after that. That is process-oriented writing.

The writing process needs to start somewhere, and screenplay writing can help us emphasize the practical. **Storyboards** are graphic organizers used in filmmaking (including animated and live-action films and television shows). They are illustrations that show the filmmakers (while film production is beginning or in-progress) how various moments and scenes could look. While a screenplay writer is unlikely to use this technique while writing the screenplay, it is a valuable tool to consider. The screenplay writer might not illustrate potential scenes with art (though they could), but this organizational strategy could inspire them to **outline** their ideas. An outline is a structured series of notes that list the intended content of a piece of writing. For a screenplay, the scenes should be listed in their proper order and explained in extensive detail.

Writers use outlines in non-creative writing (such as research-based essays), but creative writers often favor informal notes over a more structured outline. That might not be the best strategy. Indeed, a well-structured outline effectively organizes scenes and moments. There are many ways to structure an outline and, while there is no objectively right or wrong way to do it, there are essential goals to consider:

- Writers must consider and value time and structure—the most important thing an outline does is organize, so think carefully about the order in which your proposed scenes will occur.
- For a screenplay outline, *you* are the audience, outlining to guide yourself through the draft process. Use whatever type of language works best for you—sentence fragments, complete sentences, short descriptions, or highly detailed explanations. It does not matter if others do not understand this outline—it is just for you.
- An outline is not a contract—you are setting up the basic structure, but you will change things as needed to ensure the quality of the work. A rough draft is a document that asks for change, and an outline is a pre-rough draft. You should never be too attached to your outline. It is a tool.
- The traditional academic outline structure contains numbered sections (and subsections) like this:

    I. Main Idea
        a. Supporting Idea #1
            i. Additional information
        b. Supporting Idea #2

Organize a creative outline by acts and scenes. While screenplays might not have formally identified acts, you could include them in an outline for clarity, even if they are not included in your eventual draft. A screenplay outline could look like this:

    I. Act I
        a. Scene 1
            i. Specific description of scene 1
            ii. Further elaboration
        b. Scene 2
            i. Specific description of scene 2
            ii. Further elaboration.

Again, there is no single way to do this—you can use the formal outline format (as illustrated above) or keep things more informal and just make a list of paragraphs describing scenes in the intended order.

The outline is highly encouraged in screenplay writing because it creates organization and structure. Screenplays need to be structured. Even if a screenplay depicts chaotic events, the writer needs to have control. Otherwise, the screenplay will quickly evolve into nonsense and be difficult for potential collaborators to understand.

Play writers should use outlines as well. There might be a resistance to this tool because it might seem too structured and lessen a work's energy, but organization and structure do not take away energy—they help harness it. And, remember, an outline can be as thorough (or lax) as a writer needs.

Writing Practice

Think about a play or screenplay with the following elements: three characters are attempting to steal some specific item (you determine who these characters are and what exactly they are trying to get), and each has a unique reason for doing so. They each start the play or screenplay by trying to get this thing on their own but, after each fails, they decide to work together despite their apparent differences.

Using an outline and a three-act structure (meaning the work will have three parts—the beginning, the middle, and the end), plot the overall piece. Come up with basic character ideas and outline what happens. You do not have to write anything after the outline, but just practicing an outline—and seeing how pieces fit together—is an enormous benefit.

Formatting

Instead of "The Hybrid," this section will discuss formatting because screenplays and plays are formatted differently from the other genres, and knowing the basics of that formatting is essential. Throughout this book, the formatting for plays and screenplays have been informal, emphasizing dialogue and basic stage descriptions, but formal structure is required for professional endeavors. These unique formatting styles are by design—a screenplay and play must be as accessible as possible to people other than the writer for successful collaboration. Trying to make sense of a poorly formatted script with character names and lines jammed together on a page while trying to organize a performance is a nightmare. Other people will read screenplays and plays to help create the final product, whether a film or stage play. Because those final forms are different, formatting is different for each. You must know how to format screenplays and plays—if you do not know and attempt to submit an incorrectly formatted work, the recipient will likely assume you lack experience. It is critical to look professional when submitting creative work. Editors, agents, publishers, directors, and film producers read countless submissions and, as cynical as it sounds, there comes the point where they are mainly looking for reasons to say no. After all, when a reviewer has a figurative mountain of unread manuscripts, the objective can quickly go from *I want to find the next great work of literature!* to *I just need to get through this pile of submissions.* Ensure you follow the formatting rules (and individual reviewer expectations) to eliminate a seemingly unfair dismissal of your work. Do not get rejected because of a technicality—and being rejected because you did not carefully make sure your formatting was up to the reviewer's standards is losing because of a technicality.

Intersecting Genre

While this chapter will provide examples of proper formatting, it is just about the basics. This formatting guidance will increase your comfort level with formatting, but it does not profess to have all the answers. The best guide for formatting (whether plays, screenplays, and anything else) is to look at published examples that accurately follow the accepted format. Beyond that, plenty of craft books and websites are available for further assistance. Also, individuals and publishing presses (and this is true when discussing publishing across all genres) have unique expectations and guidelines. Always research what specifics are desired and make sure you follow them carefully. While the guidelines discussed in this section are common, if an individual or group has guidelines that contradict something in this book, use the guidelines provided by that group or individual.

The following sections will begin with a list of basic formatting guidelines for each genre followed by an example page for the genre under discussion.

Formatting Plays

- Use a standard 8.5" x 11"/A4 paper with black ink. When submitting something in print, make sure it is printed only on one side.
- The font *must* be Courier and 12-point. This font looks like an old-school typewriter, which is standard for the industry.
- If submitting the work formally, a play should include a title page. The title should be vertically centered, all in capital letters. Your name should follow underneath with standard capitalization. At the bottom of the page, include your mailing address, phone number, and email address. All of this information must be flush against the right margin
- Plays often follow the title page with a list of characters. The characters' names should be presented in all capital letters and listed in order of importance. After the characters' names, you can include a brief description of each character. This can include age and gender information (which can help a director with casting) and potentially brief background information. For example,

  ```
  MARGARET (Female, 40s. No-nonsense newspaper
      editor)
  ANDREW (Male, 20s. Inexperienced staffer at the
      newspaper)
  ```
- A list of the acts in the play and where each occurs can follow the list of characters. If there is an intermission in your play, you can include that information in the list of acts. If the play is a one-act, there is no need to include a list of acts.
- The main pages of your play should follow these guidelines:
  - 1-inch margins on the top and bottom of the page
  - 1 ½ inch margins on the left

- 1-inch margin on the right
- At the top of the first page, include the act and scene centered:

    ACT I, SCENE 1

    or

    ACT I

    SCENE 1

    If the play is a one-act (without scene or act shifts), there is no need to include this heading.
- When a scene or act begins in a new place, include brief information about the setting, including time and place. The setting description should be indented about halfway across the page after the word "setting" appears at the left margin, like so:

    SETTING: *A bustling office in a busy newspaper office in a major American city. It is morning, and the office is filled with staffers and editors crowded around a large conference room. MARGARET, a forty-something editor, approaches the crowd around the table with frustration. She is clenching a newspaper as she tries in vain to get everyone's attention.*

- Write dialogue with the speaking character's name (all in capital letters) centered with the line of dialogue underneath the name (with standard capitalization). If a brief action description is needed, it will be centered (with standard capitalization) directly underneath the character name. That action could be italicized. The dialogue will start at the left margin and continue to the right.

    MARGARET

    (*shouting*)

    I asked a question! Is there anybody who is going to listen to the person who is supposed to be in charge?

- Stage directions should italicized and be on their own line, indented two to two and a half inches from the left margin. Capitalize character names.

    The room is buzzing as MARGARET enters, holding a newspaper. She appears focused and frustrated. She slams

Intersecting Genre

>   *the paper on the conference*
>   *table. She expects the*
>   *chatter to stop,*
>   *but it does not.*

- Keep stage directions to only what is necessary. When a company produces your play, excessive stage directions will only hamper the eventual director's creativity. There is no rule between using complete sentences or fragments when writing stage directions—that falls to a writer's personal preferences.

- If a character is speaking from offstage (and not visible to the audience), indicate this with the direction "off":

>   TERRI
>   (*off*)
>   Don't you dare start without me!

- To emphasize particular words, use an underline (or boldface):

>   MARGARET
>   How did <u>this</u> happen?

- If two characters speak simultaneously, format it so both speakers are side-by-side. In this example, these characters are speaking their lines at the same time:

| MARGARET | ANDREW |
| How did <u>this</u> happen? | It's not my fault! |

There are other possibilities for necessary formatting—reading scripts and looking up information is a necessary tool. The previous information contains a few common approaches, but plenty of writers do things differently.

Sample Play Formatting

>   ACT I
>   SCENE 1

> SETTING: *A bustling office of a busy newspaper in a major American city. It is morning. The office is filled with staffers and editors crowded around a large conference room. MARGARET, a forty-something editor, approaches the crowd around the table with frustration. She is clenching a newspaper as she tries in vain to get everyone's attention. Among other staffers and editors is ANDREW, a young staffer. As the scene begins, he is eating a donut.*

                    MARGARET
               (*holding the newspaper*)
How did <u>this</u> happen?
               The room is still buzzing with people having
               separate conversations and eating. Margaret grows
               frustrated.
                    MARGARET
               (*shouting*)
I asked a question! Is there anybody who is going to
listen to the person who is supposed to be in charge?
               MARGARET stares at ANDREW, a young staffer. His
               donut is in his mouth. He looks guilty.
                    MARGARET
               (*sighs*)
Should we just let the donut run the meeting?
               Andrew takes the donut out of his mouth and sets
               it on the table. He chews quietly.
                    MARGARET
Put it on a napkin, for God's sake.
               Andrew looks around for a napkin. He looks
               pleadingly at others, but no one helps. STEVE, a
               writer, takes several napkins off the table and
               puts them in his pocket, smirking as he does so.
               Eventually, Andrew gives up and throws the donut
               away.
                    TERRI
               (*off*)
Don't you dare start this meeting without me!
               TERRI, a charismatic culture
               writer for the paper, enters.

Formatting: Screenplays

- Use a standard 8.5" x 11"/A4 paper with black ink. When submitting something in print, make sure it is only on one side.
- As with plays, the font must be a 12-point Courier.

Intersecting Genre

- Again, as with plays, there should be 1-inch margins at the top and bottom. The left margin should be an inch and a half, and the right should be 1 inch.
- Scenes do not need to be numbered (and there are typically no formal acts in a screenplay), but a description of the physical space should precede each scene. If it is an interior space, use INT. to set things up. If it is an exterior space, use EXT. After this provide brief information about the setting and time of day. Use all capital letters. Present them both if you envision the scene starting with an exterior shot and then moving to an interior shot.

  ```
  EXT. BUSTLING CITY - MORNING

  INT. NEWSPAPER OFFICE CONFERENCE ROOM - MORNING
  ```

- Screenplays use transitions to show shifts in scene. Use "CUT TO": to indicate a quick cut from one scene to the next and "FADE OUT": to indicate a slower transition "FADE IN" indicates a slow transition to start a scene.
- When introducing characters, present the character's name in all capital letters. Then (with standard capitalization), indicate their age and a brief description.

  ```
  MARGARET is a forty-something newspaper editor.
  She's a no-nonsense leader, but she has a soft
  spot for those who care about journalism and
  what it can accomplish. She's a great ally but a
  ferocious enemy.
  ```

- When introducing characters, present the character's name in all capital letters. Then (with standard capitalization), indicate their age and a brief description.

Sample Screenplay Formatting

```
FADE IN

EXT. CHANNEL 7 NEWS STATION - MORNING
```
The city is waking up from a long nap. The satellite above the local news station reaches into the heavens.
```
                                          DISSOLVE IN:
INT. NEWS STATION CONFERENCE ROOM - MORNING
```
Several news editors, journalists, and staffers crowd around a table. People are CHATTERING, moving about, and getting into chairs. There's chaos to the scene.

MARGARET, the morning news editor, is a well-dressed woman in her 40s. She slams a newspaper down on the conference table.

                    MARGARET
               How did this happen?

The room is still buzzing with people having separate conversations and eating. Margaret grows frustrated.

                    MARGARET
                    (Shouting)
               I asked a question! Is there anybody who is going
               to listen to the person who is supposed to be in
               charge?

CUT to ANDREW, a young staffer, donut in his mouth. He looks guilty.

CUT to MARGARET

                    MARGARET
               Should we just let the donut run the meeting?

Andrew takes the donut out of his mouth and sets it on the table. He chews quietly.

                    MARGARET
               At least put it in a napkin, for God's sake.

Andrew looks around for a napkin. He looks pleadingly at others, but no one helps. STEVE, an anchor, takes several napkins from the table and puts them in his pocket, smirking as he does so. Eventually, Andrew throws the donut away.

Summary

Plays and screenplays are similar, but it is at a writer's peril to assume them to be mere duplicates. The eventual performance and production of each differ significantly, which requires careful consideration from the writer. The stage varies dramatically from the screen. While a play audience expects scenes presented in real-time, often in a fixed location, films can move and ignore time rules. On the stage, the audience's reactions are part of the experience, but this cannot happen the same way on the screen.

Dialogue in each needs to be compelling and convincing. While recreations of absolute reality should not be the immediate goal for a writer of plays or screenplays, the work must be convincing, even if it is entirely fictional. Writers in both genres need to carefully consider formatting rules—both genres are formatted similarly, but with enough difference to confuse.

Writing Wrap-Up

Sometimes the most challenging part of writing a play or screenplay (or anything else) is knowing where to start. Often, this challenge leads writers to start at obvious moments (like the protagonist waking up) that do little to challenge the reader or audience.

For this exercise, try something different. Envision an opening scene that starts the work unexpectedly. Resist the urge to start at the beginning of a day, the beginning of action, or even in the middle of something exciting. Instead, find another way to capture your reader's attention.

CHAPTER 12
THE LYRICAL SELF
INTERSECTIONS BETWEEN CREATIVE NON-FICTION AND POEMS

One of the most important parts of poetry—and any other form of writing interested in conveying the musicality synonymous with poetry—is *lyric*. But what exactly is lyric, and why does it matter so much?

When prompted to define "lyric," the first instinct might be to consider songs, which makes sense because the term describes the words used in songs. While we do not have a word separate from "poem" to describe the specific words in a poem, we use "lyrics" to describe the words in a song, and the term indicates the divide between the melody and the song's words. We do not have a term like this in poetry or any other form of writing, as if there is no need to split musicality from the language.

Lyric is a specific style of poetry, one the American poetry writer Mary Oliver, in her essential book *A Poetry Handbook*, explains as:

> The lyric poem is brief, concentrated, has usually no more than a single subject and no more than a single voice, and is more likely to employ a simple and natural rather than an intricate or composed musicality. It is not unlike a simple coiled spring, waiting to release its energy in a few clear phrases.

So, in poetry, the lyric is a high-impact tool that gives great focus to a particular subject and does so with a dedicated musical approach. If the emphasis on a single subject reminds us of image as discussed in Chapter 9, that is no coincidence. *Image* and *lyric* go together, one in service of the other. While images exist in contexts outside of lyric poems, you will not find many lyric poems that exist without specific imagery. Focusing so narrowly on a single subject makes it impossible to imagine a lyric poem without a clear focus on imagery. Besides plays (as discussed in Chapter 6), no genre has seen more efforts to incorporate the lyric than creative non-fiction.

> ### Writing Warm-Up
>
> Before getting deeper into lyric poems, it is wise to practice what we know about the lyric (and then add more knowledge later).

Intersecting Genre

> While longer poems can contain lyric elements, the lyric, as Oliver describes, is typically short but impactful, dedicated to a single subject or theme. Without overthinking musicality (although you are more than welcome to overthink it if you are so inclined), write a laser-focused poem on a single subject—an object or an animal, for example. While lyric poems are not epic length, it would not be uncommon to find one that spans close to sixty lines. This poem can be shorter than that but challenge yourself to find out as much as possible about this subject by writing at least twenty lines.

The Lyric Essay

The **lyric essay** emerges from the intersection of lyric poetry and CNF essays. This vibrant hybrid provides new opportunities for CNF essayists to incorporate the essential traits of the lyric poem—focus on a single subject and an ear toward musicality—while still writing about personal experiences in ways that create resonance for a reader.

According to onetime *Seneca Review* editor Deborah Tall and *Seneca* associate editor for Lyric Essays John D'Agata,

> The lyric essay partakes of the poem in its density and shapeliness, its distillation of ideas and musicality of language. It partakes of the essay in its weight, in its overt desire to engage with facts, melding its allegiance to the actual with its passion for imaginative form.

The lyric essay combines the storytelling capacity of essay-writing with the musicality and experimentation of poetry. What do Tall and D'Agata mean by the lyric essays taking the "density and shapeliness" of poems? A *dense* poem implies that it carries a lot of weight for the literal space it maintains—every word matters. For a lyric essay to match the density of a lyric poem, it must do the same. For a poem (or any piece of writing) to be dense, everything needs to have purpose. There can be no unnecessary words or phrases. If anything in the lyric poem does not contribute to its argument or mission, it will lighten the poem and decrease that necessary density.

Shapeliness refers to the shape of a poem. What exactly does this mean? Is it the way a poem looks? The way it moves? Do different poems have different shapes? In some cases, the shape is unmistakable—think of a **concrete poem**, where the words form the shape of an object (like seventeenth-century English poetry writer George Herbert who shaped the words in his poem "Easter Wings" to look like wings). But shapeliness can be more subtle—a poem can look like a straight stick composed of short lines or a mass of long lines. When thinking of poetic "shapeliness," versatility should come immediately to mind. While a traditional essay is of consistent shape (namely, prose paragraphs), the lyric essay is entirely different. Lyric essays, like poems, are found in myriad shapes, and the lyric inspiration provides versatility that can drive an essay's potential forward.

The essay's potential merges an important aspect of CNF ("allegiance to the truth") with a critical part of poetry ("passion for imaginative form") to create something wholly new that overflows with possibilities.

While discussing his personal experience as a student writing essays that had neither a home in traditional non-fiction or poetry workshops, D'Agata continues:

> I liked the challenge of writing in-between the two worlds of poetry and essay, and as these things go when you're fully immersed in a new and exciting passion, I started to see everything through the lens of that hybridity.

Genre blending often begins out of necessity and challenge. The necessity comes about because a writer has a specific thing to say, and no preexisting genre allows them an easy way to say it. The challenge comes from attempting something with minimal precedent. Writing is always challenging—boldly merging genres makes things even more difficult. The lyric essay invites the best of both genres. Often, a writer can incorporate tension in prose poems—*is this a poem or a short story?* But the lyric essay is less concerned with what it is not and more interested in what it could be.

Writing Practice

The next sections will further discuss the lyric essay, but let us first take the basic information shared thus far to try out this hybrid genre.

Lyric essays incorporate poetic imagination (and the potential of various poetic forms) with honest storytelling that satisfies the needs of CNF. That is not much to go on but try your hand at what you think lyric essays could be by writing one of your own. Once you read and learn more, your thoughts may evolve, but it will be interesting to see what the expectations of the lyric essay seem to be to you now.

What CNF Teaches Us about Poems

If poems teach about the lyric side of essays, CNF shows the "essay" side of things. To begin that conversation, it helps to discuss and define an **essay**. The strict definition is a short piece of non-fiction prose about a particular topic. The *American Heritage Dictionary* adds that it "usually" gives us the writer's point of view. If an essay is a short piece of writing that focuses on the writer's feelings about a single topic, we can see how much that parallels our fundamental understanding of lyric poems. If these two terms are so closely related, is there a point to this intersection between the two? Is prose vs. poetry the only difference?

Part of our problem is that the term *lyric* is precise, and *essay* is not. To fully understand the relationship between the terms, we must further elucidate what we mean by *essay*.

Intersecting Genre

Since the focus is on creative non-fiction, it is safe to exclude *essays* that would not fit easily into our creative mindset, like more academic endeavors—a research essay on a particular topic can be interesting, but it resists the label of "creative" (though there are obviously ways to make such an essay creative). Our focus should be on learning from essays that deftly merge lyrical and narrative qualities into essays.

In Chapter 10, we looked at the first section of "Prophecy" by Eric Tran. Here is that lyric essay in its entirety:

A patient says his god is almighty and most of the staff agrees with salvation and devotion. He says his god will crush us underfoot and we have nothing to say in return.

The next day he focuses on his healing god powers: He passes me in the hall, his hands in prayer: "Be blessed, not stressed."

* * *

I admit I've been thinking a lot about comic book heroes, their movie and TV adaptations. A sentient android constructs a family of robots. A young gay couple—one alien, one wizard, both nearly omnipotent—break up again and again. A detective with super strength has PTSD from an abusive relationship. I describe them to my best friend Z, who says of them, "poorly veiled metaphors for suffering."

* * *

Almost no titular superheroes have powers to heal others. If they do, it's one tooth in a smile, alongside others like spellcasting, flight, prophecy.

* * *

To cut to the chase: Z died unexpectedly a month before I started residency. One night he texts me that he's having intractable vomiting and he's not asking for advice but I suggest ginger tea and then he's in the hospital and then he's gone.

* * *

The patient is only in his mid-twenties, but he's been hospitalized more times than my geriatric patients. In some ways it's frustrating how rote the story seems. In other ways, it's like returning to a book I haven't figured out yet, with notes bled through, a spine crack under my fingers.

* * *

In one comic series, a powerful lawyer develops an incurable neurodegenerative disease. Western medicine tells her she is doomed and in response, she frees her lover's former lover from prison because he is an alleged healer. When the healer's hands hover over her body, we don't see heavenly light or seizure, but still she trembles and sobs, her mouth broken open in bliss and surrender.

* * *

In some religions, the laying-on of hands is the act of bestowing divine favor or healing through physical touch.

* * *

Z suffered from depression and anxiety. I only ever gently pushed him to go to therapy, to stay on medication, because I thought all he needed was a little more time.

* * *

Because the patient won't take medication and threatens staff, we consider injections, euphemistically *non-emergent forced medication*. He wanders the halls proselytizing our doom; we hope for improvement, like we can will it into being.

* * *

In psychiatry we call restraining someone by physical touch a *therapeutic hold*.

* * *

The day after the lawyer is healed, we see her argue down—downright bully—superhumans. After a day of victories, she opens the door to her light-filled apartment and finds the drawers emptied out, jewelry boxes like corpses on the floor, and her would-be savior gone.

* * *

I only know of one contemporary comic hero whose main ability is to heal. The first time he heals his skin turns gold, like he's wrapped in tinsel; the first time he kills his skin becomes a metallic black. Even when he reverts there's a black spot that moves around his body, always staying a little out of sight.

* * *

I've ordered forced injections before. One patient was just hours out of a meth binge and screamed that we might as well kill her. I imagined, again and again, all the details—the needle, the security, the screaming that would live in her nightmares.

The morning after her injection the patient woke up and poured milk on her bran flakes and told me she didn't remember anything.

* * *

Sometimes patients say, "You can't help me," and I think they're right. Most doctors I know didn't go into medicine because of the field's miracles; more often it's for the loved ones who died of cancer, pneumonia, suicide, whom medicine failed.

* * *

One of Z's favorite comic book characters cast spells by speaking them backward. Once, her enemies shot a hole through her voice box and to save herself she wrote *leaH em* with the ink of her own hot blood.

* * *

We finally decide to give the patient an injection, and the patient doesn't ask us what's going on but sits calmly on the bed. He faces the window, which in the mornings shows a line of mountains holding up the sun. He asks us to pray for him and a nurse holds his hand. *Dear heavenly father, please help us get well.*

* * *

doG lpeh em, I ssim uoy os hcum.

This essay appears in a collection entitled *A Harp in the Stars: An Anthology of Lyric Essays*, edited by Randon Billings Noble. In the introduction to that book, Noble says the following about the form: "Lyric essays require a kind of passion, a commitment to weirdness in the face of convention, a willingness to risk confusion, a comfort with outsider status. When I'm writing a lyric essay, I'm not worried about what it is or what to call it." So a "weirdness" is encouraged in the form and, for some styles of the lyric essay, that weirdness is immediately evident. For example, the **hermit crab essay** borrows its structure from some other form of writing (the term, coined by Brenda Miller, refers to how a hermit crab borrows other shells). So, in a hermit crab essay, a writer can write about a personal experience but structure it as something unexpected, say a shopping receipt. Or an excerpt from a toaster's instruction manual.

Another example is the **braided essay**, where deliberately repeating sections create the essay. As Noble explains, these structures "have a repeating pattern—the way each strand of a braid returns to take its place in the center." In short, a braided essay uses separate topics or themes and "weaves" them together in an essay to make a more significant point.

These experimental and unique structures evoke creativity and excitement, and writers are constantly creating new types. But they are not the only manifestations of the lyric essay. Sometimes, a lyric essay uses an inventive form that does not seem innovative. This is the case with Tran's essay—one inspired by poetic technique but not overwhelmed by it. The poem's theme is never obscured, and the form enhances rather than dominates. In his essay "Projective Verse," twentieth-century American poetry writer Charles Olson (who credits Robert Creeley for the phrasing) explains, "FORM IS NEVER MORE THAN AN EXTENSION OF CONTENT" (the all-caps are Olson's). Olson and Creeley mean that a poetic form should not be used unless it serves the poem's message (its "content"). If the form overshadows the content, the poem will not be successful. Instead, the form needs to be a natural extension of the content. Inorganic form does not benefit a poem. While Olson specifically discusses poetry, this also informs our understanding of lyric essays.

The two main reasons Tran's essay is lyrical are its structure and language. While the structure of this poem might not seem as striking as the hermit crab essay or braided essay, it still has an apparent and deliberate structure. The essay contains seventeen short unnumbered sections (the transition between sections indicated by a single asterisk). While all of these seventeen sections overlap and some tell a narrative over sections (such as Z's death and the speaker's patient), those narratives are not linear from one section to the next (instead jumping around different narrative threads).

This technique of sections that do not complete a traditional narrative arc is used in poetry (often but not always with numbered sections). Such a poem introduces a theme (that the title may or may not establish) in several sections that serve as vignettes or meditations on that central theme. Taken individually, each section tells a complete story and potentially leaves an emotional impact on the reader, and some of the sections may connect (as do the sections in Tran's work). Taken as a whole, the sections become something more significant—a quilt of moments that elucidate the various aspects of a single theme.

As a lyric poem, the format of Tran's essay is crucial. But poetic language is still essential for an essay to be *lyric*. Both ethereal poetic language *and* straightforward, informative language comprise Tran's essay. While some moments of the essay reflect a physician's necessary distance from a situation, the piece also focuses on small details with a voice-driven speaker. A simple experiment shows how Tran's essay implements poetic language and instincts. By taking the second-to-last section of the essay and breaking it into lines, we can see that the essay transforms quickly into a contemporary lyric poem:

He faces the window,
which in the mornings

shows a line of mountains
holding up the sun.

Intersecting Genre

> He asks us to pray for him
> and a nurse holds his hand.
>
> *Dear heavenly father,*
> *please help us get well.*

When looking at the essay's sentences broken into poetic lines, a reader who has not seen the original prose essay might not know it was not a traditional poem. This does not have much to do with the specific line break choices either—the reader's response to the work changes when told it is a poem. But it is also because the language is imagistic and emotionally revealing. The audience's response to the work changes when told it is a poem. The image of "mountains/holding up the sun" is striking and fits elegantly into what we would expect from a lyric poem, as do the concluding two lines, italicized and poignantly calling out for help (before we get to the backward spelling of the final section).

A lyric essay intersects genre effectively because it deftly reveals the best of both poetry and CNF. When we find an intersection that celebrates both intersected genres but still manages to create something new, we not only hold on to it, we do what we can to find out what more it offers. While the lyric can drive both poems and CNF, CNF teaches poetry writers about the value of directness and intimacy. It is easy for craft and poetic possibilities to overwhelm a poem's potential for connecting with a reader, and CNF shows that comfortable intimacy with a reader is achievable.

Writing Practice

Take a CNF essay you have already written and focus on a paragraph within that essay. Then, using carefully considered line and stanza breaks, turn it into a poem. Think about how your line breaks can best emphasize certain words and ideas. Try to keep the words of the essay intact—just add line breaks.

When you have finished, feel free to revise or change the words. How did breaking the essay into lines change the original essay? Does it resonate more with you now? Less? Why?

What Poems Teach Us about CNF

Using the concept of the lyric narrative as a guide, thinking about poetry's impact upon CNF becomes clearer—poems can teach the importance of lyric writing. When we use the term "lyric" to describe a poem, it refers to a particular style and approach. The term is supposed to support the idea of musicality and, while we would not think of lyric poems as necessarily singable (though "lyric" can understandably evoke song lyrics), that fact would have been more common centuries earlier. The lyric poem should still elicit a sense of musicality from the reader. While this emphasis on musicality once

The Lyrical Self

defined the lyric poem against dramatic and epic poetry, in a contemporary sense, it usually has more focus than musicality. The definition from Mary Oliver earlier in this chapter serves as a guide to understanding how best to approach the lyric in and out of poetry. She mentions several aspects of the lyric poem: narrow focus, a single voice that is natural and straightforward, and quick and palpable energy.

- *Narrow Focus*: Considering completed poems are typically shorter than the other genres discussed in this book, the idea of a poem having a narrow focus is expected (obviously, there are countless long poems with multiple points of focus). This might be an epiphany for a writer who considers multiple subplots and ambitious storytelling the norm. To truly maximize the message of a work—especially a shorter work—nothing should get in the way of the primary focus.
- *Single Voice*: While non-lyric poems can have a single speaker, it would be common to see a longer poem with multiple speakers. Again, it is about focus—a lyric poem (and a lyric essay) will work most effectively with a narrow focus and a distinct and unique voice.
- *Natural and Straightforward Voice*: The voice of the lyric should be accessible and direct. That does not mean the language cannot be complicated, but convincing contemporary lyric poems should be naturally accessible. Lyric poems provide readers with points of entry. Oliver compares a lyric poem to a "simple coiled spring" and tells us that phrases should be "simple" and "clear." This, again, does not exclude the possibility of complex thought (lyric poems should be intellectually provocative), but it does mean the poem (or essay) should feel immediately accessible.
- *Energy*: The lyric should immediately and consistently contain energy that propels it forward. Lyric poems are not slow-burning—they are quick and decisive. An excellent lyric poem or essay is sharp and impactful.

While Oliver explains that the lyric poem is brief, it is worth noting that she specifies that it would typically not exceed sixty lines. On the surface, sixty lines does not feel particularly short, but if a writer stays focused on a single idea, elaborating on that one idea in detail—and does so in a way that cultivates musicality— sixty lines is still relatively brief.

Lyric poems are not uncommon. In fact, the poems most often studied in literature classrooms are lyric. American writer Edgar Allan Poe's musical rhyming poems certainly qualify, as do the narrowly focused sonnets of Wordsworth and the other Romantic poets. Most of the "great works" on university reading lists are lyric poems. As with all writing styles, there have been changes to the way writers approach the lyric, so looking at contemporary examples is valuable for the contemporary writer. The following poem by American writer Robyn Schiff is a sixteen-line lyric poem that provides several exciting examples of Oliver's basic tenets of the form:

Intersecting Genre

House of Dior

Now we are on the chapter of pleats.
The impatience to fold, the joys of having folded,
the pleasure of folding them again.
Fabric enough in the sleeve to drape the dress,
in the skirt to drape a chest of drawers,
in the dress to drape the view of trees blacked-out
along the walk from here to the next
house. Walking in the dark inside the house
this is the black we black the windows with.
I have hung the last square of cloth.
Good-bye porch. Good-bye midnight postman
with your sack of envelopes. My love sings
to himself. Each pleat steps into the seam
with a pin in its mouth. Crease upon crease,
a fan on which an embroidered rowboat sits
at the far edge of a lake. The lake is deep enough.

The poem has a narrow focus. Now, it is true that the poem deviates from its initial focus on pleats and cloth as it progresses to show what can be concealed, but it never veers far. Even when the speaker considers something else ("Good-bye porch. Good-bye midnight postman/with your sack of envelopes"), the speaker immediately moves back to the pleats. These moments challenge the poem's focus, but the poem pushes those challenges away and maintains focus.

The poem also contains a single speaker. When the speaker mentions the lover in line 12 ("my love sings/to himself"), it feels like the poem is about to let in a voice, but it is ultimately a distraction. Not only does the reader not hear this lover sing, the speaker acknowledges that he is singing is for no one but himself. There are other speakers in the speaker's world, but the reader does not get to hear them. The speaker is the poem's only voice.

At first, the poem seems complicated. A reader might be confused and find the poem ambiguous upon a first read. But a more focused second read will show how direct and forthcoming this language is—the words themselves are accessible in this first line and throughout. There are 133 words in this poem, and only three words in the poem have three syllables (and no words contain more than three syllables). The three trisyllabic words are "impatience," "envelopes," and "embroidered," none of which are particularly complicated. Monosyllabic words (containing one syllable) make up 110 of the words in the poem, and the remaining 18 have two syllables (and that includes hyphenated phrases like "good-bye" and "blacked-out"). Readers often assume a poem is difficult even when it is not—Schiff's poem is not complicated on a vocabulary level.

The poem begins with the line, "Now we are on the chapter of pleats." The words may appear to the reader unexpectedly arranged and presented. Usually, "chapter" refers to a book, and perhaps that is what Schiff is referring to, but it can also be about a chapter in one's life or experience. If we think of chapters as being self-contained, vital aspects of something, it may be surprising to see the defining characteristic of that "chapter" be something as small as a "pleat." But that is a joy of the poem. It is focused and straightforward but also unexpected.

Those unexpected moments give the poem energy. It crackles with repeated phrases that build momentum. It also creates energy with its use of sentences and sentence length. This poem is composed of nine sentences within the sixteen lines of the poem. Of those nine sentences, two are single lines, and two others take up half a line each. Of the remaining five sentences, one is precisely two lines long, two more are roughly two lines (with lines that include parts of other sentences), one is four lines and a word, and the next is about two and a half lines.

The poem is an excellent example of a lyric poem—it can use simple and straightforward language to tell a single "story" by a consistently voiced speaker. But "simple" and "straightforward" do not tell the whole story. The lyric focus and minimalism give it its power. This is true for any other genre—a lyric essay (or lyric fiction or a lyric play) can do what a lyric poem does.

Explorations

Read these two lines from Schiff's poem aloud:

> The impatience to fold, the joys of having folded,
>
> the pleasure of folding them again.

At what speed did you find yourself reading these lines? Would you say it was fast? Slow? Somewhere in the middle? Were there places in these lines where your pace quickened? Other places where you felt like you had to slow down? Read it again, conscious of how Schiff's words guide you.

Think about the word "impatience." Did you read it quickly or slowly? While not a difficult word to say, the "sh" sound in the second syllable is unhurried. The word comes quickly in the line, and readers can feel unprepared and forced to slow down. The word "pleasure" in the second line can do the same—this time affected by the "s" sound that lulls through the middle of the word and the word itself. Both "impatience" and "pleasure" create a sort of caesura, or a natural pausing place in a line of poetry.

The poem uses other techniques. The punctuation is cluing the reader into pacing—the commas are not stopping points, but temporary lulls. They also create natural pauses that accentuate the line break (which is a natural pause itself). These strategies force us to slow down and let the poem languish.

What makes a poem great? There is no one answer or formula, but it usually comes down to a cumulation of multiple objectives. Sound and words must merge (sometimes with

Intersecting Genre

an eye toward visual appeal). While this is the case in poetry, there is no reason it cannot apply to other genres. Lyric poems are excellent opportunities to show how sounds and meaning (and visual experimentation) can come together.

Explorations

While we have discussed what makes for a great poem, what about the opposite? What makes for a truly terrible poem?

Write the worst poem you can imagine. Listen to your instincts and do the opposite. Think about what things make you cringe when you hear or see them in a poem. Then do them as dramatically as you have ever seen.

When you have finished, take a look at what "rules" you have violated and why they led to such a writing disaster. Then destroy the poem and never do any of those terrible things again (unless, of course, you have good reason to revisit them).

The Hybrid: Post-Confessional Poetry

For its primary focus, this entire chapter has delved into lyric poetry, a recent hybrid, so it is reasonable to discuss a slightly older hybrid in this section. The term "confessional poetry" originated in response to American writer Robert Lowell's autobiographical poems in *Life Studies*, a book in which Lowell wrote unflinchingly of his relationships and mental illness. Writing autobiographical non-fiction was nothing new in 1959 (when American critic M. L. Rosenthal coined the phrase while discussing *Life Studies*), but it was typically the stuff of autobiography. But Lowell was not writing autobiographical prose—he was writing poems. These poems were not written in the accepted style of the time (like the poems in his great but more traditional *Lord Weary's Castle*)—they were direct and conversational. The book made it feel like Lowell was telling a difficult, personal story—and doing it with poetry.

By the 1960s, Lowell, Sylvia Plath, and Anne Sexton were known as confessional poets because of their work's personal and direct nature. Over time, confessionalism became less of a subgenre and more a part of other forms, specifically the lyric. Most critics agree that by the 1970s, strictly confessional poetry was less in fashion, but it did not disappear. It simply became engrained in the modern voice. While it was new in Lowell's time to write poems of such directness and intimacy, the approach became normalized over time, eventually becoming a standard part of contemporary work. Lyric and narrative poems today contain many aspects of the confessional. The confessional does not need to exist in the same ways it did in the 1960s. It pushed poetry in a more intimate direction and then assimilated itself into the larger body of contemporary work. **Post-confessionalism** is not a specific movement in contemporary poetry. Instead, the phrase describes how poetry has been influenced by confessionalism, and it describes most contemporary work. Most current poetry writers use personal aspects of their lives in their work, but with less candor, perhaps, than the writers of the confessional era (consider the Susan Blackwell Ramsey poem in Chapter 9).

Even still, there is much for confessional poetry to teach us. Think of a hypothetical writer who writes primarily poems. This writer mostly eschews personal intimacy in their poems, favoring image-based nature poems or non-personal narratives (perhaps with invented characters). This writer's friend suggests they write more work of a more personal nature. Maybe the friend knows of the writer's personal struggles and encourages the writer to lay those challenges out on the page. The writer hesitates, thinking readers would not want to read about their personal experiences. But the writer realizes that this rationale is untrue—they read too many autobiographically influenced writers to believe that their personal stories would not be compelling to someone else.

No, the hesitation comes mostly out of fear and vulnerability. *What if I talk about myself and my experiences, and get judged for it?* In reality, this is not an ungrounded concern. Lowell took a massive risk of alienating his loved ones with his poems, and in *Dolphin*, his 1973 sonnet sequence, he went arguably too far. The book features several lines adapted from personal letters and phone calls between Lowell, his soon-to-be-ex-wife, and others. The poems can feel uncomfortable even today because of their private and intimate nature.

So if post-confessionalism has taught anything, it is that confession has a price. Perhaps that price is personal betrayal, or less dramatically, it is writing poems that favor candor and directness over the potential concern of others. And our hypothetical writer, so averse to confessionalism, avoids betrayal and alienation.

Post-confessionalism provides avenues to confess without regret. Some writers write personal poems with discretion, something Lowell did away with in *Dolphin*. Perhaps this discretion comes through subject choices—taking on smaller private moments to build poems. Any writer can feel vulnerable regardless of the subject. Post-confessionalism also encourages mixing the confessional into the larger world of a poem. While this assessment should not invalidate the merit of the brilliant work crafted by Lowell, Plath, Sexton, and others during the confessional period, critics can argue that "confession" was at the center of those poems regardless of the craft or quality of the poems themselves. But in a post-confessional world, the confession can live side-by-side with other elements of a poem.

If we think of building a poem as we would build a brick wall, a confessional poetry wall is sealed solely with bricks representing actual experiences. While certainly a reader would imagine even the staunchest of twentieth-century confessional writers to have taken liberties when writing confessional material, these bricks are still almost exclusively the stuff of truth. But the post-confessional writer has whatever freedom they desire. The writer can mix fabricated bricks with truthful ones. Perhaps some elements in a given poem are true, and others are not. Maybe a writer adverse to vulnerable confession can find security behind fabrication—if a poem contains multiple statements and some are personal experiences, and some are not, that can buffer the writer's potential vulnerability.

Intersecting Genre

Even that comes with a risk. As discussed in Chapter 2, readers expect (with a few exceptions) creative non-fiction to be true (or, at the very least, expect it not maliciously lie). Readers and viewers mostly expect fabrication as acceptable in fiction, plays, and screenplays. Even in a biographical film, audiences seem less bothered by creative invention than they would with CNF.

But poetry lies somewhere in between. Even if readers instinctively know that the "I" in a poem is not necessarily the speaker, they still might proceed through the poem with that mindset. This is not necessarily bad, but it causes an obstacle for writers. If a poem mixes fact with fiction (which it has every right to do—there is no rule that poems must be factually accurate), a reader could feel misled if the fiction is more engaging than the fact.

Ultimately, this falls to the reader. Maybe that is the main objective in a post-confessional world: deciding to confess or simply fabricate a confession is up to the writer and not the reader. Even if a poem blends creative ideas with authentic ones, that does not devalue the poem. If a poem, regardless of content, represents the writer, it matters. No poem is a lie.

Writing Practice

The game "Two Truths and a Lie" is often used as a conversation starter for people just getting to know each other. In the game, one person says three things about themselves. Two are true and one is not. The other person must then figure out which of the statements is the lie. While the merits of this game as an icebreaker activity are suspect (since the one thing you might remember about your new acquaintance could be the lie), as a post-confessional writing exercise, it is a winner.

Write a first-person poem that contains two truths and a seemingly personal thing you have made up. Do not bother getting somebody to spot the lie however. When that "lie" becomes part of your poem, it is as true as anything else.

Summary

Poetry and CNF both pursue truth. CNF's truth might be more factual than the other, but both must value *emotional* truths. Emotional truth has less to do with facts and more with instinct. CNF deals with literal facts, but that does not mean emotional truth simply follows along obediently. Just because something is honest does not mean a reader will automatically invest. CNF and poetry must find ways to earn a reader's emotional investment.

One of the ways poetry has long earned that investment is through musicality. The rhythms and sounds of poetry create a style of language that sounds uniquely "poetic." When a person says that a piece of writing is "poetic," it typically means that the writing is musical, but it could also mean that it is a bit harder to interpret the language than it would typically be in another genre. Regardless, if a work contains "poetic language" and it is not a poem, the "poetic language" will usually be seen as a feature of the work and not the main trait.

Writing Wrap-Up

Think of a memorable time when you had to stand in line for something. Perhaps the waiting was memorable because of the goal at the end of the line, or something interesting happened in the line itself.

Now, write a poem (or lyric essay) in three sections about this experience. Perhaps all three sections are about different moments while you stood in line, or maybe the final section is about reaching that goal. However you structure it, think about what you can say about that experience to make it emotionally interesting for others.

CHAPTER 13
PLAYING TENNIS WITHOUT A NET
FURTHER GENRES

Free verse in poetry is a style that deemphasizes meter and rhyme in favor of freedom. In free verse poetry, writers can choose whatever form and style they like. By eliminating regular meter and rhyme, many writers feel liberated to explore different ideas. Without the "restrictions" caused by blank verse and other more structured forms and rhyme schemes, writers find a world of poetic possibilities.

American poetry writer Robert Frost was not a fan of free verse. He felt poems needed structure to have value. To show his disdain for free verse, he many times compared it to "playing tennis without a net" (or "with the net down"). The metaphor works if we see the net in tennis as a vital part of the sport's challenge—if a match between two people has no net, then the skill required would decrease. Any hit within bounds would be valid. The game would devolve into either chaos with two people haphazardly hitting the ball without focus, or boredom with two players hitting the ball dully back and forth, seemingly forever. For Frost, meter and rhyme make poetry interesting, and free verse removes the challenge and takes away poetry's power. Frost would tell us that anybody could write free verse, but blank verse (and other formal approaches) takes skill.

And he would be partly right. Blank verse—iambic pentameter lines written in verse—takes enormous skill. But so does free verse. Creating images and emotional connections are difficult regardless of the formal structure. Frost was right to value the difficulty and value of a well-crafted metrical poem, but we can also be correct in extolling the merits of a terrific piece of free verse.

While the Frost quote discusses poetry, his thoughts assist us in our conversations about genre. In a way, each of these genres is like Frost's net. The genres discussed in the book inherently come equipped with guidelines and "rules," even if the writer is not fully conscious of them at first—"rules" reveal themselves as they go. So creative writing in a specific genre is like playing tennis *with* a net. These discussions of intersecting genres certainly complicate our "net," but it is in place because of the expectations attached to the different genres.

But it is time to take the net away, at least in theory. Some types of creative writing do not fall specifically into these genres because plenty of styles do not snugly fit. For example, graphic novels incorporate dialogue and "stage directions" in the way that plays and screenplays do, but they do it with visual images, which make for a different genre. Songs with lyrics have plenty in common with poems, but there are so many aspects of songwriting that differ from poems that it makes sense to treat them as a separate genres. We usually consider journalism a non-creative form, but there are examples of creative prose in journalism, especially in opinion or entertainment articles. Even academic writing, a genre that encompasses research papers and reports, can be a realm for creative exploration if intersected with another genre.

These types of creative writing outside the major genres are referred to in this book as Further Genres. This book will not provide a list of Further Genres because there are too many to make such a list worthwhile. And new forms of writing that do not fit into the established framework emerge constantly. Social media posts and text messages are familiar today, but no one would have had any idea what they were a couple of decades ago. Writers are creating compelling internet articles all the time and, while text messages may seem primarily functional (and sometimes they are), they can also be places for unexpected creativity. Text messages are a genre in which proper grammar and spelling are optional, and adding images and emojis helps the writer's creative (or functional) goals. There are possibilities for creativity inherent in all these genres. So maybe we are taking away the net, as Frost claims. Or maybe we are adding additional nets to the court, creating an entirely new sport.

> ### Further Explorations
>
> While this book will not attempt to list all possible "Further Genres," that should not stop you from considering what else is possible. What are some examples of "Further Genres" that come to mind? You can think of general categories (such as those discussed in this chapter) or specific works that represent Further Genres. Can you find other interesting intersections between genres? Writing is about possibilities—you have read about many of them, and now see where else you can go.

Exploration of Further Genres is not new. Some of these less-considered forms might be relatively common, though not thought of as creative. Consider **satire**—a work that mocks certain aspects of human behavior and decision-making—as a Further Genre. It is not fiction, but it is typically not precisely CNF either. That makes it sometimes difficult for readers to grasp. Suppose first-year university students read "A Modest Proposal" by Irish writer Jonathan Swift. There is a good chance some of those students will be horrified as they realize that Swift's essay advocates selling poor children as food to feed the wealthy. A few students may realize that Swift is mocking how people discuss the poor and see the essay as a reasonably dark (but funny) joke. And others in the class might not know how to make any sense of it. After all, satire is a style of writing that does not fit into the categories to which we are most accustomed. While the themes are still relevant, Swift wrote the essay a long time ago (1729), so a contemporary reader might have difficulty finding points of connection.

Besides, as discussed in Chapter 9, readers not looking for humor can have difficulty finding it. On the stage or screen (or when someone is telling a joke), numerous cues can help the viewer or listener know a joke is coming. Written words are a different story, and the words must overcome the lack of a speaker. Satire is even more challenging because satire relies on the act of creating something that is like something else but biting and over-the-top enough to alert the reader that things are much different than expected.

Here is a satiric essay by American writer Matthew Brian Cohen that follows in Swift's footsteps:

The Safest Place for Your Kids Right Now is Inside the Scorpion Pit

Americans are locked in a heated debate: Should we close public schools due to this new wave of deadly scorpions? And while some might beg to differ, the experts all agree: there is no safer place for your kids to be than trapped inside a scorpion pit.

I get it. That sounds insane. But you have to look at the numbers. Only a few varieties of scorpions can actually kill you. Most scorpion stings will only maim the victim, with symptoms ranging from brief bouts of unbearable pain, mild convulsing, and some slight difficulty breathing. Are we supposed to disrupt our children's education just because a handful of teachers don't feel comfortable teaching in a dank pit with a bed of scorpions crawling all over everyone?

Yes, there is a nonzero risk of permanent injury or death. Yes, the scorpions are breeding at an alarming rate. And yes, science suggests their venom carries long-term effects. But you're just cherry-picking data to support your irrational fear of teaching inside a deep pit surrounded by hundreds of scorpions.

So while it may be true the number of scorpions inside each pit may be up, how many kids are actually being stung? Oh, your kid was? Sorry, but your anecdotal evidence isn't enough to convince me that we can't hold classes inside the scorpion pit safely and responsibly. Every behavior carries SOME risk, whether it's driving a car or insulating your attic with asbestos. Because what's the alternative? No more cars? A house without asbestos? Remote learning, away from the scorpion pit? That's not sustainable. What are parents who have to hurl themselves down in the scorpion pit for minimum wage and no health insurance going to do for childcare? You selfish teachers have to understand that parents are counting on overworked and underpaid teachers to not only educate their children but babysit them too.

This isn't some partisan issue, like seat belts or marginalized people having the right to vote. Both Democrats and Republicans overwhelmingly support sending your kids back to school and into the scorpion pit. You know something is a good idea when both parties support it. In-person learning with scorpions has joined the illustrious ranks of sound bipartisan policies such as "massive tax cuts for the rich" and "the Iraq war."

But it's not just the parents who are suffering. If we go back to remote learning, it's the kids who will really feel it. Every day they're not in school, they're not learning crucial answers that will be on the tests that determine their school district's funding. They're not learning a laughably distorted, exclusively white perspective on American history, leaving them unprepared to become future cable news pundits and op-ed writers. And most importantly, they're not socializing with other children, so it's likely they won't even know the name of the school shooter that kills them. These are all vital parts of growing up in America, and I'd hate for this generation to miss out on these foundational horrors.

It's not like we don't have safety protocols in place. This isn't 2020—we've learned a ton about how scorpions work and how to best prevent them from significantly harming the ruling class's stock portfolios. First, anyone stung by a scorpion will be sent home from the pit at the end of the school day. They'll be forbidden from interacting with scorpions for at least five days, unless the school administrators need them to descend back into the pit for team sports. Our contact-tracing program will inform the rest of the scorpion pit that they've been in contact with someone who's been stung, but they will still have to continue to come in to the scorpion pit unless we can visibly see symptoms, such as frequent vomiting and explosive diarrhea. If they have any questions or concerns, we have one school nurse who comes in for a half-hour every other Wednesday.

I know that none of this is ideal, but at the end of the day, we're just going to have to learn to live with the scorpion pits. Well, you all will have to learn to live with them. I'm permanently working from home, stockpiling scorpion antidote. What, you're not hoarding antidote?! That's insane. Why aren't you taking this seriously?!

This piece was written during the Covid-19 pandemic and during a period of great debate as to whether schools should resume/continue in-person learning despite the dangers of the pandemic. That context is necessary for both the effectiveness of Cohen's satire and the reason for the satire to exist in the first place. There would be no need for this satire if there were no debate on school openings during a pandemic. While a reader could find this essay without context and therefore be unsure about its tone and whether it is satire, most readers will likely be aware of its nature because of its over-the-top approach. It was published on *McSweeney's Internet Tendency*, a site known for humor and satire, so a reader will likely approach this essay assuming it will be comic.

For this type of writing to be most effective, the reader must grasp the circumstances that inspired it. A reader far into the future who lacks the context of the Covid-19 pandemic might not "get it," nor would a reader who, perhaps aware of Covid-19, does not know the tensions that went into school reopenings in the United States and elsewhere. These factors will challenge a reader's ability to fully appreciate the essay's humor and creativity. The humor is cutting and political, skewering not just Covid responses, but also policies that lead to wars and allow school shootings.

It might be difficult to sell some readers on the creative component of a work that deals with political issues. An objective article about parliamentary debate or local elections would not qualify as creative, but a satire or humorous approach to the subject would. While Cohen's insinuations about politics and polarizing topics may make some readers uncomfortable, others will applaud his ability to find an interesting way to talk about a volatile subject.

Writing Practice

Satire is difficult to write. Humor is challenging enough; with satire, you are ostensibly writing humor that is not only based on real-world experiences, but is also typically trying *not* to sound like traditional humor. If readers miss a necessary reference, they will not grasp the satire's humor or social commentary.

Satire is an essay that uses exaggeration to mock or criticize someone or something. So try this: write a love letter to a celebrity (a singer, political figure, or someone equally public) or about a concept (a political policy, for example) that you do not like. Do not be sincere—you are writing about someone or something you actively dislike. But try to be somewhat subtle. Let your dislike emerge in this essay through sarcastic praise.

Those exploring Further Genres need to think about their audiences. Often, Further Genres creative works will be aimed at narrower audiences—sports journalism is an example. And often, even within a more limited genre, the topic (and audience) can get even narrower—an essay that profiles a professional hockey player is sports journalism, yes, but not all sports fans will be interested in that specific subject, so that hypothetical article is narrow in both scope and audience. This does not mean it is less important than a work that attracts a larger audience—it just means the potential audience is small (but likely passionate).

Limitless Possibilities

When writing, dismiss no ideas. Maybe not everything you come up with will work, but anything *can* work. Anything can be creative writing. Fiction, poetry, CNF, plays, and screenplays are our main playgrounds, but there are no limits on what else can fit. Are letters creative writing? Songs? Speeches? Greeting cards? Comic strips? Video game scripts? Why not? If creative writing is a type of writing that shows the writer's imagination through inventive language or concepts, then anything is possible.

Here are a few prompts that will get you thinking in all six of the Further Genres listed above—and potentially inspire you to think about even more possibilities.

> *Letter Writing*: Write a letter to an inanimate object. The object can be something big or small. What is most important is that you think about what you want to get out of the letter. Is it merely a friendly greeting? Are you asking for something? Are you apologizing? Think about your purpose before writing, and then keep that purpose in mind.

Songs: Whether you play a musical instrument or not, think of a character from either the last book you read or some other memorable book (fiction, CNF, or any type of non-fiction). Then, come up with first-person song lyrics that capture that character's wants and needs. You can think of music to accompany if you like but primarily focus on that character's voice as they lay out their needs.

Speech: Giving speeches may seem like an uncreative endeavor, but the difference between listening to a great speech and a terrible one is vast, so clearly some creativity is in play. It is helpful to think of speech as a persuasive tool. See if you can convince a reader or listener to come with you on your persuasive journey. While there are creative ways of exploring serious topics, try something lower stakes to best find your creative argumentative voice. Think of your favorite television show and discuss what makes it great and argue why others should watch it. This is not an argumentative essay, however—you need to write something that will sound good aloud. Think carefully of what you want to say and *how* you can say it compellingly—and why that particular style will be effective.

Greeting Cards: While not the most respected form of writing, a greeting card must effectively encapsulate a feeling in very few words. Often cards have set-ups on the front that get paid off with something emotional or funny (or both) inside. In that way, greeting cards can be fascinating tools for understanding how to build suspense and deliver a payoff. First, consider an occasion—birthday, anniversary, graduation, or something similar. Then, consider an unfinished message that can appear on the front of a card for that occasion (for example, "On your birthday, I hope you know. . .," "There is one thing to say on our anniversary. . ." "You did it! Now you can. . ."). Then think of something surprising yet appropriate to include inside such a card.

Comic strips: A comic strip is a sequence of drawings that tell a story. While a comic book or graphic novel (discussed in Chapter 5) is a long narrative with potentially complex characters and subplots, a comic strip is likely no longer than three or four panels of images (usually, though not always, with words). Not much of an artist? No problem. Draw something that depicts an action as best as you can. And then, directly next to it in the second panel, draw whatever would happen a few moments later. Then, in the third panel, draw a character thinking about the action from the first two panels (give that character a thought bubble or speech bubble to say their thoughts about the action of the first two panels aloud).

Video game scripts: Video game scripts have to prepare for many possibilities. Unlike a novel, a video game can potentially go in different directions based on a player's decisions and ability. Also, a video game script is likely fragmented (because the game's actions often interrupt the narrative). A good video game narrative should have compelling and relatable characters and a world worth the challenge of interaction. Consider a character-driven video game you enjoy, and think of the primary playable character from that game. Next, think of an entirely different game, one without that character. Now, write an interaction in which that first character goes to the world of the second game. How do they interact with that world? How does this juxtaposition change the character?

Writing Practice

You have encountered many prompts in this book. Now, it is your turn to create one. Using one of the Further Genres listed in the prompts earlier (or combining more than one), come up with a prompt of your own creation. You can—and should—write a response to it later, but let this exercise be about crafting the prompt itself.

Summary

While the five major creative writing genres primarily discussed in this book provide valuable lessons for creative writing, those genres are a starting point for your writing journey, not the ending. Every genre intersection is a new possibility, and we cannot put labels on many of these exciting possibilities. Further Genres remind us that we should never stop thinking about new ways to explore creative writing.

The ideas presented in this chapter are not comprehensive. There is no way to list everything possible in Further Genres. Writers can find new genres and possibilities every day, but it is essential to remember that discovering Further Genres should not just be someone else's job—do not be afraid to take chances and find a new genre that allows you to harness your writing and creativity.

CHAPTER 14
SIXTEENTH THOUGHT
REVISION AND EDITING

Writers love the thrill of a first draft. Sure, a first draft is sometimes hard to start, and writers occasionally stumble their way through a draft, but drafting can be beautiful once things get rolling. Those early drafting stages are exciting times—a writer can see how their vision is coming to life, and the writer can shape these formative movements. An early draft is filled with ideas and potential; the writer can play with those ideas in any way they choose. A first draft is an opportunity and a judgment-free space where the author can try whatever they like without fear of criticism or failure. A draft is a safe place to play, take chances, and follow imaginative threads.

American poetry writer Allen Ginsberg was inspired by English poetry writer William Blake's thought, "First thought is best in Art, second in other matters." Ginsberg shortened the sentiment to "first thought, best thought," something that very much summed up Ginsberg's approach to writing. For Ginsberg, the creative energy of a first draft is more important than anything else a writer can do. With this phrase, Ginsberg argues that no ideas the writer can have will surpass what comes out of the idea generation stage. We have all had this instinct too. Whenever we have come up with the correct answer to a test question or at trivia night and then second-guessed ourselves and gotten it wrong, we wish we had stuck to the "first thought, best thought" mantra.

There is a lot of merit to the concept, too. "First thought" *can* be your best thought. Often an idea comes into a writer's head, and it ends up being exactly what they needed. "First thoughts" can be great thoughts.

But the way these words get interpreted devalues revision. If "first thought, best thought" is true, what about *second thought*? What is the point of revising our work if we cannot possibly eclipse what we accomplished on the first draft? Writing is not—and can never be—exclusively about first drafts. It is helpful to think of your first draft as yours and yours alone—it is your private experimentation lab. Share second drafts with trusted readers. That circle of readers can expand for subsequent drafts, but most published writers go through perhaps a dozen or more drafts (in some cases, many more) before even thinking about sending it off for publication.

A quickly rendered successful first draft is an intoxicating thing. It is tempting to leave your first draft alone, call it finished, and move on to your next project. Do not fall for this trap. No matter how successful a first draft, something in it will benefit from a second draft. Always.

> ### Writing Warm-Up
>
> There are many ways to approach a draft—a writer can take a simple seed of an idea and jump into writing, or they can be more calculated. As will be discussed, this is up to the writer. But whether jumping head first into the first draft swimming pool or just cautiously dipping in your toes, writers should set themselves up for success as early as possible.
>
> Before writing a rough draft, make a plan. There is no need to be extensive, but a little planning can make a huge difference. Answer the following four questions and then start writing.
>
> - What do I want to write about?
> - Why do I want to write this?
> - Why would someone else want to read this?
> - Why am I the person who should write this?
>
> These questions may seem hard before you have written your draft, but they are valuable. Once you have answered them, start writing your draft. When you have finished the draft, revisit these questions. You can answer them more clearly when you are ready to write the second draft.

What Is the Best Way to Write a Good First Draft?

Unsurprisingly, there is no *one* method for writing a successful draft. Everyone thinks differently—it is logical that all writers write differently. Even though there is no one way to write a successful draft, plenty of approaches exist. Each writer must try different ideas until they find strategies that work for them. Of course, what works for one writer while drafting a poem might not work for drafting a personal essay. And the strategies that work for a short story will not necessarily make for a successful novel. Here are a few strategies that are worth considering:

- Just write. It does not matter where you start. Beginning a novel and you first write chapter twelve? Perfect. Writing a poem by beginning with a single line and working backward? Great strategy.
- As best as you can, figure out what you want to write. You do not have to have a clear vision of everything you will do, but you should have some sense. Whatever basic idea you start with, make sure it is in the rough draft.
- If helpful, write notes about your ideas before you begin drafting. Have something to consult if you run out of ideas.
- Find the pace that suits you. Remember, there is no right or wrong answer to your writing process.

- Some writers write very quickly, sometimes with hour-long (or more) non-stop writing sessions.
- Some are slower, revising and editing as they go.
• Try not to let the pressure of a draft overwhelm you. It is a place to start ideas.

When writing a rough draft, it is valuable to remember this: a rough draft exists to be replaced by something better. That is a tough life. So be nice to your drafts. If your rough draft lives a short life, that means you get to start the second draft sooner.

Nothing you put in a rough draft, whether an experimental idea or a misspelled word, needs to stay. One of the significant benefits of a first draft is trying whatever you want. If it does not work, just change it. This is true in later drafts, but the first draft provides absolute freedom. Try whatever you want and then figure out what comes next in the second draft.

Going Further

Writing a quick rough draft is not for everybody. In fact, some people who practice **quick drafting** (the strategy of writing complete first drafts in a single setting) should not be doing it unless they understand a very critical aspect of quick drafting.

When you decide to quick draft, you must make a deal with yourself. In exchange for writing a start-to-finish draft in a short amount of time, you must promise to carefully revise the draft before you do anything with it. Quick drafts can never be the final product—by definition, they are energetic bursts of writing. To write this way, you must have that agreement with yourself. Otherwise, you are indeed writing (which is good), but you will not be writing anything you should share with others, at least not yet.

What Is a Successful First Draft?

What makes for a successful first draft is very different than what makes for a successful second, third, or later draft. What a writer sees as a successful first draft would be a disappointing later draft. Writing is a process, and frequent revision is an essential part.

Here are the marks of a successful first draft:

- The writer's basic ideas are on the page. This does not mean *everything* the writer hoped to share is on the page, but *something* is. Good enough.
- There is room to grow and develop the ideas introduced in the draft.
- A hypothetical reader would be able to understand the basic concepts of the ideas introduced in the draft. This does not mean you need to share the draft with an actual reader to find out if that is true—first drafts are only for you—but you can infer that the basic concept is in place.

Intersecting Genre

- A successful first draft is not necessarily going to be *good* writing. Do not be discouraged if it is not your best work. It should not be. You are just trying to write.
- When you look at what you have written, you think, *I can work with this*.
- If there are words on the page, you have accomplished something. It might not seem like much, but if you have got *anything* to work with, you are in a better place than where you started.

A first draft is not necessarily going to be good. You might hate it. You might write the draft and think, *this is the worst thing I've ever written*. Even if it is the worst thing you have ever written, does that mean it is a bad first draft? No! It means there is work to be done, and you are aware of that. You are successful if there is more on the page than when you started. Obviously, the more you have to work with, the better, but sometimes what matters most is just getting started. Once you have words, you can reach the next step of making those words better fit your vision.

Going Further

One obstacle to writing is "writer's block," a condition that prevents a writer from writing. When suffering from writer's block, a writer cannot write to their satisfaction. Not only does this create a practical problem, but it can also mentally affect a writer by hurting their confidence.

One way to prevent this is to refuse to acknowledge writer's block. This is not to say that writer's block is a myth—enough eager writers have gotten stymied by it to validate its existence. But instead of accepting that you suffer from writer's block, rethink what it means to write.

If a writer is not literally writing, that does not mean they are suffering from writer's block. Why not? Because literal writing is only a fraction of what a writer does. Thinking is part of writing, and revising is part of writing. Just because a writer is not putting words on the page, that does not mean they are suffering from writer's block. It just means their definition of "writing" is narrower than it should be.

Sometimes, there is nothing harder than staring at a blank screen. Next time, instead of blaming writer's block, think about what you want to write about, preferably away from your writing devices. Or, if thinking does not come easily, look at an earlier work of yours and review or revise. Or, if nothing feels worth revising, pick up a book. Inspiration matters, so reading is writing too. Writing is a complicated and diverse experience. Once we accept its complexity, writer's block will not stand a chance.

Successful Second Drafts

While Ginsberg would have us think that nothing can improve our "first thoughts," a good second draft will do precisely that. A good second draft begins where a successful first draft ends—by going over the first draft and figuring out what works and what could be improved. Some writers describe the first draft as "play" and subsequent drafts as "work," but that does not give second (and later) drafts enough credit. Whether it is the first draft or the sixth, you are still writing. Do not allow yourself to think, *the first draft is where I get to come up with cool ideas and have fun, and revising is just about making it sound better by doing a lot of work.* This is not true. Revising is not the opposite of drafting. It is just another stage.

Revising is the act of taking your work and making it better. It is not the last thing you do when you write—it can come much earlier in the process. It is also not just about "fixing" punctuation, grammar, and spelling. That is editing. Editing is important, but it is not revising. Revising is looking at your piece of writing from a broader perspective. Do not think small when revising—revising is not, *I bet I can replace this word,* when it should be, *I could move this entire paragraph and change the tone of the piece.* You can and should change one word to improve the piece but do not make small changes to avoid making bigger ones. Revising is impactful—think actively about moves that can improve your writing. While you should never undervalue the quality of a first draft, it is a mistake to overvalue it. You can write a good first draft that is legitimately good, but that does not mean improvement is impossible. It can be. If you think your best writing always comes in your first draft, you will be amazed at how much your writing improves when you dedicate yourself to revision.

As far as editing, you can go through and fix those sentence- or word-level issues on a second draft, but it is not a good idea to overly fixate on them. There are two reasons to not limit yourself to editing (or to do any at all) in the earlier stages of revision. First, it is easy to go through a rough draft, fix the punctuation mistakes, and feel like you have accomplished something. You have, but it is not the most important thing you can do. Editing when you ought to be revising makes you feel like you have revised even if you have not. Revision is revision. That is our goal. Second, editing at this stage simply gets in the way. When you need to rethink the type of description you have used in a specific paragraph, it can be tempting to fix that paragraph's commas instead of the more in-depth work of revision, but you do not have to, not yet. Stay focused on the overall work and how to improve it. Good revision is focused revision.

And revision is not a onetime event. When you have revised your first draft, let it sit for a while and then go back to it. When you are ready, revise it again. Then take another break and revisit it again. Revise, wait, revise, wait. Repeat. Whenever you read a published work you admire, know you are not reading the first draft. More likely, the writer has revised that piece many times to reach the point where it was ready for publication.

A lot of the writing we admire feels spontaneous. Excellent writing often has an energy that makes it feel like writing it was easy, but it likely was not. To revisit Ginsberg's take on first drafts, maybe we should not concede that the first thought is the best thought, but it is reasonable to say, "First thought, Good thought." From there, we can add "Second thought, better thought." And if the second thought is better, the writer will learn more about the piece and themselves by the third draft. And if the third draft is still better, what about the sixteenth draft? It is so important to keep revising. It is easy to undervalue revision, but if you stop too soon, you might not be able to let a piece of writing reach its full potential, and that is not fair to your or your future readers.

> ### Writing Practice
>
> Our rough drafts are often wordier than we need them to be.
>
> If you are having trouble expanding a work you would like to make longer (like a book-length collection of prose or a full-length play or screenplay), you might think, *well, I wish I was wordy*, and skip this writing practice. Do not do that!
>
> Wordiness and having trouble reaching a word count goal are not mutually exclusive. It might seem like they are, but they are not. Just because a draft is not long does not mean it is not wordy. Wordiness indicates that a writer's language is not as tight as it needs to be. When writing, whether a poem or a novel, every word needs to have a reason for being in the text. If a writer can remove a single word without affecting the meaning or voice of a piece, the writing is wordy.
>
> When talking about language-tightening, we often focus on poetry, but tightening is relevant to all genres. For this practice exercise, focus on poetry and see how the advice can apply to any genre. Take a poem you have already written. Count the number of words in the poem. Now, cut out 10 percent of those words (So if you have a 200-word poem, cut out 20 words). Whatever you cut was the most obvious stuff to remove, so try again. Now, cut out 20 percent more. You are making sure that what remains in the poem is only what is most necessary.

When to Stop?

You may have several questions at this point. When have I revised enough? Can I over-revise a creative work? Can I make my work worse if I make ill-advised revisions? How can I get help when I have run out of things to improve, but I know my work still needs help? There may be questions even beyond these. Let us start with the four above questions, which should help us feel more grounded.

When have I revised enough?

You probably will not like this response, but this is a difficult question to answer. This is not avoiding the question, either—it is true. Sometimes, a creative work will need twenty or more revisions. Sometimes a handful suffice. And, yes, as the writer, it is often hard to tell. One essential piece of advice on revising is to put the work away after completing a revision. Complete the revision and then save and close the file. Do not think about it yet, and try not to think of the work as *finished*. If you have completed a draft, you have done significant work. Take a break. Go back to it in a few days (or shorter or longer, depending on your instincts). At that time, read through it and revise it again. Eventually, you may review it after a break and think it is working well. That might be a time to share with someone or move on to something else.

Can I over-revise a creative work?
Yes, but probably not. In writing, we often worry about things that are unlikely to happen—over-revising is one of those things. Sure, you could revise a piece of creative writing so much that it becomes too polished and loses its appealing edges. But, honestly, it is much more likely that we will under-revise, and you will share the work with friends or send it off for publication before it is ready. So, while over-revising is possible, the likelihood of not revising something enough and trying to publish it or otherwise share it with others before it is ready is much more likely. So go ahead and risk over-revision. All you will likely do is make it better.

Can I make my work worse if I make ill-advised revisions?
Again, it is possible but unlikely. If a writer is making unfortunate revision choices, then, yes, making the draft worse is undoubtedly possible. Reading other work helps with this problem. The more you read similar types of creative work—and subsequently understand what makes those works successful—the more you will understand how to make *your* work succeed. And if you have written a solid first or second draft, you should trust your instincts. If they have gotten you this far, your instincts will likely take you even farther. Just let them.

How can I get help when I have run out of things to improve, even when I know my work still needs help?
There comes the point where we cannot improve a work any further because we have simply looked at it too many times. At this stage, we may need help. Finding readers to help us with revision becomes valuable. If you have friends who are also writers (and have an appreciation and experience with the type of writing you prefer to do, or are willing to step outside of their comfort zones), ask them to go over your work. And when they give you feedback, remember that you do not have to follow all of their advice, but you must consider their thoughts and be respectful of their ideas. If you disregard their ideas and dismiss their help, they likely will not want to help you again.

Summary

In many ways, creative writing is simple—you come up with a creative idea and write it down. Maybe the idea becomes a poem, perhaps a screenplay. But it starts with one of the most amazing things we humans can do—creative thinking. Writing an entire collection of poetry or a novel is difficult, but what makes you want to write those things is simple.

When we read our favorite books, poems, plays, or even watch a beloved movie, we often feel a connection to the writer and their ideas that is hard to describe. Even if

Intersecting Genre

that writer has been dead for hundreds of years, their work can still move us. That is why we write—to share what matters to us and possibly create the same deep emotional connection with reading for someone else. You have chosen to write, and that choice is wonderful and profound. There is so much you can do with your words.

But remember, writing starts with the simplest of concepts—you have an idea and want to share it with the world. Not only is writing that simple, but it is also uniquely beautiful.

GLOSSARY

Acrostic A poem where the first letter of each line spells out a message not intended to immediately be noticed by the reader.
Alliteration The use of a repeated specific consonant sound in poetry to create a musical effect. For example, the following sentence uses D-sound alliteration *David danced splendidly*.
Antagonist The character (or theme or concept) in a work of literature that serves as the protagonist's primary adversary.
Assonance The use of repeated vowel sounds in poetry to create a musical effect. For example, the following sentence uses I-sound assonance *The evening invites the wind inside*.
Autobiography A CNF work about the writer's life, beginning with events early in life and ending as recently as possible.
Blank Verse Poetry without rhyme that still follows strict metrical form (often with unrhymed iambic pentameter).
BME Story structure that prioritizes a "beginning," a "middle," and an "end."
Braided Essay A lyric essay that uses multiple repeating sections (with unique topics and themes) that intertwine like a braid so that the individual sections merge to make a larger point.
Break In poetry, where a writer chooses to end a line.
Caesura A pause that occurs within the middle of a poetic line.
Character Sketch The act of writing down specific character information (and potentially drawing a visual representation of the character) to better understand the character a writer is looking to create.
Character vs. Character A conflict that pits a protagonist and antagonist against each other.
Character vs. Nature A conflict where a protagonist must oppose difficult natural forces.
Character vs. Self A conflict where a protagonist must confront their capacity to change to fulfill personal goals.
Character vs. Society A conflict that forces a protagonist to challenge social structures and laws.
Character vs. Technology A conflict where a protagonist must oppose technological forces.
Concrete Poems Poems where writers arrange the words in a way that creates a shape that provides greater insight into the poem's message.
Conflict A struggle that defines the plot of narratively-driven creative work. Often takes the form of character vs. character, character vs. nature, or character vs. self.
Craft The formal aspects of creative writing, such as form and structure.
Creative Non-Fiction (CNF) A creative work in prose based on personal or historical events.
Cues Information in a text that gives the reader insight on how to read it. These could be subtle (implicit) or obvious (explicit).
Denouement Scene (or scenes) that occur after the resolution of the central conflict. It would typically answer outstanding questions and provide information on how characters fare after the completion of the plot.
Dialogue Tags Indications attributing a line of dialogue to a specific character. Typically, these are some expressed in a variation of "they said."
Deuteragonist A secondary protagonist in a work of literature.
Easter Egg An element in a creative work that an audience might not immediately notice but will enhance some aspect of the creative experience. Primarily found in video games, films, and television.

Glossary

Enjambment In poetry, when a sentence continues through a line or stanza break.

Epistolary A creative work composed of letters ostensibly written by characters.

Essay A prose piece of non-fiction (or CNF) of nominal length.

Establishing Shot In film, the initial visual representation of a location. For example, it may show a building before moving to a scene within that building.

Fiction A creative work in prose based on imagined scenarios and characters.

Flashback When a creative work goes backward in a timeline to reveal a scene (or scenes) that has a specific meaning to the storyline's main timeline.

Flashforward A literary device in which a work depicts a specific scene (or scenes) from after the work's primary timeline to provide information about "future" plot or character developments.

Foreshadowing The act of revealing hints of future plot or character developments before those developments occur.

Form A term that can be used synonymously with genre but can also refer to approaches within specific genres (like sonnets, lyric essays, or novels)

Found Poem A poem constructed from words and phrases the writer found elsewhere. The writer arranges these words and phrases to create a poetic artifact different from the source material.

Fourth Wall Typically from film or plays, the act of a character specifically addressing the audience.

Free Verse Poetry without rhyme or structured meter.

Further Genres A term that refers to creative writing categories outside the five primarily discussed genres (CNF, fiction, plays, poetry, and screenplays).

Genre A way of identifying a specific type within a larger category.

Genre Fiction Works of fiction that fit into subgenre categories (like science fiction, fantasy, romance, or mystery, for example)

Hermit Crab Essay A lyric essay that "borrows" its structure from another form of writing. For example, a personal essay written like a movie review.

Iamb A metrical foot that combines an unstressed syllable that is followed by a stressed syllable.

Iambic Pentameter A metrical line of five iambs. It totals ten syllables overall.

Idealized Audience The hypothetical audience that would most appreciate a specific work.

Idioms Expressions that have meanings that are not necessarily obvious by the words themselves. They are expressions that mean something other than what their literal words insinuate.

Image A literary tool that uses vivid description and detail to allow readers to "see" the events described—and therefore invest emotionally.

Imitation The act of taking the work of others and using certain aspects of its craft or meaning to write something original.

Infodump When a writer presents a vast amount of information (whether it is about the plot, a character, or something else) all at once.

Infodrizzle Instead of presenting the reader with too much information at once, this strategy encourages the writer to provide information in a gradual and approachable way.

Legato Music that moves smoothly yet consistently.

Limited Point of View A POV technique where a single character (who does not know everything that has happened or will happen) is the narrator.

Lines A poetry unit where a writer consciously ends a sentence prior to the right margin.

Lyric In poetry, a type of poem that creates emotional resonance for the reader through tightly focused imagery, typically in a musical fashion.

Lyric Essay A work of CNF that embodies aspects of poetry (like poetic language and innovative structure).

Magical Realism A fictional work that is predominately realistic (and often mundane) but also contains magical elements.

Memoir A CNF work of varying length that focuses on a specific period, theme, or relationship of the writer's life.

Glossary

Metaphor A literary device that uses a comparison between two very different things to emphasize some aspect of the first thing.

Metrical Foot Two or three syllables that compose a sound unit that creates poetry. An iamb (an unstressed syllable followed by a stressed syllable) is a common example of a metrical foot.

Mesotic A poem arranged so that a hidden message appears horizontally within the text, typically toward the center of the text.

Monologue A speech, often lengthy, spoken by a single character. Most often found in plays.

Narrative The way a given story is told.

Near Rhyme Two words that do not rhyme perfectly, but are similar enough to one another to create a pleasing sound (for example, ""ball" and "roll," and "house" and "toast")

Non-Linear Structure A storytelling structure where, instead of presenting the plot in chronological order, the events are out of order, thus surprising the reader, creating mystery, and using the new order to find unexpected relationships between events.

Omniscient Narrator A narrator that knows everything happening in the world of a work. This narrator knows everything possible in the work's world and can inform the reader of anything.

Outline A drafting tool that lists the events that will occur in a work (typically in order) to help the writer organize and subsequently write the piece.

Pace The speed at which a work moves (can be used to refer to the speed of any work in any genre).

Paraphrase Rephrasing the words of another into the speaker's own words, typically with the detail and length of the original version.

Personification Giving human traits to something that is inanimate or non-human.

Play A creative work written in a standardized format with the intent of eventually being performed on a stage.

Plot The specific sequence of events that occur within a given work of creative writing.

Poetry A creative work typically written in verse that values musicality, imagery, and compelling language.

Point of View The perspective from which a work of prose is told, often abbreviated to POV. First-person POV is from the narrator's perspective ("I did this"), second-person POV directly addresses another person ("You did this"), and third person is about another person with no "I" in the narration at all ("They did this.")

Post-Confessional Poetry after confessionalism that has taken on some of the autobiographical aspects of confessionalism but employs them to different effect.

Protagonist The primary character in a work of literature.

Quick Drafting A writing technique where a writer composes an early draft as quickly (and without stops) as possible.

Satire A humorous work that ridicules something or someone, often by pretending to be supportive of the thing being ridiculed.

Scene A recreation of a moment in creative writing—it depicts characters, dialogue, setting, and sensory details that collectively make the reader feel immersed.

Screenplay A creative work written in a standardized format with the intent of eventually being produced as a film or television show.

Set The specific physical items (big and small) that occupy the stage to create setting in a play.

Setting Where a creative work takes place, including the general physical location and time.

Shapeliness The art of discussing the physical look of a piece of writing.

Shiny Thing Syndrome When a writer is distracted from their main focus, as if by a "shiny thing" that captures their eye.

Simile A literary device that uses a comparison between two very different things to emphasize some aspect of the first thing. Unlike metaphor, this comparison uses "like" or "as."

Staccato Music in which notes move deliberately so that they are somewhat isolated. Stands in contrast to the smoothness of legato.

Glossary

Stage The physical location of a play performance.

Stanza A unit in poetry composed of lines.

Story Real or imagined events that drive a work of creative writing.

Stress In metrical poetry, a syllable or sound that receives emphasis when read aloud.

Storyboards Graphic organizers used in filmmaking to show how a work (typically an animated or live-action screenplay) will look at future stages.

Subgenre More specific categorizations within a genre. For example, if "fiction" is the genre, "western" is a subgenre.

Sublime An emotional reaction that evokes awe or gratitude, typically to art or nature.

Subtext The unstated meaning behind words. In creative writing, this typically refers to the meaning behind dialogue.

Summarize To rephrase the thought of another in the speaker's own words. This is typically much shorter than the original material, emphasizing only the original's most essential aspects.

Surrealism Literature that blurs the line between dreams and reality.

Tension Uncertainty about what will happen in a work of literature.

Unlimited Point of View There is no limit to what the speaker (typically third person) in a creative work can know or do.

Unreliable Narrator A narrator who, for various reasons, cannot be seen as entirely trustworthy. Among the reasons for this unreliability are deceit, limited knowledge, or biases toward others that affect the narrator's judgment.

Verse Play A play written in poetic lines.

Videopoetry A form that combines poetry (either original or written by others), video, and music.

Voice The personality of a piece of writing.

World-Building The act of creating a larger universe within a creative work.

WORKS CITED

"All-Time Box Office Hits (Domestic Gross) by Decade and Year." *Filmsite*. https://www.filmsite.org/boxoffice2.html.
Beers, H.A. *The Connecticut Wits and Other Essays*. HardPress Publishing, 2012.
"Best Adapted Screenplay." *Oscars Wiki*. https://oscars.fandom.com/wiki/Best_Adapted_Screenplay.
"Best Original Screenplay." *Oscars Wiki*. https://oscars.fandom.com/wiki/Best_Original_Screenplay.
Boswell, James. *The Life of Samuel Johnson*. Edited by David Womersly. Penguin Classics, 2008.
Bronte, Emily. *Jane Erye*. Norton, 2016.
Carroll, Tobias. "Making the Case for the Surreal Memoir." *Literary Hub*, April 2, 2019. https://lithub.com/making-the-case-for-the-surreal-memoir/.
"Character." *The American Heritage Dictionary of the English Language*, Fourth Edition. Houghton Mifflin Harcourt, 2008.
"Creative Writing." Lexico.Com. www.lexico.com/en/definition/creative_writing.
Crichton, Michael. *Jurassic Park*. Ballantine Books, 2012.
"Composing Free Verse Is like Playing Tennis without a Net." *Quote Investigator*, April 1, 2022. https://quoteinvestigator.com/2021/05/24/poem-tennis/.
D'Agata, John. "Might as Well Call It the Lyric Essay." *Seneca Review*. https://www.hws.edu/senecareview/dagata_le.pdf
"Definition of Art." Google Search, *Google*.
Dickinson, Emily. *Selected Letters*. Edited by Thomas H. Johnson. Belknap Press, 1986.
"Essay." *The American Heritage Dictionary of the English Language*, Fourth Edition. Houghton Mifflin Harcourt, 2008.
Fitzgerald, F. Scott. *The Great Gatsby*. Collier Books, 1992.
Frow, John. *Genre*. Routledge, 2014.
Ginsberg, Allen. "Mind Writing Slogans." *The Allen Ginsberg Project*, November 17, 2019. https://allenginsberg.org/2016/02/mind-writing-slogans/.
Goldstone, Richard H. "Thorton Wilder, Art of Fiction, No. 16." *Paris Review*, Winter 1956. https://www.theparisreview.org/interviews/4887/the-art-of-fiction-no-16-thornton-wilder.
"Graduate Class in American Fiction, Tape 1." *Faulkner at Virginia*, February 21, 1958. https://faulkner.lib.virginia.edu/display/wfaudio21.html.
Gruenwald, Mark. "Mark's Remarks." *Quasar* 1, no. 59 (1994): 24. Marvel Comics.
Haley, Heather. "Heather's Artist Statement—'Where Sins Are More Sinful.'" *Atticus Review*, February 27, 2012. https://atticusreview.org/where-sins-are-more-sinful/.
Jurassic Park. Directed by Steven Spielberg. Universal Pictures, 1993.
Konyves, Tom. "Videopoetry: A Manifesto." *Issuu*, September 6, 2011. https://issuu.com/tomkonyves/docs/manifesto_pdf.
Kooser, Ted. *The Poetry Home Repair Manual*. University of Nebraska Press, 2005.
Lawrence, D.H. *The Bad Side of Books: Selected Essays of D.H. Lawrence*. New York Review Books, 2019.
Lech, Kasia. *Dramaturgy of Form: Performing Verse in Contemporary Theatre*. Routledge, 2021.
Le Guin, Ursula K. *Steering the Craft: A Twenty-First-Century Guide to Sailing the Sea of Story*. Houghton Mifflin Harcourt, 2015.
Lowell, Robert. *Collected Poems*. Farrar, Strauss, & Giroux, 2003.

Works Cited

Lusty, Natalia, ed. *Surrealism*. Cambridge UP, 2021.
Malamud, Bernard. *The Natural*. Farrar, Strauss, & Giroux, 2003.
McClintock, Pamela. "Global Box Office Revenue Hits Record $41B in 2018, Fueled by Diverse U.S. Audiences." *The Hollywood Reporter*, The Hollywood Reporter, March 21, 2019. https://www.hollywoodreporter.com/news/general-news/global-box-office-revenue-hits-record-41b-2018-fueled-by-diverse-us-audiences-1196010/.
The Natural. Directed by Barry Levinson. Tri-Star Pictures, 1984.
Noble, Randon Billings, ed. *A Harp in the Stars: An Anthology of Lyric Essays*. University of Nebraska Press, 2021.
O'Connor, Flannery. *Mystery and Manners: Occasional Prose*. Farrar, Strauss, & Giroux, 1970.
Oliver, Mary. *A Poetry Handbook*. Harcourt Brace & Company, 1994.
Olson, Charles. "Projective Verse by Charles Olson." *Poetry Foundation*. https://www.poetryfoundation.org/articles/69406/projective-verse.
"Paul Thomas Anderson's Advice on Writing." *YouTube*, December 3, 2019. https://www.youtube.com/watch?v=myrRBNHswfQ.
"RFID Machines in British Libraries Are Producing Charming Found Poetry." *Electric Literature*, July 25, 2019. https://electricliterature.com/rfid-machines-in-british-libraries-are-producing-charming-found-poetry/.
Rosanoff, Martin André. "Edison in his laboratory." *Harper's Magazine*, September 1932.
Rosenthal, M.L. "Nation." 189, no. 8 (September 1959): 154–5. EBSCOhost. https://search.ebscohost.com/login.aspx?direct=true&db=nih&AN=13392865&site=ehost-live.
Shakespeare, William. Othello. Edited by Tom McAlindon. Penguin, 2015.
Spenser, Stuart. *The Playwright's Guidebook: An Insightful Primer on the Art of Dramatic Writing*. Farrar, Straus, and Giroux, 2002.
"Stanley Kubrick." *IMDb*. https://www.imdb.com/name/nm0000040/bio?ref_=nm_dyk_qt_sm#quotes.
Swift, Jonathan. *Irish Political Writings after 1725: A Modest Proposal and Other Works*. Edited by David Hayton, and Adam Rounce, Cambridge University Press, 2018.
Tall, Deborah, and John D'Agata. "The Lyric Essay." *Seneca Review*. https://www.hws.edu/senecareview/lyricessay.aspx.
Tate, James. *The Route as Briefed*. The University of Michigan Press, 1999.
"The Tony Award Nominations." *The Tony Award Nominations—The American Theatre Wing's Tony Awards*. https://www.tonyawards.com/nominees/year/any/category/play/show/any/.
Welty, Eudora. *One Writer's Beginnings*. Scribner, 2020.
Whitman, Walt. *Leaves of Grass and Selected Prose*. Edited by Lawrence Buell. Modern Library, 1981.
Wordsworth, William, and Samuel Taylor Coleridge. *Lyrical Ballads*. Taylor & Francis Group, 2005.
Wright, Michael. *Playwrighting in Focus*. Focus, 2009.

Permissions

Chong, Eileen. "Green Grief" from *Dark Matter* © 2018. Reprinted with permission of Recent Works Press.
Cohen, Matthew Brian. "The Safest Place for Your Kids Right Now is Inside the Scorpion Pit" © 2021. Originally appeared on *McSweeney's Internet Tendencies*. Reprinted with permission of the writer.
Croggon, Alison. "The Poet Has No Identity" from *New and Selected Poems, 1991–2017*. © 2017. Reprinted with the permission of the author.

Works Cited

Jackson, Penny. "Before" (fiction version) © 2017 by Penny Jackson. Reprinted with permission of the author.

Jackson, Penny. "Before" (play version) © 2017 by Penny Jackson. Reprinted with permission of the author.

Khelawan, Rajni Mala. From *Kalyana* by Rajni Mala Khelawan. Printed with permission from Second Story Press, Toronto. www.secondstorypress.ca.

Kove, Torill, director. *Me and My Moulton*. © 2014 written and directed by Torill Kove. Discussed with permission of the National Film Board of Canada.

Makoha, Nick. *The Dark*. © 2018 by Nick Makoha. Reprinted with the permission of Oberon Books, an imprint of Bloomsbury Publishing Plc.

McLindon, James. "Choices" © 2020 by James McLindon. Reprinted with the permission of the author.

Mockler, Kathryn. "The Séance" from *The Purpose Pitch* © by Kathryn Mockler. Reprinted with the permission of Mansfield Press.

Norris, Denne Michelle. "Audition." © 2020 by Denne Michele Norris. Reprinted with the permission of the author and SLL/Sterling Lord Literistic, Inc.

Ramsey, Susan Blackwell. Reproduced from *A Mind Like This* by Susan Blackwell Ramsey by permission of the University of Nebraska Press. © 2012 by the Board of Regents of the University of Nebraska.

Reeher, Rachel. "Lobster" © 2020 by Rachel Reeher. Reprinted with the permission of the author.

Sampson, Fiona. "Take, Eat" from *Common Prayer* © 2007. Reprinted with the permission of Carcanet Press.

Sanders, Scott Loring. "Bee Man." © 2018 by Scott Loring Sanders. Reprinted with the permission of the author.

Schiff, Robyn. "House of Dior" from *Worth* © 2002. Reprinted with the permission of University of Iowa Press.

Seale, Derin, director. "The Eleven O'Clock" © 2016, directed by Derin Seale, Screenplay by Josh Lawson. Discussed with the permission of Derin Seale.

Shapley, Maggie. "Change" from *Proof* © 2017 by Maggie Shapley. Reprinted with the permission of Recent Work Press.

Thompson, Hildegard, translator. "Coyote and Rabbit." From *Navajo Coyote Tales,* collected by William Morgan, translated into English by Hildegard Thompson. Copyright © 2007 by Gibbs Smith, Publisher. Reprinted with the permission of Gibbs Smith Books.

Tran, Eric "Prophecy" © 2021 by Eric Tran. Reprinted with the permission of the author.

INDEX

alliteration 17, 38, 73, 75–6
assonance 17, 75–6
audience 2, 10, 46, 51, 56, 65, 95, 96, 113, 139–43, 164
    Easter eggs and 120–1
    idealized 16
    performing in front of 52–3, 126
    in screenplays and film 25–6, 83–5, 89, 118, 170
    in theater and plays 21–3, 43, 45, 69–70, 76–80, 97–100, 102–3, 106–9
    writer perceptions of 15, 30, 130, 148, 177
autobiography 19–20, 168

backstory 49, 57, 104
beginning-middle-end (BME) 93–4, 127, 129–31

characters 29, 47–50, 53, 55–8, 83–4, 88–9, 97–100, 107, 109, 123, 126–7, 129, 135, 137, 178–9
    in creative non-fiction 20, 45–7
    and dialogue 62–5
    in fiction 15, 32, 34–5, 38
    in plays 22–3, 43–5, 103, 143–6
    in poems 114
    and point of view 103–7
    in screenplays 67, 86, 117–20, 144
Chaucer, Geoffrey 32, 118
Chong, Eileen 40
closet drama 107–9
Cohen, Matthew Brian 175–7
collaboration 122
    in film 23–5, 51, 55, 83, 148–9
    in theater 22–3, 43
comic books 30, 65–6, 173, 177–8
confessional poetry 168–70
conflict 99, 135, 145–6
Croggon, Alison 38–9

dialogue 58, 60–6, 80–1, 85–6, 97–100, 117, 155
    in plays 21–3, 43, 76, 143–6
    in screenplays 25, 55, 59–61
Dickinson, Emily 4, 32

Easter Eggs 120–1
editing 1, 88, 183, 185
The Eleven O'Clock 59–62

enjambment 73–5

Faulkner, William 47–8
Fourth Wall 22, 78, 106
free verse 173

Ginsberg, Allen 181, 184–6
graphic novels, *see* comic books
The Great Gatsby 104–5

humor 19, 25, 37, 57, 61–2, 88, 116, 118–20, 127, 174–7

iambic pentameter 23, 71–2, 89, 173
images 18, 31, 79, 111–14, 116, 121–3, 157, 173–4
imitation 36–7

Jackson, Penny 100–3

Khelawan, Rajni Mala 33–5
Kooser, Ted 117
Kove, Torill 88–9

Lawson, Josh 59–62
lines 9, 16–18, 32, 38, 71–5, 79, 86–7, 164
    and break 1, 7–8, 16–17, 35, 164
live performance storytelling 51–3
Lowell, Robert 168–9
lyric essays 5, 20, 127–8, 158–65
lyric poetry 29, 37, 111, 157–9, 163–8

McLindon, James 142–5
magical realism 6, 136
Makoha, Nick 76–9
Me and My Moulton 88–9
memoir 7, 11, 19–20, 46, 78, 84–5, 90, 135–7
metaphor 4, 32, 39, 76–9, 116
Mockler, Kathryn 36–7
monologue 79, 103, 108–9
music 5–6, 55, 95, 178
musicality 7, 16–17, 31, 35, 37–9, 71–7, 80–1, 111, 115, 157–8, 164–5, 170

narrative poetry 37
Navajo 30–1
Norris, Denne Michele 56–8

Index

O'Connor, Flannery   92–3
Oliver, Mary   35, 157–8, 165
oral tradition   29–31, 69
outlines   147–9

pacing   39, 59, 134–5, 167
plot   9, 15, 23, 29–30, 35, 38, 40, 47, 87, 89, 91–5, 100, 133, 136
podcasts   94–6
point of view   65, 98, 102–7, 128, 134–5
post-confessional poetry   168–70
prose poems   31, 38–41, 159

Ramsey, Susan Blackwell   114–16, 169
Reeher, Rachel   131–4
revision   1, 16, 50, 88, 129, 181–7

Sampson, Fiona   72–5
Sanders, Scott Loring   90–4
satire   174–7
scenes   20, 23, 50, 86–7, 118, 125, 130–1
    pacing and   133–5
    structure of   147–8
Schiff, Robyn   165–7
Seale, Derin   59–62
setting   1, 23, 59, 86, 97, 125–6
    in formatting   149–54
    and plays   7, 22, 139, 143
    and screenplays   21, 24, 111, 117
    and set   50–1, 53
Shakespeare, William   32, 62, 70, 79–80, 97
Shapley, Maggie   112–14

Sonnets   5–8, 23, 75, 165
stage   21–5, 43–5, 50, 52, 69–70, 107–8, 129, 146
    directions   151–2
stand-up comedy   52
stanza   9, 16–17, 35, 37
story   6–7, 15, 21–2, 32–5, 40, 51–3, 55, 61, 83, 86–7, 94, 102, 114, 125–31, 134
    and dialogue   65
    and plot   29, 91
    and point of view   103–6
    and structure   90–1, 99, 129–31
storylistening   29–30
storytelling   3, 21, 26, 30–1, 37–8, 59, 62, 66, 69, 77, 83, 95, 97, 109, 125, 137, 158
subtext   62, 65
surrealism   133, 135–7
suspension of disbelief   43, 76, 78, 103

tension   61–2, 73–4, 97, 99, 102, 136, 145–6, 159
text messaging   10, 27, 106, 140, 174
Tran, Eric   128–9, 160–4
true stories   84–5

verse plays   79–81
videopoetry   121–3
voice   3, 27, 30–1, 35–7, 61, 80–1, 115–16, 126–9
    and dialogue   63–5
    in lyric poetry   165–7

Wordsworth, William   4, 71–2, 76, 165
world-building   15, 125
writer's block   184

www.ingramcontent.com/pod-product-compliance
Lightning Source LLC
Chambersburg PA
CBHW051644230426
43669CB00013B/2434